DEDALUS IN HARLEM

The Joyce-Ellison Connection

Robert N. List

UNIVERSITY
PRESS OF
AMERICA

University Press of America, Inc."

P.O. Box 19101, Washington, D.C. 20036

Printed in the United States of America

Library of Congress Cataloging in Publication Data

List, Robert N.
    Dedalus in Harlem.

    Includes bibliographical references and index.
    1. Ellison, Ralph--Criticism and interpretation.
2. Joyce, James, 1882-1941--Influence--Ellison.
I. Title.
PS3555.L625Z76 1982   818'.5409   81-43837
ISBN 0-8191-2630-6
ISBN 0-8191-2631-4 (pbk.)

For my wife, Vicky, who endured.

ACKNOWLEDGMENTS

The research and initial drafts of the book were completed at
the Robert R. Moton Memorial Center in Capahosic, Virginia
while I was a scholar-in-residence there from 1979-1980. I
wish to thank Dr. Broadus Butler and the staff of the Center
for very generous support. I also wish to thank Dr. Estus
Smith, Vice President for Academic Affairs, Jackson State
University, Jackson, Mississippi, for his encouragement.

Also, grateful acknowledgments are made to the following for
permission to use quotations from their publications:
Edmund R. Brill for Totem & Taboo in The Basic Writings of
Sigmund Freud by Sigmund Freud, Translated by A. A. Brill,
Copyright 1958 (excerpts pp. 811, 914, 915, 923, 925).
Doubleday & Company, Inc., for The Long Dream by Richard Wright,
Copyright 1958 (excerpt p. 102). White Man, Listen! by Richard
Wright, Copyright 1957.
Harper & Row, Publishers, Inc., for The Outsider by Richard
Wright, Copyright 1953 (excerpts from pp. 102, 123, 134-35,
140, 244, 357-58, 358, 424-25). American Hunger by Richard
Wright, Copyright 1944 & 1977, (excerpts pp. 26-27). Black Boy
by Richard Wright, Copyright 1937, 1942, 1944, 1945 (excerpts
pp. 33, 89, 215). Native Son by Richard Wright, Copyright 1940,
1968 (excerpts pp. 58, 101, 155, 256, 354, 391-92).
Pantheon Books, a Division of Random House, Inc., for White
Racism: A Psychohistory by Joel Kovel, Copyright 1971,
(excerpts pp. 127-265).
Random House, Inc., for Invisible Man by Ralph Ellison, Copyright
1972. Shadow & Act by Ralph Ellison, Copyright 1972. Ulysses
by James Joyce, Copyright 1961.
Society of Authors, Literary Representative of the Estate of
James Joyce for Stephen Hero by James Joyce, Copyright 1963.
(excerpts pp. 64, 64-65, 116-117, 146, 177-78, 194, 213).
Viking Penguin, Inc., for Dubliners by James Joyce. Originally
published in 1916 by B. W. Hueback, Copyright 1967 by the Estate
of James Joyce.
Portrait of the Artist As a Young Man by James Joyce, Copyright
1916 by B. W. Hueback, right renewed by Nora Joyce. Definitive
copyright 1964 by the Estate of James Joyce.
Finnegans Wake by James Joyce, Copyright 1939 by James Joyce.
Copyright renewed 1967 by George Joyce and Lucia Joyce.
Reprinted by permission of Viking Penguin Inc.

CONTENTS

I think that he [Joyce] has a lot to teach
us, especially in Finnegans Wake. It's
annoying at first, but when you get into it
you begin to see how he plays with rhythms,
how he will extrapolate from popular songs
and everything else.[1]

Ralph Ellison

Loss of identity, sleeping and blindness are
the figures that express the invisible man's
confusion and despair as his world disintegrates. Then, after the cultural malaise
climaxes in the riot, the final phase of the
anti-hero's progress begins, a descent into
the tomb--the netherworld across the Styx
where heroes went: 'Its a kind of death
without hanging, I thought, a death
alive. . . . I moved off over the black
water, floating, sighing . . . sleeping
invisibly!' So he remains immortal and
waiting, like the heroes of myth who disap-
pear and are believed to wait should the
world require them--like King Arthur and
Finn MacCool, sleeping giants blended into
the landscape. The invisible man, now
grown into Jack the Bear, turns to New
York's sewer system, a black and labyrinthine underground--a fitting anti-hero's
mausoleum.[2]

William J. Schafer

Amen! But though they took us like a great
black giant that had been chopped into
little pieces and the pieces buried; though
they deprived us of our heritage among
strange scenes in strange weather; divided
and divided and divided us again like a
gambler shuffling and cutting a deck of
cards. Although we were ground down,
smashed into little pieces; spat upon,

1

stamped upon, cursed and buried, and our
memory of Africa ground down into powder and
blown into the winds of foggy forgetfulness.
. . .[3]

                    Ralph Ellison
                    "Juneteenth"

CHAPTER I

In "The Little Man at the Chehaw Station" Ellison
angerly denounced the enemies of the melting-pot
concept:

During the nineteenth century, an attempt
was made to impose a loose conceptual order
upon the chaos of American society by
viewing it as a melting pot. Today that
metaphor is noisily rejected, vehemently
disavowed. In fact, it has come under
attack in the name of the newly fashionable
code word 'ethnicity,' reminding us that in
this country code words are the linguistic
agencies for the designation of sacrificial
victims, and are circulated to sanction the
abandonment of policies and the degrading of
ideals. So today, before the glaring
inequities, unfulfilled promises, and rich
possibilities of democracy, we hear heady
evocations of European, African, and Asian
backgrounds accompanied by chants proclaim-
ing the inviolability of ancestral blood.
Today blood magic and blood thinking, never
really dormant in American society, are rampant, among us, often leading to brutal
racial assaults in areas where these seldom
occurred before. And while this goes on,
the challenge of arriving at an adequated
definition of American cultural identity
goes unanswered.[4]

Never one to doubt the value of the cultural contri-
butions of the various ethnic groups to the larger
whole of the American experience, Ellison nonetheless
attacked the artificial assertion of ethnicity that
might serve as a wedge between the present and the
ideals of the Founding Fathers:

The proponents of ethnicity--ill concealing
an underlying anxiety, and given a bizarre
bebopish stridency by the obviously American
vernacular inspiration of the costumes and
rituals ragged out to dramatize their claims
to ethnic (and genetic) insularity--have
helped to give our streets and campuses a

3

rowdy, All Fool's Day, carnival atmosphere. In many ways, then, the call for a new social order based upon the glorification of ancestral blood and ethnic background acts as a call to cultural and aesthetic chaos. Yet while this latest farcical phase in the drama of American social hierarchy unfolds, the irrepressible movement of American culture toward the integration of its diverse elements continues, confounding the circumlocutions of its staunchest opponents.[5]

These lines could just as well have been written by Richard Wright who held similar views concerning ethnic insularity and blood-thinking. And beyond the influence of American egalitarian idealism it will become clear that James Joyce's conclusions regarding the negativism of blood thinking deeply saturated the literary projects of these two American writers.

Integrative images such as Blake's Albion and Emerson's giant Transcendentalist or Ireland's vanquished Finn concerned Joyce especially in Finnegans Wake where he dismantled and x-rayed motives for ethnic and racial chauvinism, a process which culminated in his cataloging the universal archetypes and urges of the collective unconscious. In partial homage to their Irish mentor, Ellison and Wright declared intellectual war on the negativism inherent in the racial net and in the several other Joycean nets that would hold down intellectual freedom. At the same time they deconstructed the "diseased conscience," the "paralysis," and "confusion" of the racially obsessed in their corresponding milieus. For the main burden of each writer would be to offer strategies for the transcendence of the nightmare of history that such chauvinism helped to sustain, to forge a cosmopolitan, international identity.

Indeed, Joyce grew up in an era bathed in ethnic consciousness. The Irish Catholics of his day were considered by many Englishmen and Protestant Ulstermen to comprise a separate race of Celtic outcasts deemed incapable of "civilized" behavior, to say nothing of self-rule. The torrid and puerile debates that raged over the concepts of "race" and "blood," debates which so intrigued imperialist England, have been summarized by L. P. Curtis:

4

The vast majority of Irishmen were. . . considered to be Celtic as well as Catholic, these two categories being taken as almost but not quite independent. Those Englishmen who insisted that the Irish belonged to a distinctly different or alien race took it for granted that they possessed a set of permanent traits which marked them off from all the non-Celtic peoples or races of the world.[6]

So pervasive was this sentiment that even young James Joyce could give credence to it, although he would later repudiate and burlesque its extreme positions in Finnegans Wake. In his essay "Ireland, Island of Saints and Sages" (1907) Joyce argued:

Do we not see that in Ireland the Danes, the Firbolgs, the Milesians from Spain, the Norman invaders, and the Anglo-Saxon settlers have united to form a new entity, one might say under the influence of a local deity? And, although the present race in Ireland is backward and inferior, it is worth taking into account the fact that it is the only race of the entire Celtic family that has not been willing to sell its birthright for a mess of pottage.[7]

So faddish was the ideology of race that Disraeli could argue in Tancred:

But England flourishes. Is it what you call civilization that makes England flourish? Is it the universal development of the faculties of man that has rendered an island, almost unknown to the ancients, the arbiter of the world? Clearly not. It is her inhabitants that have done this; it is an affair of race. A Saxon race, protected by an insular position, has stamped its diligent and methodic character on the century. And when a superior race, with a superior ideal to Work and Order, advances, its state will be progressive, and we shall perhaps, follow the example of the desolate countries. All is race; there is no other truth.[8]

5

The maturer Joyce would reevaluate such cries for ethnic purity and "racial" superiority that were proclaimed on both sides of the Irish channel. He would enter the incest-ridden nightmare of HCE and concede just how ethnically "confused" the perennially invaded Irish really were. For Joyce, Disraeli's assertion that "All is race" added terror to the nightmare of history from which we are still feebly trying to awake. Race must be partially transcended; but the universal in man, and the explication of the universal in the conscious and unconscious experience of characters would form the bulwark of an artistic conscience. For an unconscious, mysterious, universally shared and mostly repressed humanity, that "confused music" Stephen Dedalus counterpoints with the "diseased conscience" not only of the "gratefuly oppressed" Irish but of "The Europe" that "lay out there beyond the Irish Sea, Europe of strange tongues and valleyed and woodbegirt and citadelled and of entrenched, and marshalled races," was a humanity that had to be cultivated.[9] No wonder a confused Davin asks Stephen in A Portrait: "Are you Irish at all?"

Ellison and Wright were profoundly influenced by Joyce's treatment of "race" and ethnicity when they observed unsettling analogies existing among oppression in Ireland, in the United States, and in Africa. Intrigued by Joyce's pioneering inquiries into the psychology of oppression, they hoped to construct their own inventory of the peculiar psychological effects fostered by racial myths in both oppressed people and in the oppressors. They wished to play variations on Joyce's "wake" from this nightmare of history while they continued to sort out the pathological effects of racism from that contrary ambiguous riddle of human personality, that inner urge to defy the definition of one's self by others in the quest for self-realization and freedom.

In his introduction to Drake's and Cayton's Black Metropolis, Wright would say in 1945: "What would life on Chicago's South Side look like when seen through the eyes of a Freud, a Joyce, a Proust, a Pavlov, a Kierkegaard?"[10] In the coming years Ellison and Wright would look through those eyes and many more including those of Vico, Marx, Engels, Twain, Conrad, Melville, Dostoevsky, Hegel, Malraux, Sartre, Camus, Otto Rank, and assorted sociologists,

in their attempts to chart the mental landscape
forged by that sickness unto death, that diseased-
conscience, which partly resulted from the race
mythologies here and abroad. But Joyce's psychological vision would be the profoundest influence of all.
For Ellison and Wright concluded that the psychoanalytical approach was needed to probe the pathology of
race in an oppressor-oppressed set. And they helped
to pioneer such an approach through fiction and
essays.

Although Ellison disregarded many of the
reductive, stereotyped observations of the sociologists who studied race, both he and Wright could not
have overlooked E. Franklin Frazier's early protest.
Frazier argued quite bluntly in 1927 that racism is a
form of insanity: "the Negro Complex" is "an
acquired psychological reaction, and there is no
scientific evidence that it represents the functioning of inherited behavior patterns."[11] Ellison
and Wright would partially disagree. For racism
seemed to be enmeshed in the "return of the
repressed," in the return of unconscious wishes right
off the pages of Freud's Totem and Taboo: those
latent desires for incest, parricide and fratricide,
as we shall discover in Chapter IV. Nevertheless,
Ellison's and Wright's obsessive use of disease imagery aligned them with Frazier's overall "insanity"
thesis which argued that a variety of infantile
sexual and sadistic projections could go on almost
unchecked in the racist:

> Like the lunatic, he refused to treat the
> repugnant desire as a part of himself and
> consequently, shows an exaggerated antago-
> nism toward the desire which he projects
> upon the Negro. . . .[12]

And that racist, like the severely disturbed, cannot
face change, cannot rationally discuss prejudices,
and cannot transcend the many defense mechanisms that
inhibit mental health and growth.

Joyce's literary approach to the diseased
conscience was less reductive and more multifaceted
than the many formula studies of the sociologists,
and his Hegelian-Freudian task of x-raying the Irish
and British consciences from Dubliners through
Finnegans Wake fired the imaginations of these two

7

Americans. Joyce's task was finally completed in _Finnegans Wake_ where he blueprinted several pre-oedipal and oedipal-sadistic forces in the unconscious, in the "ding idself," forces which emerged to form the daylight world of conscious history. The vicissitudes of Irish history certainly provided Joyce with a dramatic microcosm of the nightmare of history. For Ireland has been a battleground of conflicting cultures and religions culminating in endless wars: Norman, Plantagenet, Brucite, Marian, Elizabethan, Jacobean, Cromwellian, Willamite, French Revolutionary, Napoleonic, Black and Tan, but worst of all, the internalized war of a plundered, sundered, emasculated Irish psyche against itself which continues still in Ulster. Joyce confessed of his plantation culture:

> . . . the economic and intellectual con-
> ditions that prevail in his own country do
> not permit the development of individuality.
> The soul of the country is weakened by cen-
> turies of useless struggle and broken
> treaties, and individual initiative is para-
> lysed by the influence and admonitions of
> the church, while its body is manacled by
> the police, the tax office, and the garri-
> son. No one who has any self-respect stays
> in Ireland, but flees afar as though from a
> country that has undergone the visitation of
> an angered Jove [CWJJ, p. 171]

And in a less sympathetic moment, Joyce would write to Stanislaus:

> I loathe Ireland and the Irish. They them-
> selves stare at me in the street though I
> was born among them. Perhaps they read my
> hatred of them in my eyes. I see nothing on
> every side of me but the image of the
> adulterous priest and his servants and of
> sly deceitful women.[13]

Yet despite Joyce's "political" obsession with the alleged devastation of the Irish psyche, paradoxi-cally, he refrained from writing fiction that would serve primarily as a mouthpiece for the Sein Fein, the IRA, the socialists, or for any other would-be liberation group. He praised the Irish writer Mangan for literary detachment from political diatribes:

8

. . . he refused to collaborate with the
English newspapers or reviews; although he
was the spiritual focus of his time, he
refused to prostitute himself to the rabble
or make himself the loud speaker of politi-
cians. He was one of those strange abnormal
spirits who believe that their artistic life
should be nothing more than a true and con-
tinual revelation of their spiritual life,
who believe that their inner life is so
valuable that they have no need of popular
support, and thus abstain from proffering
confessions of faith, who believe, in sum,
that the poet is sufficient in himself, the
heir and preserve of a secular patrimony,
who therefore has no urgent need to become a
shouter, or a preacher, or a perfumer [CWJJ,
p. 148].

In A Portrait of the Artist as a Young Man, frus-
trated Stephen echoed Joyce's sentiments to Cranly:

. . . I will not serve that in which I no
longer believe whether it call itself my
home, my fatherland or my church: and I
will try to express myself in some mode of
life or art as freely as I can and as wholly
as I can, using for my defence the only arms
I allow myself to use--silence, exile, and
cunning [p. 519].

Ellison's dogmatic refusal to write protest
literature stems partly from this Joycean cunning,
but, in actuality, both Joyce and Ellison were
writing more complex protest novels which focus not
only on the politics of one culture but on the
"unconscious politics" of the universal human urge to
dominance that crisscrosses all races. For both
writers, the racism that was closest to their lives
only served as a microcosm of that unconscious politics. And for the maturer Joyce, as for Ellison and
Wright, political change and transcendence of the
nightmare of history could only be adjunct to existential transformations of individuals who could
articulate and purge their regressive impulses from
the unconscious, who could escape the stereotyped
roles which defined them at the expense of their
inner drive for self-realization: roles which cast

them on the bill of the dramatis personae of the
nightmare. Ellison depicts Stephen (although not
Joyce) as a misguided egoist who must discover this
existential truth as Jack recalls his own school
days:

Perhaps it was something that Woodridge had
said in the literature class back at
college. I could see him vividly, half-
drunk on words and full of contempt and
exaltation, pacing before the blackboard
chalked with quotations from Joyce and Yeats
and Sean O'Casey; thin, nervous, neat,
pacing as though he walked a high wire of
meaning upon which no one of us would ever
dare venture. I could hear him. "Stephen's
problem, like ours, was not actually one of
creating the uncreated conscience of his
race, but of creating the uncreated
features of his face. Our task is that of
making ourselves individuals. The
conscience of a race is the gift of its
individuals who see, evaluate, record . . .
We create the race by creating ourselves and
then to our great astonishment we will have
created something far more important. We
will have created a culture. Why waste time
creating a conscience for something that
doesn't exist? For, you see, blood and skin
do not think!" [IM, pp. 345-46][14]

Ellison, whose anti-hero Jack nearly kills a man
for ignoring him, and Wright, with his chilling
portraits of men such as Bigger and Fred, who seem
reduced to the bare id, both moved to the concept of
universal man because they knew that the brutal urges
for dominance, the "general paralysis of the insane,"
as Joyce put it, were latent in all men. For these
writers, it was these innate or acquired urges that
drew the bottom line of history. Stephen's admission
of his own inner drives serves as an epiphany of this
universality in Ulysses. In "Proteus" Stephen
realizes: "Famine, plague and slaughters. Their
blood is in me their lusts my waves. I moved among
them on the frozen Liffey, that I, a changeling among
the spluttering resin fires."[15] In "Scylla and
Charybdis" Stephen contemplates Shakespeare's
creative genius and the stuff of the human mind in
general:

10

Every life is many days, day after day. We
walk through ourselves, meeting robbers,
ghosts, giants, old men, wives, widows,
brothers-in-love. But always meeting ourselves. The playwright who wrote the folio
of this world and wrote it badly (He gave us
light first and the sun two days later), the
lord of things as they are whom the most
Roman of catholics call dio boia, hangman
god, is doubtless all in all in all of us,
ostler and butcher, and would be bawd and
cuckold too but that in the economy of
heaven, foretold by Hamlet, there are no
more marriages, glorified man, an
androgynous angel, being a wife unto
himself. [p. 213]

As we shall discover, these writers realized that
true morality could only come out of a downward
descent into universal man. Possible transcendence
of the violent urges of the "ding idself" could
result only after the existential and introspective
descent and not before, only after a leap largely
motivated by the systems of Hegel and Freud.

If Freud argued finally that urges for parricide
and incest appeared to be innate archetypes, Hegel
before him x-rayed the heart of darkness from a
slightly different position. Hegel's famous and
tremendously influential division of man as well as
classes of men into the polarities "master and
servant" in the "Lordship and Bondage" section of The
Phenomenology of the Spirit, greatly influenced 20th
century writers including Joyce, Ellison and Wright.
This dialectical man came to replace Prometheus as
the dominant image of human desire. Gunther Anders
explains:

. . . What is decisive in this new symbol is
the "pluralization" and its inherent
"antagonism": that "Man" is now seen as a
pair of men; that the individual (who, as a
metaphysical self-made man, had fought a
Promethean struggle against the Gods) has
now been replaced by men who fight each
other for domination. It is they who are
now regarded as reality; for "to be" now
means "to dominate" and to struggle for

11

domination; and they alone are seen as the "motor of time": for time is history; and history, in the eyes of dialectical philosophy, owes its movement exclusively to antagonism (between man and man or class and class); so exclusively, that at the moment when these antagonisms came to an end, history itself would cease too.[16]

So the struggle between the master-servant pair not only symbolized the class stuggle of history, but it was put forth as a microcosm of the warring antagonistic impulses of the individual as well. The oppressed, then, can put on the hat of the oppressor; the gentle individual can suddenly emerge as a tyrant. Yet for Joyce, Ellison and Wright, as for Hegel, the tendency toward dominance inherent in the individual can be neutralized, transcended, through introspection. In "Lordship and Bondage" Hegel described four stages which the "bonded self" must ideally encounter in the journey of self-discovery.

He must first experience stoicism and resist being crushed emotionally by the dominance that is directed toward him; secondly, he must experience skepticism as he doubts the right of the dominating party to relegate him to inferiority; thirdly, the skepticism he has directed outward at his master must be directed inward while he introspects his own urges; and then his own desires for revenge must be examined objectively. In himself he finds all the urges of the master and the servant. Fourthly, the hero must strive for transcendence of negative urges, toward Hegel's "rational consciousness," which obviates that he control the urge to dominance and accept, as Stephen has it, that he is "all in all."[17] The reader's understanding of this introspective process is crucial to interpret the ordeals of many fictional heroes of Joyce, Ellison and Wright, as we shall discover in Chapter IV.

The impact of Joycean themes on the fiction of Ellison and Wright began to emerge during Ellison's and Wright's early association. Michel Fabre, one of Wright's biographers, mentions that Wright studied both **A Portrait** and <u>Ulysses</u> in 1935.[18] Ellison acknowledged that Wright advised him to read Joyce's

12

works. He took the advice and studied Joyce in
Dayton, Ohio in 1937.[19] Fabre describes the early
days of Ellison's and Wright's friendship:

> Ralph Ellison had just graduated from
> Tuskegee Institute and, despite his interest
> in contemporary literature, was then most
> drawn to sculpture and music. In Wright's
> work he had been able to discover for the
> first time in a black poet's writing the
> sensitivity and technique of modern poetry.
> After reading "I Have Seen Black Hands" and
> "Between the World and Me," he asked
> Langston Hughes to put him in touch with
> Wright. They met almost as soon as Wright
> reached New York and began a literary
> friendship that lasted for years. Surprised
> by Ellison's intellectual curiosity and
> talents, Wright was only too happy to act as
> mentor to this slightly younger man so pre-
> disposed to admire him. Ellison had studied
> literary technique for some time and had
> even written some poetry, but he had never
> dreamed of becoming a writer. The two met
> often that year to exchange views on litera-
> ture. Wright recommended his own favorite
> authors--Conrad, Joyce, James, Eliot and
> Malraux--but he was perhaps less of an ini-
> tiator than a stimulus, since Ellison had
> already read a great deal.[20]

Wright had enjoyed extensive discussions of
Joyce's Ulysses at John Reed Club meetings in
Chicago, and in a 1944 article in New Masses Ellison
chided most of the writers of the Harlem Renaissance
for ignoring American folklore, and the philosophical
and stylistic innovations introduced by Joyce and
the then, avant-garde American writers:

> Aside from ignoring the folk source of all
> vital American Negro art, the fiction of
> this group was chiefly lyrical, and for the
> most part was unaware of the technical
> experimentation and direction being taken by
> American writing as the result of the work--
> itself a product and symptom at the breakup
> of a world--of such writers as Joyce, Stein,
> Anderson, and Hemingway. It was not

addressed to Negro readers, but to a white audience that had recently "discovered" the Negro in its quest to make spiritual readjustments to a world in transition.[21]

In an interview with Richard J. Stern in Shadow and Act, Ellison reminisced over his first contact with Wright in New York City:

Stern: "At that time were you dissatisfied with the sort of work Wright was doing?"

Ellison: "Dissatisfied? I was too amazed with watching the process of creation. I didn't understand quite what was going on, but by this time I had talked with Wright a lot and he was very conscious of technique. He talked about it not in terms of mystification but as writing know-how. 'You have to go about learning to write consciously. People have talked about such and such a problem and have written about it. You must learn how Conrad, Joyce, Dostoievsky get their effects. . . ." [p. 15]

During his short appointment with the Federal Writers' Project, Wright discussed the impact of Joyce on several black artists. He certainly included Ellison and himself among them, as Fabre notes.[22] In 1941 Ellison was pondering Stephen Dedalus' zeal in A Portrait "to forge in the smithy of my soul the uncreated conscience of my race" when he wrote of Native Son: "There must be no stepping away from the artistic and social achievements of Native Son if the Negro writer is to create the consciousness of his oppressed nation." [23] In the same article Ellison called for a new Negro consciousness in a new American society:

The new Negro consciousness must of necessity go beyond the highest point of bourgeois consciousness and work toward the creation of conditions in which it might integrate and stabilize itself; it demands new institutions, a new society.[24]

In his 1945 essay "Richard Wright's Blues," Ellison compared Richard's rejection of the provincialism of

14

black American life to "Joyce's rejection of Dublin in A Portrait of the Artist." [SA, p. 78] Black Boy was also contrasted to Stephen Hero in the same essay:

Thus the drama of Black Boy lies in its depiction of what occurs when Negro sensibility attempts to fulfill itself in the undemocratic South. Here it is not the individual that is the immediate focus, as in Joyce's Stephen Hero, but that upon which his sensibility was nourished. [SA, p. 82]

Fabre notes the influence of A Portrait on Wright's Black Boy and Lawd Today:

The power and sincerity of Black Boy had few predecessors, and the quality of the writing made it a new Portrait of the Artist as a Young Man. The influence of Joyce may not have been obvious, as with Lawd Today, but the parallel immediately noted between his concerns and those of Wright was justified by many common features in their work: the protagonists' realization of belonging to a minority; the horror of a religion haunted by sex, and the difficulty of escaping from it; the conflict between obedience and liberty.[25]

Direct testimony from Ellison reveals how he continued to incorporate Joycean themes into his own artistic vision. Ellison candidly admitted his own debt to A Portrait in the creation of Invisible Man: "Look at it this way. The book is a series of reversals. It is the portrait of the artist as a rabble-rouser, thus the various mediums of expression" [SA, p. 179]. In the same interview he acknowledged the influence of Eliot, Joyce and Hemingway in his own attempt to reveal mythic level of modern life:

I learned a few things from Eliot, Joyce and Hemingway, but not how to adapt them. When I started writing, I knew that in both The Waste Land and Ulysses ancient myth and ritual were used to give form and significance to the material; but it took me a few years to realize that the myths and rites which we find functioning in our everyday lives could be used in the same way. [SA, p. 174]

As we shall discover in Chapter IV, Ellison and Wright were intrigued by the skill of both Joyce and Eliot to employ a "double vision," to intuit ancient, universal archetypes in the pedestrian events of modern life. And Ellison, more so than Wright, was fascinated in their musical, syncopated uses of language. Responding to John Hersey's observation that Ellison has himself cited his debt to "Joyce, Eliot, Dostoevski, Hemingway, Stein, Malraux and others," Ellison has explained:

> It is best, of course, when they don't show themselves directly, but they are there in many ways. Joyce and Eliot, for instance, made me aware of the playful possibilities of language. You look at a page of Finnegans Wake and see references to all sorts of American popular music, yet the context gives it an extension from the popular back to the classical and beyond. This is just something that Joyce teaches you that you can do, and you can abstract the process and apply it to a frame of reference which is American and historical, and it can refer to class, it can refer to the fractions and frictions of color, to popular and folk culture--it can do many things.[26]

This study will present more direct acknowledgements of Joycean influences as we proceed, but for now it is necessary to examine the many ties which Joyce, Ellison and Wright discovered between the ordeals of the oppressed in America, Ireland and Africa--the complex black-Irish connection.

Ellison's and Wright's interest in Irish history and in the Joycean, fictional, Celtic melancholy blues appears to have been rewarded by endless analogies with the American and African predicaments. And such an interest by historians, as well, helps to clarify these analogies. Indeed, the dreaded Penal Laws, first passed in the 16th Century and continuously resurrected by England to throttle the Irish, also helped to serve as a blueprint for future European slave codes and England's general imperialistic attitude toward future colonies.   Donald S. Connery summarizes some of the more drastic repressions in the Penal Laws of 1695:

Catholics were deprived of the right to vote or hold office. They were forbidden to bear arms. They were barred from teaching, trading and entering the professions. Catholic estates, because of new restrictions on ownership and inheritance, were broken into ever smaller portions. A Catholic owning a house worth more than five pounds could have it taken from him at that price by any Protestant. Catholic schools were forbidden and the Catholic clergy outlawed. Any bishop found in the country was liable to be hanged, drawn and quartered. The Catholic Church went underground. Priests said Mass in the fields while lookouts kept watch for the authorities, and children were taught clandestinely in the "hedge schools." More than ever, the Irish became dodgers of the law, ingratiating talkers and masters of deception.[27]

A Lord Chancellor of the period concluded that "the law does not suppose any such person to exist as an Irish Roman Catholic."[28] Indeed, de Toqueville could say in the 19th Century that many of the Irish Catholics he observed lived in more pitiful conditions than black slaves in America. The Penal Laws, which were modified over the centuries, became the backbone of the English "experiment" in Ireland. The experiment would be tried over and over again with varying degrees of severity by many European countries in their relations with Africa, America and Asia.

Joyce followed the ongoing experiment as it surfaced in the Congo Free State:

I find it rather naive to heap insults on England for her misdeeds in Ireland. A conqueror cannot be casual, and for so many centuries the Englishman has done in Ireland only what the Belgian is doing today in the Congo Free State, and what the Nipponese dwarf will do tomorrow in other lands. [CWJJ, p. 166]

Joyce would continue to link European imperialism in Africa with English policies toward Ireland. Perhaps the best example is the African Alaki of Abeakuta parody in "Cyclops":

A delegation of the chief cotton magnates of Manchester was presented yesterday to His Majesty the Alaki of Abeakuta by Gold Stick in Waiting, Lord Walkup on Eggs, to tender to His Majesty the heartfelt thanks of British traders for the facilities afforded them in his dominions. The delegation partook of luncheon at the conclusion of which the dusky potentate in the course of a happy speech, freely translated by the British chaplain, the reverend Ananias Praisegod Barebones, tendered his best thanks to Massa Walkup and emphasized the cordial relations existing between Abeakuta and the British Empire, stating that he treasured as one of his dearest possesions an illuminated bible, the volume of the word of God and the secret of England's greatness, graciously presented to him by the white chief woman, the great squaw Victoria, with a personal dedication from the august hand of the Royal Donor. The Alaki then drank a lovingcup of firstshot usquebaugh to the toast <u>Black and White</u> from the skull of his immediate predecessor in the dynasty Kakachakachak, surnamed Forty Warts, after which he visited the chief factory of Cottonopolis and signed his mark in the visitor's book, subsequently executing an old Abeakutic wardance, in the course of which he swallowed several knives and forks, amid hilarious applause from the girl hands. [p. 334]

F. L. Radford has discussed the black-Irish linkage in this double-edged parody noting not only that the African King is a reflection of King Edward VII, but also that the obsequiousness of the black king toward the English is not unlike the obeisance of the Irish toward their own conquerers:

. . . on one side, the Alaki is a comic Edward on tour: on the other, his messages

18

of loyalty and gratitude are not very different from those presented to Edward by various Irish officials. The implied judgement is also dual, the imperial monarch is merely an Alaki of Abeakuta writ large; and the Irish have no right to ridicule the African Chieftain for they too treat Edward as a great white father. . . .[29]

The barflies in "Cyclops" continue to discuss the plight of Africa, and the name of Roger Casement is brought up:

> "Well," says J.J., "if they're any worse than those Belgians in the Congo Free State they must be bad. Did you read that report by a man what's this his name is?"
> "Casement," says the citizen. "He's an Irishman."
> "Yes, that's the man." says J.J. "Raping the women and girls and flogging the natives on the belly to squeeze all the red rubber they can out of the them."
> [p. 335]

Casement had exposed atrocities committed in the Congo under King Leopold of Belgium, and, as Radford notes, the implication is that similar atrocities have been committed in Ireland, and Casement's martyrdom in the Easter Rising of 1916 will add yet another.[30]

If oppression denied civil rights and fostered a slave mentality in many of its Irish victims, it did so with the aid of psychological reinforcements, those ubiquitous anti-Irish stereotypes, which to Ellison and Wright must have resounded with an analogous, off beat rhythm. The formation of these anti-Irish stereotypes resulted partly from the clash of two different value systems. Patrick O'Farrell describes the culture the British conquerors discovered in Ireland:

> They [the Irish] cultivated no land. They were nomadic. They had no money system. Their relationship one to another was highly personalized. They had no towns. They slept in the open, or in wretched huts. They talked in Gaelic. Their appearance,

half-naked, long hair, clad in animal skins, always armed, was wild.[31]

To the British, the rude qualities of Irish life beyond the Pale became equated with the life-styles of African cultures and American Indians. Margaret Hodgen explains:

> While sovereigns of the realm were struggling to pacify the tribal Celts and the Puritan colonies in North America were wrestling with the Red Indian for his soul and his lands, all frontier antagonists looked more or less alike. . . they were enemies, they were ignorant, and they were animal-like. . . the epithets used to describe the folk on Britain's Celtic border were interchangeable with those applied to the Negroes in Africa or to the Indians across the Atlantic.[32]

In "Cyclops" the citizen argues that if it weren't for Irish resistance "there would soon be as few Irish in Ireland as redskins in America" [p. 329]. L. P. Curtis reveals too that the British distortions involved in their perception of Irish Celts

> resembled in some respects the ways in which Englishmen formed their "image of Africa" before 1850. In both cases they mixed small fragments of reality with large amounts of what they wanted to believe about the indigenous peoples in order to arrive at a foregone conclusion based on their particular needs at the time.[33]

Unable to accept Irish, African or Native American culture as worthy of respect and of autonomous existence, the English sought to impose their culture and their stereotyped definitions of these alien cultures onto their new subjects.

Early in the dominance game, Sir William Fitzwilliam regarded his tenure of rule in Ireland as a form of banishment from civilization itself. He perceived himself as exiled "among unkind people, a people most accursed, who lusted after every sin. Murder and incest were everyday matters, and a lying spirit brooded over the land."[34] In 1567 Sir Henry Sidney reinforced the bestial/sexual stereotype:

Matrimony among them is no more regarded in effect than conjunction between unreasonable beasts. Perjury, robbery, and murder counted allowable. Finally, I cannot find that they make any conscience of sin...[35]

The psychology of racism, which Ellison and Wright would explore in their fiction and essays, was well developed in the 16th Century. The projection of the oppressor's repressed sexual fantasies and desires onto the oppressed to solve the oppressor's half acknowledged guilt for his own desire had started in Ireland and would be exported throughout the colonial world. And these British rulers rarely understood that much of the behavior they observed resulted from their own destabilization of the once intact cultures. The Irish were asked to conform to English standards, and yet they were judged as inadequate to do so. A double bind had begun.

The stereotyping continued. Disraeli wrote in The Times in April 1836 that the Irish

... hate our free and fertile isle. They hate our order, our civilization, our enterprising industry, our sustained courage, our decorous liberty, our pure religion. This wild, reckless, indolent, uncertain and superstitious race have no sympathy with the English character. Their fair idea of human felicity is an alternation of clannish broils and coarse idolatry. Their history describes an unbroken circle of bigotry and blood.[36]

In 1860 Charles Kingsly likened the Irish to "white chimpanzees," revealing a variation on a stereotype that occurred obsessively in the British press:

... I am haunted by the human chimpanzees I saw along that hundred miles of horrible country. I don't believe they are our fault. I believe there are not only many more of them than of old, but that they are happier, better, more comfortably fed and lodged under our rule than they ever were. But to see white chimpanzees is dreadful; if they were black, one would not feel it so much, but their skins, except where tanned with exposure, are as white as ours.[37]

21

Stephen recalls this stereotype combined with that of
the "stage Irishman" in Stephen Hero as "the drunken
Irishman, the baboon-faced Irishman that we see in
Punch."[38]

Ellison and Wright may have discussed the stage
stereotype, which Wright argued was frequently projected onto the oppressed of the world. In 12
Million Black Voices he compared its occurrence in
black America and in Ireland:

> We lose ourselves in violent forms of dances
> in our ballrooms. The faces of the white
> world, looking on in wonder and curiosity,
> declare: "Only the Negro can play!" But
> they are wrong. They misread us. We are
> able to play in this fashion because we have
> been excluded, left behind; we play in this
> manner because all excluded folk play. The
> English say of the Irish, just as America
> says of us, that only the Irish can play,
> that they laugh through their tears. But
> every powerful nation says this of the folk
> whom it oppresses in justification of that
> oppression.[39]

In Chapter III the complex issue of the theater/
cinema consciousness among the oppressed will be examined. It will be revealed that Joyce's metaphor of
the filmic, dreamy consciousness of the Irish
influenced Ellison's description of Harlem's
"actors," for in Finnegans Wake Dublin becomes "A
phantom city, phaked of philim pholk, bowed and
souled for a four of hundreds of manhood. . . ."
where actors, film folk, role play through life in
search of an identity.[40] And, indeed, we shall
discover that Ellison's description of Jack's
surreal, cinematic consciousness is partly derived
from Finnegans Wake.

The Irish ordeal, then, did not go unnoticed by
Ellison and Wright, for their fiction and essays
include frequent Irish references. Both seemed to
have felt that the Irish Catholic could come closest
to understanding the black experience in America. If
Ellison questioned the validity of the black-Jewish
connection, he would show less skepticism toward
black-Irish parallels. In "A Very Stern Discipline"
Ellison objected to a close comparison of the
experience Jews and black Americans:

22

I think, however, that the parallel is much too facile. Jewish writers are more familiar with literature as a medium of expression. Their history provides for a close identification with writers who were, and are, Jewish, even when they wrote or write in languages other than Yiddish or Hebrew; and this even when that identification rests simply on a shared religious tradition and hardly on any other cultural ground whatsoever. It reminds me of our attempts to claim Pushkin and Dumas as Negroes. By contrast, neither Negro American expression nor religion has been primarily literary. We are by no means, as is said of the Jews, "people of the Book"-- not that I see this as a matter for regret. For we have a wider freedom of selection. We took much from the ancient Hebrews and we do share, through Christianity, the values embodied in the literature of much of the world. But our expression has been oral as against "literary."[41]

Sartre had tried to link the Jewish and black ordeals in "Black Orpheus," but Ellison and Wright revealed less inclination. In a 1972 interview Ellison reinforced his apparent choice of the Irish as candidate for the most analogous of oppressed groups to suffering black masses in America:

In order to have a human society you are going to have to have some form of victimization. Somebody is always going to be designated as the symbol of evil. They may be lynched in a realistic rite of scapegoating, or scapegoated verbally, or scapegoated in terms of where they can live, how high they can rise in the society. This is the human way. I suspect that as this society matures we're going to find ways of designating the scapegoat on a basis other than race. We no longer designate him on the basis of his late entry into the society, as with the Irish migrants in the late nineteenth and early twentieth centuries. Just as the Irish are no longer designated as scapegoats and have even become a cult because of the Kennedys, you

are going to have other modifications. And
I am hoping as this society matures that
whatever the scapegoat is going to be, he's
not going to be black and it's not going to
be based upon race. And I think that as
that happens we are going to come to grips
with the fact that we are a class society
but that the possession of culture is much
more important in the scheme of things than
a man's skin or his background.[42]

Invisible Man goes on to designate Native Americans,
Blacks and Irish-Americans as the dispossessed of
America in a brotherhood propaganda poster:

It was a symbolic poster of a group of
heroic figures: An American Indian couple,
representing the dispossessed past; a blond
brother (in overalls) and a leading Irish
sister, representing the dispossessed
present; and Brother Tod Clifton and a young
white couple (it had been felt unwise simply
to show Clifton and the girl) surrounded by
a group of children of mixed races, representing the future, a color photograph of
bright skin texture and smooth contrast.
[p. 376]

The poster projects an integrated future of which
Brother Jack could never approve in smoke-filled
rooms. Earlier, in Ellison's short story "Slick
Gonna Learn," Slick Williams is roughed up by several
policemen for assaulting one of them. An Irish truck
driver picks him up and Slick feels a nervous
brotherhood with him.

Wright pushed this possible brotherhood further.
In American Hunger he recalls an Irish friend he met
in a Chicago post office:

While sorting mail in the post office, I met
a young Irish chap whose sensibilities
amazed me. . . . The Irish chap and I had
read a lot in common and we laughed at the
same sacred things. He was as cynical as I
was regarding uplift and hope, and we were
proud of having escaped what we called the
"childhood disease of metaphysical fear."
I was introduced to the Irish chap's friends

and we formed a "gang" of Irish, Jewish, and Negro wits who poked fun at government, the masses, statesmen, and political parties.[43]

In Black Boy the Irish-American Falk is the only white man who is decent to Richard at The Commercial Appeal in Memphis. Falk gives Richard a library card so that Richard can check out H. L. Mencken's works from the library. Richard describes him:

There remained only one man whose attitude did not fit into an anti-Negro category, for I had heard the white man refer to him as a "Pope lover." He was an Irish Catholic and was hated by the white Southerners.[44]

In Native Son Wright continued to solidify a black-Irish connection when he revealed the sentiments of the Dalton's maid Peggy to Bigger: "'I'm Irish you know,' she said. 'My folks in the old country feel about England like the colored folks feel about this country. So I know something about colored people.'"[45] The promise of communication and identification between Irish and black Americans was perhaps made more likely in the imaginations of Ellison and Wright because of Joyce's world-wide exposé of the oppression of blacks and because of more analogies Joyce noted, often with a bluesy humor, between the Irish and blacks in Africa and America.

In A Portrait Joyce chose to use the Greek myth of Daedalus and Icarus to provide a comic interface with Stephen and the "dead all of us" Irish. But Stephen is no Daedalus; he's a "lap-wing" Icarus instead, which he painfully admits in Ulysses. [p. 211] In any case, this myth recalls the Ethiopian myth of Phaethon. According to Winthrop Jordan, this Ethiopian myth offered one of the explanations of the way in which the Negro acquired his dark, sunburnt complexion.[46] Joyce's probable awareness of the analogies between these myths, their variations of flying too close to the sun, might be glossed over if it were not for the many often comic innuendoes that type Stephen, Bloom, HCE and Shem, and by extension the Irish, as the Negro of Europe. The Phaethon - Daedalus - Dedalus link is a comic metaphor that threads through Joyce's fiction and reaches its bluesy denouement in Finnegans Wake. In

25

Ulysses the all-purpose scapegoat Bloom is likened to
a black panther in black clothes, the dark cat who so
unsettles the dreams of the Englishman Haines.
Haines would kill such panthers in his sleep. Bloom
appears also as a "bloody dark horse" to the intol-
erant Dubliners, and his devilish dress raises the
question ". . . who the sooty hell's the johnny in
the black duds?" [pp. 335, 427] Bloom is part Jewish
and this somewhat accounts for his association with
blackness and "evil" in the minds of many anti-
Semitic Dubliners, but Bloom's geneology is such a
confused Irish stew of religions and nationalities
that his lingering Jewishness cannot alone account
for his darkness. To confuse matters more, William
York Tindall notes that the panther is a symbol for
Christ according to Medieval bestiaries.[47]   Black
Bloom becomes a most chameleon, slippery, Chaplinesque figure while he lives "quadruple" in "Doublin."
This "black sheep" comes to symbolize all the
scapegoats of the world.

The ballad of the Croppy Boy is another motif
which unites Irish and black suffering in *Ulysses*.
Harry Blamires explains:

The ballad tells a story of betrayal. The
Croppy Boy has lost his father at the Siege
of Ross and his brothers at Gorey. The
"last of his name and race," he seeks a
priest in order to make a final confession
before himself going to join the rebels at
Wexford. He is tricked into confessing to a
redcoat in priestly disguise, and executed
on the strength of his own statements.[48]

Bloom is also the last of his race since his son
Rudy has died. Blamires further notes the analogy
between the Croppy Boy and the burned American
"Sambo" who appears in "Cyclops."[49] The racist Irish
barflies relish the newspaper story:

And another one: Black Beast Burned in
Omaha, Ga. A lot of Deadwood Dicks in
slouch hats and they firing at a sambo
strung up on a tree with his tongue out and
a bonfire under him. Gob, they out to drown
him in the sea after and electrocute and
crucify him to make sure of their job.
[p. 328]

In Finnegans Wake Shem takes over Bloom's mask of
the black sheep. Shem "passed for baabaa black sheep
til he grew white woo woo wooly . . . ." [p. 133]
For notorious Shem is known as "this hamboned dog
poet" and the Ireland of his father, "his joawdry's
purgatory was more than a nigger bloke could bear,
hemiparalysed by the tong warfare and all the
shemozzle. . . ." [p. 177] Adeline Glasheen notes
that Hambone is a black character out of an American
comic strip.[50] And the "bear" pun would not go unnoticed by Ellison. Shem and HCE are also described as
"nigger blokes" whom Ireland would like to
incarcerate. [p.177] Shem, as his predessesor Bloom,
is of indeterminate identity--a "semi-semitic seren-
dipitist, you . . . Europasianized afferyank.'"
[p. 191] Africa, Europe and Asia are all combined in
this thin portrait both of internationalized Joyce
and the chromosomologically diverse Irish in his
comic portrait of Shem, the "faynix coalprince," who
will one day rise from his coalhole, who is condemned
to sing the "night blues" of the improvisational
Wake. [pp. 113, 475, 608] Shem is also "this vague
of visibilities" in "the wake of the blakesheep,"
when William Blake, who probed racism in "The Little
Black Boy" and who wrote of human apocalyptic rebirth
through mystical experience, is combined with the
invisible scapegoat black sheep. [p. 608] The ethnically mixed-up characters of Ulysses and the Wake
may have also influenced Ellison's portrait of
Senator Sunraider in Ellison's chapter "And Hickman
Arrives" for his forthcoming novel. This confused
Southerner, who finally acknowledges Daddy Hickman as
his foster-father after the assasination, is as confused as any Joycean character.[51] He persecutes
blacks, and yet his speech and mannerisms are derived
from a forgotten emulation of Hickman. Susan L.
Blake has noted Sunraider's similarity to Joe
Christmas in Faulkner's Light in August, but his
comic-pathetic likeness to HCE, Bloom, and Shem echo
as well in Ellison's portrait of this confused white
racist politician who represents a New England state.
Of the symbolic meaning of Sunraider, Blake
concludes: His "apparently bizarre relationship with
Hickman is actually the archetypal relationship of
white America to the black: something more than a
brotherhood--an identity, perhaps--denied."[52]

    Indeed "Funnycoon's wake" occurs in the dream
landscape of Dublin, a town earlier known as

27

"Blackpool" as well as "Vieus Von DVbLin" which "twas one of dozedeams a darkies ding in dewood," when the hibernating oppressed of Dublin are linked to the dreamy blacks of the American South and the sexual stereotype of the oppressed ("ding" is German for "penis" and it also stands here for "dream"). [pp. 309, 293] Shem or "Old Sooty" sings the blues of the Irish Negro of Europe, the blues of Finn, who, as Ellison's Jack the Bear, or as the Wakes' "Furbear" totem god, must bear the indignities of hibernation until the day arrives when blacks and Irishmen fail to serve as scapegoats. For Shem is comically likened to a scapegoat in a mock letter from Stanislaus. Stanislaus charges that Shem, with his "africot lips," is a "Negoist Cabler, of this city, whom tis never to name, my said brother, the skipgod. . . ." when Stanislaus likens his brother to a black cabinet-maker, a black Christ and scapegoat-figure. [pp. 488-89] Lastly, HCE is given the title of Negro of Europe which is not so subtly combined with the sex drive of a chimp: "Hip champouree! Hiphip champouree! O you longtailed blackman, polk it up behind me! Hip champouree! Hiphip champouree!" [p. 236]

It is doubtful that Ellison failed to discover these puns and the black-Irish analogy in general when he carefully studied the Wake. Ellison's "bear" pun in Invisible Man, especially, may have been derived from American folklore as well as from the bear image in Irish folklore. Glasheen explains how St. Patrick drove out the snakes from Ireland when he introduced the Christian suppression of idolatry, but the bear, or Mahan (the "man servant") would keep alive the spirit of the snakes, of the Pagan-Celtic world view, much as Shem and Jack the Bear nurture the inner self with its jazzy syncopation in their respective coalholes.[53] For they hear a music of invisibility that defies the patterning urges of the mechanizers of consciousness, the modern day St. Patricks.

An etymology that echoes the Phaethon-Daedalus link as well, and the etymology of the name "Shem," must have also intrigued Ellison. For "Shem" is derived from Cham or Ham, the dispossessed, exiled son of Noah. Curious Ham, who caught Noah with his "ark open" as Joyce puts it, is comically reincarnated in the Wake as Mohammed, Ishmael, Hamlet,

Satan, Telemachus, and, of course, poor Mahan, the oppressed Irish bear.[54]   Could Ellison have missed the arrest of Shem (Sham) in Ireland by a KKK man? Shem, the comic "hambone" of Europe, must record the psychological damage resulting when the British helped turn the Hill of Howth into a KKK "Hoodie Head." [p. 4] And could Ellison have overlooked the still prevalent slur on the Irish of Spanish descent as the "Black-Irish"?

This summary does not exhaust the black-Irish linkage in Joyce's last novel; instead it tries to simulate a reading that Ellison and Wright may well have given the Wake. The black-Irish connection is a powerful one in Ireland that extends beyond litera- ture.   It appeared in Ulster on the streets of Derry when Bernadette Devlin and the civil-rights fighters, both Catholic and Protestant, joined to sing black American protest songs such as "We Shall Overcome" in homage to Martin Luther King and to his battle for human decency.

The Joyce-Ellison connection reveals more of its complexities and rewards when it is understood that both Ellison and Wright fashioned the following sen- timents of Stephen Dedalus into the ordeals of many of their heroes:

"The soul is born," he said vaguely, "first in those moments I told you of.   It has a slow and dark birth, more mysterious than the birth of the body. When the soul of man is born is this country there are nets flung at it to hold it back from flight. You talk to me of nationality, language, religion.   I shall try to fly by those nets." [P, p. 469]

Stephen adds yet another net when he discusses aesthetics with Lynch:

"Let us take woman," said Stephen.
"Let us take her!" said Lynch fervently.
"The Greek, the Turk, the Chinese, the Copt, the Hottentot," said Stephen, "all admire a different type of female beauty. That seems to be a maze out of which we can- not escape." [P, p. 475]

Ellison and Wright would also entrap their characters
in all of these nets, and in still another which
Joyce, too, had set everywere in the robot city of
Dublin: the net of the lingering 18th century mechanistic world view. Much as Stephen, Bloom, Molly,
Shem and the other Dubliners would attempt to
transcend these nets, so also would the heroes of
Ellison's and Wright's short stories and novels opt
for freedom.

The first net, nationality, is dangerously
interwoven with religious and ethnic chauvinism.
Stephen confesses bitterly: "I am the servant of two
masters. . . . The Imperial British State . . . and
the holy Roman and apostolic church." [U, p. 20]
Much has been written of Joyce's and his heroes'
repudiation of the negative side of nationality and
religion, of the quest to rediscover a primal, positive sexual base in an otherwise blood-drenched
primitive religion, of the desire to escape the negative forms of repression by priest and king so that
human autonomy and authenticity might be restored to
the artist and to the Irish. So much commentary has
been generated, in fact, that a selective discussion
of the Joycean hero's struggle with this conglom-
erate, and the apparent impact of this struggle on
the imaginations of Ellison and Wright is needed.

For Joyce, Irish Catholicism, British imperialism
and the confused heroics of much Irish nationalism
were all haunted by a grim specter: the dio boia, or
Hangman God, that jealous, vengeful, anti-sexual,
infantile projection of the father who demands the
sacrifice of free thought and sexual release as well
as blood sacrifice and martydom when fused either
with imperialism or defensive Irish nationalism. For
Joyce, Irish culture revealed a shared infantilism
that was riddled with an often repressed oedipal and
fratricidal rage. Much as Freud in Totem and Taboo
(1913), Joyce viewed the Christ story as a projection
of the family drama: the son rebels against the
father in order to destroy the Old Law with the
spirit of the New Covenant. Fearing castration, the
father must castrate the son in the symbolics of
crucifixion. Hence, the son's triumph over the Old
Law is marginal. The death of Christ does not ade-
quately remove the shared guilt over the parricidal
wish for the Christian. Despite the fact that Christ
hoped to end blood sacrifice, the oedipal drama con-

tinues in the hearts of men: The father fears the
maturity of the son, a son who would replace the
father not through identification and emulation, but
through the enactment of a repressed, parricidal
wish. At bottom, God is but an "exalted father,"
Christ, a rebellious son. Freud argues:

> In the Christian myth man's original sin is
> undoubtedly an offence against god the
> father, and if Christ redeems mankind from
> the weight of original sin by sacrificing
> his own life, he forces us to the conclusion
> that this sin was murder. According to the
> law of retaliation which is deeply rooted in
> human feeling, a murder can be atoned only
> by the sacrifice of another life; the self-
> sacrifice points to a blood guilt. And if
> this sacrifice of one's life brings about a
> reconciliation with god, the father, then
> the crime which must be expiated can only
> have been the murder of the father.[55]

If Christianity, on the psychological level, revealed
an attempt to neutralize parricidal wishes in the
hearts of men, Christ's symbolic rebellion and
castration could not sublimate these wishes and end
the oedipal struggle. Masochistic self-sacrifice
would continue through the centuries of the Christian
nightmare: guilt resulting from the unacknowledged
parricidal wish would fuel history. Old Yahweh would
demand his tribute.

Far from symbolizing the New Covenant, the Irish
Catholic Church was for Joyce the quarters of the dio
boia, the icy, Irish version of the Old Law
refashioned into that unique Irish puritanism. For
in Irish Catholicism Joyce saw the ironic triumph of
the father over the son and curiously enough over the
flesh and blood fathers of Ireland, over the
patriarchal family itself. A chilling conspiracy had
coddled the Irishman into projecting his own power
and authority onto that icy God. In Stephen Hero
Stephen tries to convince a bland Cranly that the
Christ story is really a primitive survival of the
scapegoat ritual celebrated now by an infantile
church, presided over by the Hangman God who holds
the sexuality of Irish women hostage. For Stephen,
Christ is really:

"An ugly little man who has taken into his
body the sins of the world. Something
between Socrates and a Gnostic Christ--a
Christ of the Dark Ages. That's what his
mission of redemption got for him: a
crooked ugly body for which neither God nor
man have pity. Jesus is on strange terms
with that father of his. His father seems
to me something of a snob. Do you notice
that he never notices his son publicly but
once--when Jesus is in full dress on the top
of Thabor?"
      "I don't like Holy Thursday much,"
said Cranly.
      "Neither do I. There are too many mam-
mas and daughters going chapel-hunting. The
chapel smells too much of flowers and hot
candles and women. Besides girls praying
put me off my stroke." [pp. 116-17]

Paradoxically, then, for Joyce and his Stephen the
Irish-Catholic Church was the territory of the
father, not the son, a father who would demand many
sacrifices from his children, a father who would
indeed insist that children remain children, that
fathers remain siblings.

      Richard Ellmann convincingly argues that Joyce
formed many of his judgments against church and state
after reading Michael Bakunin's God and the State
(1910) which lumped both nationalism and religion
together as vestiges of the sacrificial altar. Of
religion Bankunin argued:

      All religions are cruel, all founded on
      blood; for all rest principally on the idea
      of sacrifice--that is, on the perpetual
      immolation of humanity to the insatiable
      vengeance of divinity. In this blood
      mystery man is always the victim, and the
      priest--a man also, but a man privileged by
      grace--is the divine executioner.[56]

Joyce concurred. The triumph of the father image
survived in religion, imperialism and Irish nationalism; each was determined to usurp the authority of
men, to displace it onto the father's hatchet men,
the priest and king. In a hot exchange with Madden,
Stephen weds these usurpations with the Irish
priesthood, a holy police force:

"But Irishmen are fond of boasting that they are true to the traditions they receive in youth. How faithful all you fellows are to Mother Church! Why would you not be as faithful to the tradition of the helmet as to that of the tonsure?"

"We remain true to the Church because it is our national Church, the Church our people have suffered for and would suffer for again. The police are different. We look upon them as aliens, traitors, oppressors of the people."

"The old peasant down the country doesn't seem to be of your opinion when he counts over his greasy notes and says 'I'll put the priest on Tom an' I'll put the polisman on Mickey.'" [SH, p. 64]

Bloom echoes the sentiments of Stephen and Bakunin in "The Lotus Eaters":

The priest bent down to put it in her mouth, murmuring all the time. Latin. The next one. Shut your eyes and open your mouth. What? Corpus. Body. Corpse. Good idea the Latin. Stupifies them first. Hospice for the dying. They don't seem to chew it; only swallow it down. Rum idea: eating bits of a corpse why the cannibals cotton to it. [p. 80]

Bloom's morbid reflections continue when he contemplates the horrors of religion and a most recent embodiment of those horrors, the American Elijah Dowie, hustler-evangelist of the apocalyptic "sacrifice":

His slow feet walked him riverward, reading. Are you saved? All are washed in the blood of the lamb. God wants blood victim. Birth, hymen, martyr, war, foundation of a building, sacrifice, kidney burntoffering, druid's altars. Elijah is coming. Dr. John Alexander, restorer of the church in Zion, is coming. [pp. 151]

Later Bloom gives mock tribute to the dio boia in like manner. God is simply a "collector of prepuces" or foreskins. [p. 201] It is the vengeance of the

33

threatened father-god, complimented by the "son's" need for punishment for his unconscious parricidal wish, that are the central unconscious fantasies propping up the paternalistic church and state. Fearing the eventual surrender to the son, the paternal energy in government and religion must keep the son forever a dependent child, even if the act requires two unsynchronized police forces. The zeal with which the masochistic Dubliners regard martyrdom either for Church or political revolution really comes to symbolize for Joyce the unacknowledged wish to be punished by the dio boia whether god appears in the guise of the Pope or of King Edward VII. F. L. Radford has revealed how the sexually deflected "sacrifice" of the Croppy Boy serves as an epiphany for this immolation and for the representative attitude of Lynch that "Death is the highest form of life."[57] Joyce burlesques the sacrifice in the stage directions of "Circe":

> He jerks the rope, the assistants leap at the victims's legs and drag him downward, grunting: the croppy boy's tongue protrudes violently.
> . . . .
> He gives up the ghost. A violent erection of the hanged sends gouts of sperm spouting through his death clothes on to the cobblestones. Mrs. Bellingham, Mrs. Yelverton Barry and the Honourable Mrs. Mervyn Talboys rush forward with their handkerchiefs to sop it up. [p. 594]

Throughout Joyce's fiction, we discover that the Irishman has surrendered his authority as lawgiver, as father, as initiator of his children to the debased projection of true fatherhood, the dio boia. The payoff for this surrender, which has been managed by women and priests, becomes the false security of perpetual adolescense, intellectual and political servitude: the formula for paralysis, for the "unsubstantial father." Robert Scholes explores the results of religious usurpation in Joyce's delineation of the Irish character:

> Joyce felt--and his letters support the evidence of the works themselves--that it was precisely their religious orthodoxy,

34

combined with other sorts of "belatedness," that made the Irish so conscienceless. They had turned over the moral responsibility for their lives to their confessors and religious leaders. Thus their ability to react sensitively to moral problems, to make ethical discriminations--to use their consciences--had atrophied. In Dubliners he offered his countrymen his own counterpart to St. Ignatius' Spiritual Exercises. The evaluation of motive and responsibility in these stories--the histories of "painful" cases for the most part--must inevitably lead the reader beyond any easy orthodoxy. These case histories encourage us to exercise our spirits, develop our consciences: to accept the view that morality is a matter of individual responses to particular situations rather than an automatic invocation of religious or ethical rules of thumb.[58]

Against this vampire god, this collector of prepuces, Stephen and Joyce declared artistic war, as we shall see in detail in Chapter III.

The church guaranteed the permanence of infantile dependence among its flock through rigid puritanism and the confessional. It made inroads to the Irishman's role of father, a role that should have been respected and emulated by his children. Then, too, imperialism succeeded in reducing the Irish colony to the condition of an emotionally and economically dependent child. Angry Stephen laments this double oppression in Stephen Hero:

These wanderings filled him with deep-seated anger and whenever he encountered a burly black-breasted priest taking a stroll of pleasant inspection through these warrens full of swarming and cringing believers he cursed the farce of Irish Catholicism: an island (whereof) the inhabitants of which entrust their wills and minds to others that they may ensure for themselves a life of spiritual paralysis, an island in which all the power and riches are in the keeping of those whose kingdom is not of this world, an island in which Caeser confesses Christ and Christ confesses Caeser that together they may wax fat upon a starveling rabblement which is bidden ironically to take to itself this consolation in hardship 'The Kingdom of God is within you.' [p. 146]

For Joyce, Irish Catholicism and British imperialism neutralized the healthy strength of family life. The Irish father in Joyce's fiction is a shadowy figure, robbed of much of his power by church, state and the women of Ireland, often a sibling rather than a father. For Joyce, the church is female, full of meddling priests who are sexually repressed and perverse, who wish to nullify the minds and bodies of women through an unduly repressive morality, and, in turn, teach the women to do the same within the family as the surrogates of priestly power. The priests and the Irish women collude in a corrosive pact which all but annihilates healthy heterosexual relations and perpetuates a frigid matriarchy. Stephen's repudiation of the church reaches a crescendo in Stephen Hero:

The deadly chill of the atmosphere of the college paralysed Stephen's heart. In a stupor of powerlessness he reviewed the plague of Catholicism. He seemed to see the vermin begotten in the catacombs in an age of sickness and cruelty issuing forth upon the plains and mountains of Europe. Like the plague of locusts described in Callista they seemed to choke the rivers and fill the valleys up. They obscured the sun. Contempt of (the body) human nature, weakness, nervous tremblings, fear of day and joy, distrust of man and life, hemiplegia of the will, beset the body burdened and disaffected in its members by its black tyrannous lice. Exultation of the mind before joyful beauty, exultation of the body in free confederate labours, every natural impulse towards health and wisdom and happiness had been corroded by the pest of these vermin. [p. 194]

While Stephen laments this double servitude to church and state, he predicts the arrival of a "new humanity" free from the excessive repression of

36

sexuality, from the urge to blood sacrifice and
martyrdom, and from the reduction of manhood to servitude. Rather than worship a god wielding undue
repression and sublimation of the body, Stephen would
worship the mirror image of god, the goddog, the
animal nature of man, a benign erotic energy of the
unconscious which Joyce hoped to abstract from the
otherwise violent impulses of the Freudian id, the
"ding idself." As dogsbody, Stephen, Bloom, Shem,
and Kevin refuse to bark and wag their tails to the
priest, to the Irish mother, or to the dio boia. Art
would be the holy text for this new humanity, and to
become dogsbody the Joycean character would have to
use art and its weapon, the pen, to probe his
unconscious and his cultural mores in order to kill
the priest and king within himself. The Joycean
character must uncover and confess his own regressive
tendencies toward brutality, and restore in himself a
fallen authority. He must end the reign of the gods
in his own psyche. Stephen drunkenly confesses in
"Circe":

> "Struggle for life is the law of existence
> but modern philirensists, notably the tsar
> and the king of England, have invented
> arbitration." (He taps his brow.)"But in here
> it is I must kill the priest and the king."
> [p. 589]

Kill or be killed by death in life.

Both Ellison and Wright creatively imitated much
of the Joycean assault on the curiously parallel
forces of religion and imperialism. Like Joyce,
Ellison celebrates the goddog, a primal energy for
self-determination, that he locates in jazz and in
black folklore. The dog possesses Peter Wheatstraw
(a character who resembles Bloom in many ways) when
Peter tries to initiate Jack the Bear into the spirit
of the dog:

> "She's got feet like a monkey
> Legs like a frog--Lawd, Lawd!
> But when she starts to loving me
> I holler Whoooo, God-dog!
> Cause I loves my baabay,
> Better than I do myself. . ."
> . . . .

"What I want to know is," he said, "Is
you got the dog?"
"Dog? What dog?"
"Sho," he said, stopping his cart and
resting on its support. "That's it. Who--"
he halted to crouch with one foot on the
curb like a country preacher about to pound
his Bible--"got. . . the. . . dog," his head
snapping with each word like an angry
rooster's.
I laughed nervously and stepped back.
He watched me out of his shrew eyes.
"Oh goddog, daddy-o," he said with a
sudden bluster, "who got the damn dog? Now
I know you from down home, how come you
trying to act like you never heard that
before! Hell, ain't nobody out here this
morning but us colored--Why you trying to
deny me?"
Suddenly I was embarrassed and angry.
"Deny you? What do you mean?"
"Just answer the question. Is you got
him, or ain't you?"
"A dog?"
"Yeah, the dog,"
I was exasperated. "No, not this
morning," I said and saw a grin spread over
his face.
"Wait a minute, daddy. Now don't go
get mad. Damn, man! I thought sho you had
him," he said, pretending to disbelieve me.
And suddenly I felt uncomfortable. Somehow
he was like one of the vets from the Golden
Day. . .
"Well maybe it's the other way around,"
he said. "Maybe he got holt to you."
"Maybe," I said.
"If he is, you lucky it's just a dog--
'cause, man, I tell you I believe it's a
bear that's got holt to me . . ."
"A bear?" [IM, pp. 170-171]

Peter's jive talk brings back to Jack's mind an
earlier childhood self molded by such folk individu-
alists as Wheatstraw, "back to things I had long ago
shut out of my mind." As Gene Bluestein has noted of
this passage: "Joyce has a similar motif in A
Portrait of the Artist in which a play of language is
associated with Stephen's name and relationship to

Ireland."[59]   Stephen's   earliest   memories   in   the
opening pages of A Portrait reveal this Joycean motif
clearly, and Ellison was probably influenced by them.
Wheatstraw's   goddog,   then,   is   a   fusion   of   the
"sacred" and "profane," as well as an echo of the
Egyptian, Lemnian-Greek, and Dogon doggod Anubis.   It
represents a sensual force that wards off the bear
claws of history, a part of the assertive folk tradition of black Americans which expresses a tough
spirit of contrariness against any form of domination, a dogged energy found especially in rural black
church.   Jack retains that force as a mental seed
that Wheatstraw would water with his bluesy jive.

For   despite   Joyce's   assault   against   Irish
Catholicism, Ellison refused to damn the black church
in the rural areas of this country with any compli-
mentary Joycean rage.   Wright's attack on the
puritanical spirit of the Adventist Church in
Mississippi, however, would echo Stephen Dedalus'
non serviam. Instead, Ellison would counterpoint the
country church sensed in Wheatstraw's pose as "the
country preacher about to pound his Bible" with the
atrophied religion of the college chapel service and
the "business of religion" hustled by Rinehart.   To
be sure, the college chapel is a place of collusion.
The humble Booker T. Washington mentality of feigned
submission to the expectations of black behavior
imposed by the white power structure block free
transit with the human form divine:

Around   me   the   students   move   with   faces
frozen in solemn masks, as I seem to hear
already the voices mechanically raised in
the   songs   the   visitors   loved.   (Loved?
Demanded. Sung? An ultimatum accepted and
ritualized, an allegiance recited for the
peace it imparted, and for that perhaps
loved. Loved as the defeated come to love
the symbols of their conquerors. A gesture
of acceptance, of terms laid down and
reluctantly approved.) [IM, p. 109]

The militant, marshalled church is triumphant in the
Irish milieu, but in Ellison's Harlem, the folk survivals of the country church, symbolized and carried
by the Mary Rambos, are losing to urban dehumanization. The degenerate religion of the future is being
preached by B. P. Rinehart, a literary reincarnation

of Joyce's Elijah Dowie, who sells the religious
opiate to the people when he is not engaged in the
numbers racket, who hustles an invisible god to an
invisible people. This Melvillish confidence man
advertises his guarantee of salvation through hand-
bills which resemble Dowie's throwaways:

> Behold the Invisible
> Thy will be done O Lord!
> I See all, Know all, Tell all,
>   Cure all.
> You shall see the unknown wonders.
>   --Rev. B. P. Rinehart
>   Spiritual Technoligist

> The old is never new
> Way Stations in New Orleans, the
>   home of mystery,
> Birmingham, New York, Chicago,
>   Detroit and L.A.

> No Problem too hard for God.

> Come to the Way Station

> BEHOLD THE INVISIBLE!
> Attend our services, prayer
>   meeting Thrice weekly
> Join us in the NEW REVELATION of
>   the OLD TIME RELIGION!

> BEHOLD THE SEEN UNSEEN
>   YE WHO ARE WEARY COME HOME!

> I DO WHAT YOU WANT DONE!
> DON'T WAIT! [IM, p. 484]

If Joyce would expose the usurpation of the
father and of the autonomy of the family by religious
and imperialistic oppression, Ellison, too, would
present his version of the unsubstantial father.
Fatherhood in Invisible Man and in various short
stories appears to be as invisible as Rinehart's god,
as sad as a Walter Mitty caricature. Emerson's son
retorts to a "confused" Jack: "Identity! My God!
Who has any identity any more anyway?" [p. 184] The
demise of fatherhood occurs across racial boundaries.
In Chapters II and V we shall see how the pathetic

search for a viable father and for meaningful
initiation rites takes place in an America which
reaches its epiphany in the Brotherhood, a complex
symbol not only of dehumanized organizations such as
the Communist Party, but of the tendency toward
fascism in American life in a culture nearly without
viable fathers. Indeed, the Brotherhood sells itself
both as a substitute father and as a religion.
Ironically, much as Joyce's Jesuit fraternity, this
atheistic fraternity demands infantile dependence
among its followers and ostracizes them for free
thought. Wright also characterized organizations
such as the Communist Party as being analogous to a
priesthood. In The Outsider Hilton's face is
described as "ascetic" and Wright goes on to
describe Cross' reaction to Hilton:

> Men like Hilton did not spend their days
> scheming how to get hold of dollars; they
> worked at organizing and expoiting the raw
> stuff of human emotions. In being close to
> the common impulses of men, in their cynical
> acceptance of the cupidities of the heart,
> in the frank recognition of outlandish
> passions, they were akin to priests.[60]

In Ellison's Brotherhood scientific engineering
of human life replaces religious metaphysics; apocalyptic theories of political salvation replace
apocalyptic Jesuit sermons, as this new army of
celibates descends, like a politicized priesthood,
upon Harlem. The paternalism of a debased religion
resurfaces in the new secular world view of the
Brotherhood, an organization quartered appropriately
"in a converted church structure" above a "pawnshop."
[p. 351] The Brotherhood ultimately reveals itself
as a band of brothers, of siblings, caught up in a
political sibling-rivalry, brothers who institution-
alize childish zeal. Jack the Bear rejects one-eyed
Brother Jack in a scene reminiscent not only of
Homer's Odyssey but of Bloom's mock battle with a
Joycean Cyclops and nationalistic citizen, Michael
Cusak, in the fraternal pub which so resembles the
headquarters of a secret society, complete with
password.

If the Brotherhood revives negative religious
instincts, so does the death of Tod Clifton, exam-

41

ined in detail in Chapter IV. For Tod's death is presented through the Frazerian mythic frame as an enactment of a scapegoat ritual right off the pages of The Golden Bough or Totem and Taboo. Ellison uses a double perspective to depict both in Tod's death and funeral vestiges of primitive behavior which convert a tragic act into a scapegoat ritual, the resultant Harlem riot into a Freudian "holiday." For Ellison as for Joyce, the state, maintained in this case by the fascist policeman who kills Tod, can become an altar of "sacrifice," on a deeper level.

Although Ellison did not find Stephen's "agenbite of inwit" or his flirtation with the role of priest and his final denunciation of the Irish Church and its servile women so applicable to his own portrait of Jack, Wright did find Stephen's ordeal analogous to Richard's struggle with the Seventh Day Adventist exposure. And if Ellison would link maternal Mary Rambo to a dying folk-church in Harlem, he chose not to let Jack battle dying Ramboism, for it had its redeeming qualities. However, Ellison notes the influence of Joyce's style and of Stephen's non-serviam to both mother and church in Wright's Black Boy:

> in its use of fictional technique, its concern with criminality (sin), and the artistic sensibiity, and in its author's judgement and rejection of the narrow world of his origin, it recalls Joyce's rejection of Dublin in A Portrait of the Artist. [SA, p. 78]

Also, the sulphur and brimstone Jesuit sermon is echoed in Black Boy as are the sermon's apocalyptic catalogues:

> Granny was an ardent member of the Seventh-Day Adventist Church and I was compelled to make a pretense of worshipping her God, which was her exaction for my keep. The elders of her church expounded a gospel clogged with images of vast lakes of eternal fire, of seas vanishing, of valleys of dry bones, of the sun burning to ashes, of the moon turning to blood, of stars falling to earth, of a wooden staff being transformed into a serpent, of voices speaking out of

42

clouds, of men walking upon water, of God
riding whirlwinds, of water changing into
wine, of the dead rising and living, of the
blind seeing, of the lame walking, a salvation that teemed with fantastic beasts
having multiple heads and horns and eyes and
feet; sermons of statues possessing heads of
gold, shoulders of silver, legs of brass,
and feet of clay; a cosmic tale that began
before time and ended with the clouds of the
sky rolling away at the Second Coming of
Christ; chronicles that concluded with the
Armageddon; dramas thronged with all the
billions of human beings who had ever lived
or died as God judged the quick and the
dead. . . . [p.89]

And Wright echoes Stephen's rejection of his mother's
religion and Stephen's refusal to pray with Richard's
painful rejection of Granny and her command that
Richard must fall on his knees before God. Indeed,
for David Bakhish, Wright's self-imposed exile from
Mississippi became for Wright an American reenactment
of Joyce's (and Stephen's) initial exile to Paris:

Like the mature James Joyce, the mature
Wright came to realize that he could not
broaden his artistic and personal freedom
without leaving the oppressive soil from
which he had sprung. In order to make
effective use of his roots he had to
supplement psychic distance with physical
distance. Joyce left his home, his religion, and his country to "discover the mode
of life or of art whereby your spirit could
express itself in unfettered freedom. . . ."
"I will not serve that in which I no longer
believe, whether it calls itself my home, my
fatherland, or my church." Wright had to
leave home for the alien North, and later,
for the East that was Europe. He had
already left Christianity and Communism.[61]

In **The Outsider** Wright continued to reveal
Joycean influences. For when Cross recalls his
childhood memories, he associates his cold mother
with the invisible, violent God, the "NO-face" of her
puritanical, anti-sexual faith, a faith he must

reject in order to escape that dread he associates
with both mother and God. He painfully recalls how
the frigidity of God's love that "seemed somehow like
hate" extended even into the icy, maternal care his
mother gave him as an infant. [p. 18]

Bloom's linkage of the Mass with cannibalism also
may have echoed in Wright's memory. When Cross
observes a priest, he regards "him as a kind of
dressed-up savage intimidated by totems and taboos
that differed in kind but not in degree from those of
the most primitive of peoples." [p. 123] Like many
existential rebels, Cross must kill the priest in
himself so that he can create his own superego. For
Wright, as for Joyce, such a murder would lead to the
birth of individual autonomy, of conscience.
According to Houston (and Nietzsche), Cross is
without the myths and rituals of the Greeks and the
Jews; he is a pre-Christian man, a man ready to
create himself. The creation largely fails for
Wright's hero; it succeeds marginally for Stephen,
Bloom, and Shem.

If a benign goddog could emerge out of a battle
with church and state, then this goddog must learn to
speak. Hugh Kenner describes the speech of Joyce's
Dublin, speech which forms yet another net the goddog
must transcend. For Kenner's Joyce, the philosophical legacy of Kant, Descartes, Locke and Hume divided
the human mind from the alien, reified "other" world
of objects and refashioned direct speech into artificial discourse. For if the mind could not "know" the
objective world of objects, but only see or invent
its surfaces, then the daft, post-Cartesian man must
contemplate what he could know, the workings of his
brain, its associations, its speech, a speech largely
independent of the things it denotes. For Joyce,
Descartes had set up a net, and Dublin, steeped in
such mechanistic philosophy, had sterilized its
language. Words no longer were wedded to their
referents in the schizoid, Lewis Carroll, Dublin
psyche. Kenner argues:

Things are before we know them, that is the
first condition; they doubly are after they
are known, that is the second. The mind is
nourished and impregnated by things, the
mind affirms the existence of things. The
mind by thousands of successive acts of con-

44

ception, generates an intellected order in more or less exact analogy of the intelligible order with which it copulates. It builds a hierarchic city of the known. The very "to be" is a copula in every sense. "First came the seen, then thus the palpable." Words flourish in the soil of known things. The civilization in which the act of coition has been steril.zed shuffles its hoarded phantasms and generates nothing.[62]

Dublin's sterile, cold, philosophical exegesis resulted in an obsession with dreams, with word games, and with the cliche's of discourse at the expense of a rapport with the phenomenal world. Kenner insists:

> The comparable progression from **A Portrait** to **Finnegans Wake** leaves behind a drama of daftly autonomous words, language, not persons in action, convoluting in a world of non-communication, but, by virtue of its tenacular contacts with things and traditions, richly epiphanic of the fragmented mind of Europe.[63]

So Dublin mulled over its discourse, saw the world through its clichés, became "a city full of haunted talk, littered with hulks of public rhetoric. . . ."[64] If this were not enough to embalm language and thought, Dublin also imitated the imposed language of its conqueror, and often described the world with stodgy cliche's of England's jingoist speech.

Dublin, however, did not accept this net totally. Rumblings were heard from the Gaelic League to abandon the imposed language and return to Gaelic. Stephen would reject this strategy. For if speech represents a world view, the world view of Gaelic was to Stephen a fossil, and a sentimental return to Gaelic would be a return to the Middle Ages. Such a strategy would exchange one net for another. Rather than limit himself only to British expression or to Gaelic and the "cultic twalette," Joyce would expose the petrified, inauthentic rhetoric of both the working and the dream language of Dublin, and in **Finnegans Wake**, especially, further expose unconscious archetypes universally shared by peoples everywhere, archetypes that promulgate world languages.

For Joyce much as for Vico, a common mental language underlie the babel of world speech, and such an archetypal language, not unlike Jung's archetypal purée, could reveal the inner workings of the mind and the origin of the nightmare of history itself. Vico argued:

> There must in the nature of human things be a mental language common to all nations, which uniformly grasps the substance of things feasible in human social life, and expresses it with as many diverse modifications as these same things may have diverse aspects.
> This common mental language is proper to our Science, by whose light linguistic scholars will be enabled to construct a mental vocabulary common to all the various articulate languages living and dead.[65]

Once this inner language could be made articulate, once the unconscious could be dredged, the archetypes themselves might, paradoxically, be transcended; and an inner sanctum, a deeper layer of the unconscious, that "grandfather self" in Invisible Man, the "strange music" in Stephen's reverie, might emerge.

Joyce's psychoanalytical and anthropological zeal to chart the dream language boiling from the word cauldron of the unconscious revealed an inner language of inauthenticity and deceit which curiously paralleled the cloned, daylight discourse of Dublin. For according to Margot Norris, dream language in the Wake amounts to a pale of Freudian defense mechanisms such as distortion, displacement and condensation that attempt to block the artist's transit with his ambiguous and elusive innerness. Norris discusses this night language:

> Finnegans Wake is not merely the "illusion" of a dream, or the "surface" of a dream, as it were. The work, in fact, explores the relationship between the conscious and the unconscious, and the strange, cunning, antagonistic communication that is effected between them in dreams. A special language had to be forged for this purpose, as Joyce explained to Harriet Shaw Weaver. "One great part of every human existence is

46

passed in a state which cannot be rendered
sensible by the use of wideawake language
cutanddry grammar, and goahead plot."[66]

The quest of Wakean characters according to Norris is
for "the truth of their own being, the answer to the
question that lies at the heart of the Oedipus myth:
'Who am I?'" But the answer to this question is
unknowable in the Wake, argues Norris.[67]

The question of Oedipus is a central question
posed by both Ellison's and Wright's heroes. They
too will discover an ambiguous, chameleon unconscious, which is not unlike the "cloud incertitude"
of the Wake. Yet Joyce and Ellison will sustain
their conviction that beneath all the narcissism and
uncontrollable oedipal-sadistic passions of the human
unconscious there lies an urge for self-determination
and love, an essential, shared, human essence, an
energy that both writers attempted to tap in their
creative processes. Beneath inauthenticity, then,
lay an authentic, universally shared essence, ambiguous and indecipherable, to be sure, a playful spirit
not unlike the spirit Fred discovers in Wright's
underground, and not unlike the garrulous ambiguity
of the grandfather's final deathbed statement in
Ellison's novel. Campbell and Robinson explain these
Joycean ethics: "He believed . . . that somewhere in
the non-cerebral part of man dwells an intelligence
that is the most important organ of human wisdom."[68]
And Jack tells us in the Epilogue:

There is, by the way, an area in which a
man's feelings are more rational than his
mind, and it is precisely in that area that
his will is pulled in several directions at
the same time. You might sneer at this, but
I know now. I was pulled this way and that
for longer than I can remember. And my
problem was that I always tried to go in
everyone's way but my own. [p. 560]

On less grand, linguistic scale than Joyce, Ellison
attempted to expose the stilted, daylight rhetoric of
his role-playing characters as well as their chameleon, elusive language of dreams in hopes of
intuiting a benign, authentic and universal core of
self that Eastern philosophers and American Transcendental writers of the American Renaissance have also

sought. As a result, the more dense and profound
passages of <u>Invisible Man</u> and of Joyce's works are
those introspections into the unconscious: Stephen's
diary in <u>A Portrait</u>; Jack's opening Danteian, layered
dream of miscegenation in the Prologue; the "Circe"
section of <u>Ulysses</u>; the dreams of incest and parricide which reverberate throughout the <u>Wake</u>; the
grandfather's advice and Jack's periodic possession
by his "grandfather" self; Trueblood's dream; Jack's
dream of castration; and more. Trueblood's dream,
especially, with its sexual symbolism itemizing the
uterine canal and the fetal return to the womb with
Trueblood as penis, reveals a universal language of
displaced sexual symbols. Following the lead of
Joyce and of depth psychology, Ellison could conclude
that the symbolic, universal language of the
unconscious was the primal material of the artist.
In <u>Shadow and Act</u> Ellison speculated on dream
language and on the concern of African poets as to
whether they should write in French, English, or in
their native tongue:

> When it comes to the poet the vagueness of
> the term "Negro" becomes truly appalling,
> for if there is a "Negro" language I am
> unacquainted with it. Are these people
> Bantu, Sudanese, Nigerian, Watusi, or what?
> As for the poets in question, it seems to me
> that in a general way they are faced by the
> problem confronted by the Irish, who for all
> their efforts to keep their language vital
> have had nevertheless their greatest poets
> expressing themselves as English, as in the
> case of Shaw, Yeats, Joyce, and O'Casey.
> Perhaps the poet's true language is that in
> which he dreams. At any rate, it is true
> that for some time now poets throughout
> the world have drawn freely from all the
> world's tongues in order to create their
> vocabularies. One uses whatever one needs,
> to best express one's vision of the human
> predicament. [p. 266]

In "Circe" Stephen reflects on a primal gesture
language which is not unlike Vico's description of
the speech of giants. Such language might surpass
the universality of music:

> (<u>Looks behind.</u>)   So that gesture, not
> music, not odours, would be a universal

language, the gift of tongues rendering visible not the lay sense but the first entelechy, the structural rhythm. [p. 432]

For both Joyce and Ellison the acquisition of such a language would involve an exposure of the inauthenticity of all rhetoric, of all scripts. The goddog might be speechless.

Like Dostoevsky before them on the daylight level, Joyce and Ellison wished to illuminate language systems which created robot people who spoke "rote words in rite order," who covered up the search of Oedipus with clichéd noise. Joyce attacked British English because it imposed a way of seeing the world upon the "gratefully oppressed" that reflected the values of imperialism. Frantz Fanon explains how language can superimpose cultural values on the oppressed in any culture by examining his Antilles sample:

> To speak language is to take on a world, a culture. The Antilles Negro who wants to be white will be the whiter as he gains greater mastery of the cultural tool that language is.[69]

Stephen's trauma over language surfaces when he reflects on his native word "tundish" or "funnel" during his debate with the "English convert," the dean of studies:

> The little word seemed to have turned a rapier point of his sensitiveness against this courteous and vigilant foe. He felt with a smart of defection that the man to whom he was speaking was a countryman of Ben Jonson. He thought: "The language in which we are speaking is his before it is mine. How different are the words home, Christ, ale, master, on his lips and on mine! I cannot speak or write these words without unrest of spirit. His language, so familiar and so foreign, will always be for me an acquired speech. I have not made or accepted his words. My voice holds them at bay. My soul frets in the shadow of his language." [p. 453]

Stephen's sentiments were shared by his creator in a letter: "I'd like a language which is above all languages, a language to which all will do service. I cannot express myself in English without closing myself in a tradition."[70] Ellison would satirize the rhetoric of Homer Barbee much as Joyce debunked the speech of the Dean, for Barbee's speech attempts to elevate itself above the language of the folk as it assumes the world view of the white power structure. For Ellison, the language of the folk that is preserved in American folklore presents an authentic discourse which reflects desires for self-definition and transcendence. Indeed, in America Ellison was able to construct a language that was multi-ethnic through a combination of the foreign idiom preserved in folklore with English, a language which would serve everyone, a language which combined "all the world's tongues," as he argues in Shadow and Act. A universal language could be realized in America on the daylight level at least. At West Point Ellison revealed:

> But, nevertheless, part of the music of the language, part of the folklore which informed our conscious American literature came through the interaction of the slave and the white man, and, particularly so in the South. Mr. Faulkner, who has lectured here, had no doubt about that, and some of our most meaningful insights into the experience of the South have come through his understanding of that complex relationship. And because he did (understand) he has been responsible for some of the real glories of our literature.[71]

To soften and vitalize American English Ellison used several ambiguous puns such as those for characters' names: Jack the Bear, Supercargo (Superego), Norton (Northern), Tobbit (Two-Bits), Wrestrum (Rest Room), Ras (Race), Tod (the German "tot" or "death"), along with black speech and the syncopated, improvisational style of the blues and jazz in order to move daylight language closer to the language of the elusive grandfather self. Bluestein discusses Ellison's synthesis of language, music, and folklore elements. He notes Ellison's observation that the improvisation of African music humanized the rigid military beat of marching music in Louis Armstrong's art and affirmed "the ability to overcome oppression through the creation of art. . . ."[72] Bluestein goes on to explain Ellison's love of jazz:

> In more positive terms, jazz provides one with a new sense of time; again it is not the rhythm of a military march in which everyone must be in step, for despite the regular-pulsing beat of a jazz band, there is always the offbeat or offbeats which are characteristic of jazz style.[73]

Ellison may well have embarked on his language synthesis with Joyce's similar attempt in mind: to combine music and prose, to flesh words with musical puns: "That's the point of eschatology our book of kills reaches for now in so and so many counterpoint words. What can't be coded can be decoded if an eary aye sieze what no eye are grieved for." [FW, p. 482]

Joyce undertook a Homeric task in the Wake, a task which Ellison would pursue through far less experimental prose, but with similar purpose. Like Homer, who mixed dialects to create national unity, Joyce blended world languages into a "panaroma of all flores of speech" to foster a "holy language soons to come" where "sense and soundsense" could become "kin again" in musical prose. [pp. 143, 256] "Subsubstantiation"--the creation of a body language dominated by a play principle, words loosened from their referents, words not unlike the objects loosened from connotative levels in Wright's underground, would smash the "etym" and offer a freer transit for men with their innerness. And this inner speech would emanate not from the Viconian thunderclap of god, but from the inner flashes and thunderclaps of the "ding idself." Norman O. Brown has correctly argued that Joyce wished to end language as we know it so that it would become protean, so that men could intuit their inner polymorphous energy by means of "The map of the soul's groupography."[74]

To reach in for this language both Joyce, and, with less complexity, Ellison had to modify constricting language systems and employ their softened language synthesis. The petrification of the daylight rhetoric of their literary characters had to be exposed and burlesqued. If Joyce revealed in

Dublin speech an abstract, sterilized, cliched discourse punctuated by imitations of British affectation, so, too, Ellison would zero in on the pretensions of Barbee's and Bledsoe's rhetoric, on the "automatic" speech of young Jack, on the subliminal stutterings of Norton in the face of his half-acknowledged incestuous desires, on the scientific, dehumanized rhetoric of Brother Jack and his comrades, on the mamby-pamby discourse of the white women, and counterpoint this rhetoric with the rumblings of the inner self intuited in the puzzling dream of Jack's grandfather, in the possession of the brown girl by the spiritual at the college chapel service, in Vet's chaotic harangues, in Trueblood's directness in recounting his dream, in Peter Wheatstraw's folk jive, in the emergence of the grandfather self during Jack's speech on dispossession, in Jack's marijuana dreams in his coalhole.[75]

The language net must be cut. The mechanizers of consciousness might well stand in awe of this maneuver of the Joyce-Ellison connection, and, like Shaun, respect Shem's "root language" from the depths which reverberates with a modified Viconian thunder, a thunder that echoes throughout Invisible Man as well.

Of the fourth net, the Irish woman, Stephen confesses to Lynch: "that seems to be the maze out of which we cannot escape." Stephen is railing not only against his frigid sweethearts, but ultimately against his mother and the incest bond, the "eatapus complex," he is emotionally locked into. Stephen, in fact, is an apt case study for so many of Joyce's Dubliners, who fail to transcend the regressive incest bond with the mothers of Dublin, who can only love their spouses or lovers incestuously. And much of this soured love results from a catastrophic failure of mother love. As we have seen, for Joyce some sources for the failure of Irish family life emerged as a compact: the usurpation of the Irish father's authority by imperialism and the collusion of Irish women with the priests. This usurpation devalues the father and places the Irish mother in command of the crippling matriarchy that results. In a recent study of present day familial problems in a rural western Ireland sample, Nancy Scheper-Hughes reveals just how far this collusion between women and the priests has gone. She examines the impact of a "monastic, ascetic, Augustinian, Jansenist, puritanical Irish Catholic world view" on childrearing patterns.[76] She reveals that the mother frequently represses the normal sensual desires and needs of the child, born, allegedly, into original sin; that "the devoutly religious Irish mother acts as though she were obligated to ignore her baby's wants for sucking, stroking, and rocking and to view these human needs as unnecessary demands."[77] Her study links such harsh childrearing to the formation of Stephen's "diseased conscience," - a pseudonym for Irish schizophrenia. In light of this family failure, Joyce's marginalia in Stephen Hero does not appear too strong, for "Stephen wished to avenge himself on Irish women, who, he says, are the cause of all the moral suicide in the Island." [p. 200] The "unsubstantial father," who haunts the households of Dublin from Dubliners through Finnegans Wake, can hardly serve as a model to be emulated by his children. As a result, the successful operation of the classical Oedipus complex: the son's repression of his parricidal wish and his subsequent identification with the father after the superego is internalized, breaks down or is thwarted altogether.

In Chapter II the failure of successful pre-oedipal and oepidal development will be examined among several of the Dubliners in Joyce's psychoanalytically conscious fiction. The ubiquitous and paralysing incestuous tinge in Irish sexual relations, a tinge that becomes a lietmotif in Joyce's works, resurfaces in the fiction of Ellison and Wright where variations on this theme emerge. Parallels will be made between the Irish and black fictional family constellations in the works of each writer, and another important aspect of the Joyce-Ellison connection will reveal its complexities.

The devaluation of the father reduces him to the status of a sibling in Joyce's Dublin, a rival with his sons for the incestuous love of the mother. Mark Schechner explains the unique, Irish oedipal bond:

As opposed to classical oedipal paradigms which Freud discovered in the patriarchal, Germanic family, the patterns of childhood devotion and jealousy in Joyce's life and fantasies were more of the fecund and matriarchal Irish household. In such a

household, the libidinous bonds between
husband and wife are tenuous and a child's
primary rival for the mother's love is not
the father but a sibling. Love is at a pre-
mium in such a family, and brotherhood is a
zero-sum game which one wins only when one's
brother loses. The problem of the father in
Ulysses is that he is missing.[78]--

or, for that matter, that he is reduced to sibling
status as the infantile Little Chandler of Dubliners.

Stephen's sexual ordeal in A Portrait, his
insatiable and incestuous sexual desires, his
tormented fantasies, his multiple personalities, all
of which Wright more so than Ellison would improvise
upon, result from entrapment in a primitive incest
bond common to the oral stage. As a result he fails
to form a mature superego, a "conscience," through an
emulation of the father, an emulation that might
allow him to transcend the primitive, persecutory
fantasies he experiences which recall similar trauma
suffered by the patients of Melanie Klien, W. R. D.
Fairbairn and other clinical psychologists special-
izing in schizoid behavior.

Stephen suffers a "cold, cruel, loveless lust"
which reduces him to the state of a "baffled prowling
beast." He must have sex with whores in order to
block his incest desires through thingifying women,
and he must form intellectual relationships with
madonna-like mother figures with whom sex is forbidden. The undue repression of sexuality by the church
works together with the withheld yet desperately
needed love of the mother to place Stephen in a
spiritual refrigerator where he is haunted by icy
dreams of vampire mother images.

Ellison and Wright would also reveal the failure
of love relationships in their fiction, but Ellison's
heroes, at least, do not always recall Stephen's
Irish adolescent rage. Nevertheless, the fetish-
ridden bird-girl image is retained and refeathered in
Invisible Man. In A Portrait Stephen, charged with
adolescent exuberance, experiences a vision of a
strange creature:

A girl stood before him in midstream, alone
and still, gazing out to sea. She seemed

54

like one whom magic had changed into the likeness of a strange and beautiful seabird. Her long slender bare legs were delicate as a crane's and pure save where an emerald trail of seaweed had fashioned itself as a sign upon her flesh. Her thighs, fuller and softhued as ivory, were bared almost in the hips where the white fringes of her drawers were like featherings of soft white down. Her slateblue skirts were kilted boldly about her waist and dovetailed behind her. Her bosom was as a bird's soft and slight, slight and soft as the breast of some darkplumaged dove. But her long fair hair was girlish: and touched with the wonder of mortal beauty, her face. She was alone and still gazing out to sea; and when she felt this presence and the worship of his eyes her eyes turned to him in quiet sufferance of his gaze, without shame or wantonness. [p. 433]

When she turns from his hypnotic stare and stirs the water of the sea with her foot, Stephen journeys inward and discovers a buried self: "some new world, fantastic, dim, uncertain as under sea, traversed by cloudy shapes and beings."--the repressed Eros of the unconscious that Stephen, as artist, must mine. [p. 435] To be sure, Joyce partially satirizes Stephen's ecstasy at his vision of this phallic girl, whose long legs, feathery drawers, dovetailed skirts, and long hair quite consciously on Joyce's part represent the penis.[79] Indeed, several critics have compared this girl to other Joycean women including Gerty McDowell, with her feathery drawers and limp, and to fetish ridden Bella-Bello, the phallic mother who reigns in the male unconscious of sado-masochistic Dublin, a character who recalls the bad maternal objects identified by Klein.[80] And the fetish fantasy often allows the child or adult to bind his desire for incest with the mother, for if the mother has the penis, she cannot be ravished in fantasy.

The Joycean-bird-girl motif appears twice in Invisible Man: as the forbidden white stripper at the Battle Royal: "She seemed like a fair bird-girl girdled in veils calling to me from the angry surface of some gray and threatening sea"; and as Rinehart's girl, remembered by Jack and intwined in fantasy: "I lay there unmoving, and she seemed to perch on the bed, a bright-eyed bird with her glossy head and ripe breasts, and I was in a wood afraid to frighten the bird away." [pp. 19, 500] He muses over possible love:

> Then I was fully awake and the bird gone and the girl's image in my mind. What would have happened if I had led her on, how far could I have gone? A desirable girl like that mixed up with Rinehart. [p. 500]

We never know, for Jack, like Stephen or Wright's male characters, is notoriously unlucky in love; indeed, they all must go it alone as they reach out for a new humanity. The "confused" sexuality of their respective milieus will provide clues to their loveless states in Chapter II.

For Joyce the collapse of the patriachal Irish family creates a ripple effect throughout Irish society. If the Irish family comes to resemble a fraternity of siblings, this pattern is duplicated in Irish institutions such as the fraternal priesthood, the male world of Clongowes, and the pub in "Cyclops." Similar fraternal ripples occur throughout Invisible Man, in the college administration, in the Union at Liberty Paints, in the Brotherhood, and in Barrelhouse's Jolly Dollar bar that recalls Barney Kiernan's Dublin pub. Each of these "institutions" resemble male secret societies comprised of fatherless men, men who were never able to internalize a superego, men who must huddle together in fascist power-systems.

Although Ellison located a fraternal substructure in American life that recalls Joyce's fraternal Dublin, he did not go so far as Joyce or Wright in denigrating the family in his mature fiction. For in America, family life appeared matriarchal across ethnic lines, and rather than join the attack of sociologists on the black, stereotyped family, Ellison, unlike Wright, chose to challenge the sociological type and opt for greater character ambiguity. Ellison's reluctance to stereotype the black mother, with the exceptions of Trueblood's hatchet swinging wife and the puritanical matrons of his short stories, his general reluctance to slight black family life, is a hesitation he explains:

But if a Negro writer is going to listen to
sociologists--as too many of us do--who tell
us that Negro life is thus-and-so in keeping
with certain sociological theories, he is in
trouble because he will have abandoned his
task before he begins. If he accepts the
cliches to the effect that the Negro family
is usually a broken family, that it is
matriarchal in form and the mother dominates
and castrates the males, if he believes that
Negro males are having all of these alleged
troubles with their sexuality, or that
Harlem is a "Negro ghetto"-- . . . well,
he'll never see the people of whom he wishes
to write.[81]

In the same interview Ellison argues that although
the stereotypes of sociological formulas "are drawn
from life," he denies "that they define the
complexity of Harlem."[82] Ellison goes on to reveal
that he looks at his material not through the eyes of
sociologists but "through literature; English,
French, Spanish, Russian--especially 19th century
Russian literature. And Irish literature, Joyce and
Yeats. . . ."[83] Ellison may well have been thinking
of the character ambiguities of Bloom and Molly,
whose "family" appears to be a typical Irish
matriarchy but which winds up breaking many of the
suppositions and stereotypes of the "typical" Irish
marriage. Nonetheless, for Ellison as for Joyce,
family collapse generates cultural paralysis, a
fraternal, fascist odor to life. But an attack on
the causes of this family collapse rather than on the
family itself would increasingly occupy Joyce and
Ellison when their writing matured.

The strains of family life, however, do lead to
other shared and borrowed themes in the fiction of
each writer. The failure of initiation rites in each
cultural milieu, a failure that will concern Chapter
V, haunts nearly all of their heroes who resolve that
they must provide their own rites into sexuality and
adulthood. Their heroes also attempt to be fathers
to themselves, autonomous possessors of a self-forged
conscience, as Ellison and Wright creatively imitate
the self-originating fantasies of the hero myth and
of Joyce's adaptations of that myth.

It will become clear, however, that the
usurpation of the father and the resulting family

dislocations are caused by one other powerful
undercurrent: the general mechanization of modern
life and human consciousness, which forms yet another
net obstructing the "slow and dark birth" of
conscience.

In Ellison's many epiphanies concerning the
mechanization of modern life from the Alabama cotton-
fields to the industrial nightmares of New York, he
appears once again to have been more than casually
influenced by Joyce's picture, found in Dubliners
through Finnegan Wake, of the then freshly dawning
yet clattering, humming, mechanized 20th century.
Kenner locates one of the great epiphanies of
Ulysses:

> The medieval metaphor of the Body Politic
> hovers over every episode, Lungs in the
> newspaper office, Blood in the corpuscular
> citizens circulating the streets, Stomach in
> the crowded eating-houses. . . . The Body
> that emerges from Joyce's epic is that of a
> gigantic robot. . . .[84]

Alarmingly, the dialectic between the human and the
mechanical threatens to collapse as robotized
Dubliners, much like R. D. Laing's schizoid patients,
attempt, precariously, to retain a human core of self
in the face of the mechanical jungle of conformist,
gamey Dublin. Kenner refers to the coarse narrative
voice in Ulysses as the voice of the "god of
industrial man."[85] He goes on to reveal, with
excessive harshness, that the mentality of Bloom is a
product both of 18th century mechanical models of
human consciousness a la Locke and Hume and of their
warmed over 19th and 20th century philosophical
disciples.[86] For the tendency of these psychologies
is to negate any human essence, any innerness.
Locke's formula for the mind, a tabula rasa, an empty
vessel, is a mirror image for the Cartesian world of
dead objects, a world decipherable only as a glit-
tering maze of surfaces, seemingly devoid of essence
or inner dynamism. Kenner explains the results of
this world view, a model which Joyce would parody and
largely denounce:

> Lockeian thought seemed "true" because the
> mechanical brain repeated the structure of
> the Newtonian clock-work universe. . . .

Hence the "reasonable" man, like the well-regulated watch, exhibits a high degree of conformity with his fellows, and the Blake, the maverick, can be safely excommunicated. When reality is regarded as inaccessible, consistency is to be sought rather between mind and mind than between minds and things; hence conformity of thought as a guarantee against anarchy, and the mechanization of the community as well as of the brain.[87]

Buck Mulligan neatly summarizes the Lockeian ice-grip on Dublin when he confesses to Stephen, "I remember only ideas and associations." Mechanistic models of human thought and perception were yet another net leading to paralysis. How could conscience be born, how could an art call up the essential self of men, if Joyce's Dubliners shared Buck's view of the mind as a stimulis-response machine? Ellison would ponder this Joycean question and create ubiquitous human cogs in Invisible Man.

The mechanization of 20th century life made other inroads to conscience among the Irish. Joyce may very well have reflected on observations of Marx and Engels concerning the demise of the patriarchal family in an industrial, capitalist state. For they argued that the removal of the means of production from the home to the factory effectively removed the father and his labor from the scrutiny of his children. The results: Children understood the father's daily work only as abstraction; they were not "initiated" into the world of work by a "missing" father. Then too, imperialism, with its economic colonialism, helped to create a new indigenous native class of Irish bureaucrats who would reveal "confused" loyalties as they emulated the values of a mother country that largely regarded them as inferior. As imperial rule solidified overseas, companies solidified as well throughout Ireland, companies which would demand the loyalty of those it exploited and initiated into England's industrial state.

All three writers create characters that suffer under this mechanical pale. Dickensian-like cogs come to imitate the machines and industral rhythms they must endure. Vet's warning to Jack at the Golden Day applies to America as well. Vet dresses down Jack and Norton:

"He registers with his senses but short-circuits his brain. Nothing has meaning. He takes it in but he doesn't digest it. Already he is--well, bless my soul! Behold! a walking zombie! Already he's learned not only to repress his emotions but his humanity. He's invisible, a walking personification of the Negative, the most perfect achievement of your dreams, sir! The mechanical man!" [IM, p. 92]

Joyce, Ellison and Wright pursued the collapsed dialectic further when they wedded the dangerous, slapstick space of the reified Cartesian city, the space of which long ago Descartes confessed: "I have been able to live as solitary and withdrawn as I would in the most remote of deserts," the space most poignantly revealed in the films of Chaplin and Keaton, with their own fictional portraits of Dublin, Harlem and Chicago.[88] Frank McConnell describes a representative scene from the silent film era, an era which so heavily influenced these writers, that typifies the tragic-comic struggles of Chaplin against a dangerous, inimical world of Cartesian objects:

In Modern Times Charlie, showing off for Paulette Goddard, rollerskates blindfolded through a deserted department store. He cannot see the central shaft, plummeting down many stories, whose edge he again and again skirts. But as soon as he takes the blindfold off and sees the abyss, he is drawn to it, almost into a whirlpool. Flailing his arms, frantically backpedaling, he cannot keep away from the edge. Surely there has never been--not in Descartes, not in Milton, not in Blake--a more more powerful imagination of the impingements of matter upon the human will, of our panicky awareness that the void, sheer space, once we see it for what it is, can kill.[89]

An admitted aficion of Chaplin (Lucia was charmed by him), Joyce meant Bloom on one level to parody cinema heroes such as Chaplin, when Bloom, a befuddled hero, tripped and tramped through the tram-laden streets of Dublin, recoiled from the hungry jaws of the printing press, mused over the mechanization of the body and human fertility, and generally tried to survive in the mechanical vagina dentate of the robot city, in its amniotic sea of matter that clutters and nearly drowns the pages of Ulysses. In "Aelous" he muses next to the printing press: "Machines. Smash a man to atoms if they got him caught. Rule the world today." [p. 118] Stephen fears that the machine may already be in his guts:

The whirr of flapping leathern bands and hum of dynamos from the powerhouse urged Stephen to be on. Beingless beings. Stop! Throb always without you and the throb always within. Your heart you sing of. I between them. Where? Between two roaring worlds where they swirl, I. Shatter them, one and both. But stun myself too in the blow. [p. 242]

Ellison fashioned Peter Wheatstraw as a Chaplin figure, for Peter is seen "Pulling the seat of his Charlie Chaplin pants" to warn Jack of the bear in oppressed, urban Harlem, that "bear's den," where you can be clawed from behind. [IM, p. 171] Jack's perception of Harlem becomes slapstick on several occasions, but most comically in the scene where Sibyl, staggering, keeps reappearing in taxis and on street corners while Jack tries to escape her claws. And Harlem actually sucks Jack up into a Chaplinesque abyss when he tumbles into a manhole during his retreat from the Harlem riot as Trueblood's dreamlake and Brockway's industrial hell in the basement of Liberty Paints are improvised upon in this slapstick episode.

To develop the collapsed dialectic further, Joyce likened Stephen's frequent, passive perception of geometric surfaces to the optics of a still camera. Much as the photograph flattens and embalms space into a two dimensional continuum, so Stephen is in danger of surrendering to a schizoid perception that records only the surfaces while it neglects to intuit the innerness of things, plants, people, to a perception voyeuristically detached from the world. Joyce also scored much of the tempo of Ulysses to parody the jerky, truncated tempo of the silent film, when many Dubliners, appearing as actors and viewers, playing inauthentic roles, wandering through Dublin as voyeuristic watchers of the cinematic scenarios of

61

modern life, reading off scripts by rote as so many automatic Irish Frankensteins, peopled his frequent filmic scenes. Indeed, these cinematic themes resurface in <u>Invisible Man</u> as we shall see in Chapter III.

Yet Joyce had to offer a way out of this mechanical net. He proposed a synthesis. For Chaplinesque, gadget-loving and obsessed Bloom, Kenner's hard line to the contrary, is a humane reconciliation of man and machine. Bloom, much as Peter Wheatstraw, hopes to use the mechanical sea of matter as grist for his creativity. As Bloom to Stephen, Wheatstraw imparts his wisdom to Jack the Bear:

"What is all that you have there?" I said, pointing to the rolls of blue paper stacked in the cart.
"Blueprints, man. Here I got 'bout a hundred pounds of blueprints and I couldn't build nothing!"
"What are they blueprints for?" I said.
"Damn if I know--everything. Cities, towns, country clubs. Some just buildings and houses. I got damn near enough to build me a house if I could live in a paper house like they do in Japan. I guess somebody done changed their plans," he added with a laugh. "I asked the man why they getting rid of all this stuff and he said they get in the way so every once in a while they have to throw 'em out to make place for the new plans. Plenty of these ain't never been used, you know."
"You have quite a lot," I said.
"Yeah, this ain't all neither. I got a couple loads. There's a day's work right here in this stuff. Folks is always making plans and changing 'em."
"Yes, that's right," I said thinking of my letters, "but that's a mistake. You have to stick to the plan." [<u>IM</u>, pp. 171-72]

As "bricoleurs" Bloom and Wheatstraw would harmonize with their environment rather than attempt to escape it or allow it to absorb them. They would take the time to study the plan rather than become the plan.

McConnell cites an essential, ontological fact about the film medium which further amplifies the struggle against the mechanical in the works of these writers. Since film itself presents a two-dimensional depiction of space, actors on celluloid tend to become thingified, democritized with the inorganic objects in the film frame, literally embalmed in celluloid. Film acting at its best for McConnell involves the attempt of the actor to assert a human/mechanical dialectic within the filmic space in order to escape this illusion of being ontologically equal to objects. A good film actor, then, must essentially struggle with the mechanical nature of the film medium itself. Hence the exaggerated pace and speech of Cagney, the stamina of Paul Robeson.[90] For Joyce, the film medium served as an apt symbol, along with the printing press, of the threatened 20th century. McConnell describes Chaplin's power, a power not lacking in Bloom and Wheatstraw:

> Chaplin's greatness is, simply, to have incorporated within his film personality a crucial, archetypal aspect of all film personality: that struggle of the human to show itself <u>within</u> the mechanical. . . . Slapstick is the purest structural version of this struggle, the manifestation of the mechanical opening of <u>City Lights</u>--trying to survive among the marmoreal, mythicized versions of the self with which tradition has surrounded and nearly strangled us.[91]

In the works of these three writers, the image of the city is presented in terms of a reified, slapstick space. Sometimes merciless as in the scenarios of Wright's drab Chicago where the folk consciousness of the Southern black transplants is threatened. A great anxiety in many of the works we will examine results from the possible triumph of the machine and of the alien slapstick space of the city over the minds and bodies of characters.

The need to articulate and transcend the nets that would retard the slow dark birth, the formation of conscience, in these Irish and American heroes will occupy much of this study when themes inherent in the Irish-black American connection are delineated. But now we need to examine the peculiarily Irish qualities of Ellison's and Joyce's concepts of invisibility.

Indeed, the complex experience of invisibility in Ellison's novel derives not only from Ellison's own indigenous experience as a black American, but also from many literary, religious and philosophical sources which span centuries. From the story of Ham where Ham is punished by banishment and condemned to bear a black, literally unseen progeny as a result of his viewing his naked, drunken father Noah urinate, Ellison discovered one of the earliest myths of exclusion and invisibility, a myth where blackness is equated with the state of being unseen. From Homer, Ellison, as Joyce before him, observed the peculiar anxiety of Penelope, Telemachus and Ulysses' court in determining the certitude of the identity of Ulysses. Indeed, Ulysses must reveal his scar, for personality is protean; Ulysses, a changed man. From Sophocles, Ellison adapted the quest of Oedipus to uncover the mystery of his origins in a milieu of family intrigue. From European folklore Ellison discovered the myth of the sleeping or dead warriors of middle earth, warriors who one day would rise and resume the rule of their invaded country. From Hegel and William James, Ellison learned the importance of recognition by the Hegelian "other" during successful identity formation. Failure of recognition, rejection, was a cause for "invisibility."[92] From Kierkegaard, Ellison discovered a dialectic between an individual's false selves and the realization of a more authentic inner self that might be nurtured through an existential leap. From Dostoevsky and other 19th century Russian writers, Ellison discovered that in a Hegelian world the roles dictated by the Hegelian "master" can, if accepted by the "servant," create an inauthenticity of self, a series of "false-self systems" in the subsequent words of R. D. Laing, that could eventually obscure the core of self, the drives for self-realization, and lead to a pathological diffusion of identity. From Melville, Ellison found that the irrational, ego-splitting process outlined in "The Whiteness of the Whale" created abstract, unreal self-images of whiteness and blackness in the races which ultimately reduced both races to invisibility.[93] From the American Transcendentalists and their Eastern influences, Ellison sounded an elusive yet benign oversoul that

could be located in the otherwise fallen minds of
men. From Malraux's Man's Fate, came the protean
Baron Clappique, a myth and mask ridden character, a
figure who would serve as one source both for the
estranged hero of "King of the Bing Game" and for
Rinehart. From Camus and French Existentialism,
Ellison was able to learn how to fine tune the concepts of Hegelian man and to discover that all men,
not only the oppressed, are related to the master/
servant pattern, that all men are guaranteed a degree
of "bad faith," and that the defiance of bad faith
must become a moral thrust of the healthy individual.
From Wright's "The Man Who Lived Underground,"
Ellison discovered an invisible anti-hero who was
reduced phenomenologically to the bare id, who
resembled a naked, primal man-embryo, virtually
without false-selves, in a "green-lemon," uterine
underground which itself is filled with the symbols
of civilization--clocks, money, diamonds, electric
lights, radios--symbols which the anti-hero detaches
from cultural connotation and hierarchy, much as he
himself is detached from society.[94] And from African
and Caribbean folklore, Ellison may have recalled the
invisible spirits and zombies that populate various
folk legends--legends which often refer to the native
as being possessed by the curse of oppression.

But from Joyce, more than from these diverse
sources, Ellison gleaned the most. He eagerly
studied Joyce's complex improvisations on the invisibility of the Irish. Dubliners revealed to Ellison
the ways in which bad faith, "Bovaryism," the assumption of social masks, could lead to "paralysis," a
word and a state of mind that echoes through
Invisible Man as do other Joycean words such as
"confused," "confess," "apologize," "betrayal,"
"wake," and "hesitate," words that all reinforce the
invisibility theme. Ellison may also have noted
Stephen's contempt for the gaminess of life in
Stephen Hero, a quality further amplified as Stephen
assumes and rejects the various roles of student,
priest, and "artiste" in A Portrait. Stephen must
name himself, define himself, act on his inner music
and form an authentic selfhood in order to cure his
"diseased conscience" and free himself from the
spirits of the dead, the masks, the artifical roles
that have possessed his fellow Dubliners.

In Ulysses the concept of invisiblity is further
developed. Mulligan mocks Stephen and links him to

Caliban, the slave of Prospero, a monster enraged "at not seeing his face in a mirror. . . ." [p. 6] Sensing the drift, Stephen says of his shaving mirror and of the Irish artist: "Its a symbol of Irish art. The cracked looking-glass of a servant." [p. 6] The theme accretes when Stephen recalls lines from Edwin Hamilton's pantomine:

> "I am the boy
> That can enjoy
> Invisibility." [p. 10]

Invisibility, accompanied with distorted mirror images, resurfaces when Stephen and Bloom nervously view their reflections at Bella's brothel. They see not themselves, but: "The face of William Shakespeare, beardless . . . rigid in facial paralysis, crowned by the reflection of the reindeer antlered hatrack in the hall." [p. 567] Of the reflection, Shakespeare ironically tells Bloom, "Thou thoughtest as how thou wastest invisible. Gaze." [p. 567] Indeed, Bloom, with his sado-masochistic fantasies, finds safety in self-consciously manipulated masks which allow him to confound both the Watch in "Circe" and the threatening nighthags of the brothel. Protean Bloom, a Ulysses trickster type to be sure is also a cultural potpourri, a genealogical fact that further adds to his invisibility. Morton Levitt notes that Bloom was baptised as Protestant and later converted to Catholicism for his marriage with Catholic Molly.[95] Bloom's father, Rudolph, also converted from Judaism to Catholicism before his suicide. To add to this Irish stew, Bloom's mother, Ellen Higgins, may have had a Jewish father.[96] Joyce uses Bloom's "confused" geneology to emphasize a positive aspect of invisibility. For Bloom is able to transcend the narrow aspects of a national identity and strive for human universals through his unprejudiced acceptance of the family of man. Unlike the provincials of Dublin, he is catholic in his tastes but not in his prejudices. He is able to exploit his confused ethnic background and at the same time symbolize the intertwined lineages in Ireland which have resulted from almost continuous invasions and occupations of the country by diverse nationalities.

    Self-conscious, chameleon Bloom is a genesis for HCE in _Finnegans Wake_, for this confused Wakean character serves as an invisible composite of all native/invader mixes. "Here Comes Everybody" (HCE) resembles a cultural Irish stew so stocked with nationalities that he ceases to have a precise lineage. In fact, much of the <u>Wake</u> reveals variations of the theme of Oedipus, when the search rages on for the true identity and paternity of this possessed character. The search is carried out in the pub and resembles the act of staring into a double mirror. It is learned the HCE is a "spoof of visibility in a freakfog." [p. 48] His unconscious spews out the confession that he has "centuple selves" which "by coincidence of their contraries reamalgamerge in that identity of undiscernibles. . . . ." [pp, 49-50] Understanding the "low visibility" of HCE and of the Irish is indeed "a slopperish matter," for a stew of all the introjections of past personalities possess the Irish unconscious where "<u>one is continually firstmeeting with odd sorts of others at all sorts of ages</u>" amid the "nomanclatter" of the <u>Wake</u>. History, with its invasions and assimilations, is, for Oedipus-HCE, "a fog of invisibility." [pp. 51, 147]

The frantic search for the identity of HCE and the Irish reaches an impasse. He is "not at all, man. No such parson. No such fender. No such lumber. No such race." [p. 63] Wakean characters, in general, come to resemble Laing's descriptions of states of schizophrenia where the prevalence of introjected false-self systems in individuals break down the core of self into splinters, into invisibility.

Indeed, Jack-the-Bear has a wakean experience when he gazes at his own multiplied mirror image in the white woman's bedroom. She has stereotyped him unwittingly as a black stud and this false definition prompts a confused glimpse:

And in the mirrored instant I saw myself standing between her eager form and huge white bed, myself caught in a guilty stance, my face taut, tie dangling; and behind the bed another mirror which now like a surge of sea tossed out images back and forth, back and forth, furiously multiplying the time and the place and the circumstance. [<u>IM</u>, pp. 405-406]

Another Joycean ingredient to the stew of
invisibility was also picked up by Ellison. For
Joyce, those who stereotype the Irish or any other
group in negative terms ultimately wind up subtract-
ing humanity from themselves. For the British projection of sexuality and animalism onto their
colonial subjects, ironically, robbed the British
psyche of much of its own sexual confidence and
identity. Anglo-Saxons cultivated "sex in the head,"
as D. H. Lawrence put it, or "angelsexonism," as
Joyce punned it in the Wake. This disease is shared
by Norton in Invisible Man. He must also bear the
shame and bad faith of adhering to the stereotypes of
white purity because he secretly envies Trueblood's
incestuous act.

Joyce's x-ray views into the Irish unconscious
directly influenced Jack's dream in the Prologue
where Jack, too, discovers the lineage of the Negro
to be confused and varied, the result of the long
history of American burrowings, of rape and miscegna-
tion. Both Joyce and Ellison, however, seek a comic
and paradoxical transcendence from this aspect of the
nightmare of history. They regard the loss of
"ethnic purity," finally, as a strength, invisibility
as an asset. Ellison's statement echoes the Joycean
conscience:

First, we came from Africa. We had to
learn English. We had, in other words, to
create ourselves as a people--and this I
take right down to the racial, the bloodlines, the mingling of African blood with
bloodlines indigenous to the New World. A
few people can trace their connections back
to a given African tribe, but for most of
us, no. We can't even trace our blood back
only to Africa because most of us are part
Indian, Spanish, Irish, part any and every
damn thing. But culturally, we represent a
synthesis of any number of these elements.
And that's a problem of abstraction in
itself; its abstraction and recombining.
When we began to build up a sense of
ourselves, we did it by abstracting from the
Bible, abstracting the myths of the ancient
Jews, the early Christians, modifying them
as we identified with these people, and projecting ourselves. This was an abstract

process. We knew that we were not white; we knew that we were not Hebrews; but we also know something else: we knew we didn't <u>have</u> to be in order to make these abstractions and recombinations. This was a creative process, one of the most wonderful things which ever happened on the face of the earth. This is one of the great strengths which now people seem to want to deny. But this was the <u>reunification</u> of a shattered group of people.[97]

The theme of invisibility, then, is for both writers multifaceted and paradoxical, for invisibility offers the hope of transcendence, the "abstraction and recombining" that creates a more diversified identity. The theme includes the myth of Ham, a myth of exclusion; it embraces the stereotyping process whereby false roles and false selves are subtly ingrained into personality, false selves which either fog or block inner drives for self-definition. It involves the recognition of the fact that those who attempt to define others wind up cementing themselves into inauthenticity. It involves the examination of the burrowings of history, the miscegenation, that confuse lineages and prevent a certain blood identity, that ethnic purity upon which so much is foolishly stacked. And it involves the recognition that sham roles will generate bad faith if individuals acquiesce. But here lies the road to the transcendence of history's nightmare. "When is a nam nought a nam" asks Shaun. "When he is a sham," replies Shem. The formation of "the culture of the universal," as Fanon put it, and the shedding of gaminess and false social roles lurking in the nets Stephen and Jack must fly over become the ultimate avenues to humanity for these writers. To be sure, Ellison learned some of his existentialism from Joyce.

Intricately connected to the whole theme of invisibility in Ellison's novel are the image of the coalhole and the broader theme of "middle earth," which, as in the case of invisibility, he derived from several sources but primarily from Joyce's adaptation of Celtic folklore. Wright first drew upon the imagery in "The Man Who Lived Underground" where a definite Joycean influence is also evident.

Ellison took Wright's uterine, womb-like underground
and transformed it into a symbol of untapped psychic
energy issuing from the elusive innerness of man.
Ellison also learned of "The Legend of the Dead
Warriors," which relates the plight of conquered
heroes who lie in their omaphalos, through Lord
Raglan's The Hero.[98] Katherine Briggs' study of
European folklore reveals the variations and
complexities of the legend especially as it was told
among Celtic people. She recounts a tale of Oison,
which Ellison may have studied along with the Wake.
In the legend, Oison, mounted on a white steed,
returned from another land only to discover that his
native Ireland had been transformed: the forests had
shrunk, and little was left at Tara, the Celtic place
of kings, except a rounded green hill packed with
stunted men who were singing and dancing in their
brilliantly illuminated mound. The end of the heroic
age in Ireland resulted from the spread of
Christianity and the rise of foreign invasions after
which myths of "shians" or fairymounds were born.[99]
Briggs reveals that the inhabitants of these mounds
were varied: they could be a conquered race; they
could be called "Bogies"; they could be black fallen
angels hurled to earth by Satan during the war in
heaven; and they could inhabit mines: gold, silver,
iron and even coal mines, as well as fairymounds.[100]

Ellison apparently discovered an image from
folklore, then, that he could refashion for the
American milieu. The brightly illuminated, raucous
omaphalos became a source of Jack's underground, a
place subversively lit with by a magical 1369 lights
fed by Monopolated Light and Power, a place filled
with the loud, dissonant music of invisibility that
wails beneath the jungle of a fringe area of Harlem
instead of beneath Oison's plundered forest.

Both Ellison and Wright must have noticed the
recurrence of the mythology of middle earth when they
eagerly discussed Joyce's works. Middle earth
appears in A Portrait during Stephen's troubled
dreams:

    25 March, morning: A troubled night of
dreams. Want to get them off my chest.
    A long curving gallery. From the floor
ascend pillars of dark vapours. It is
peopled by the images of fabulous kings, set

in stone. Their hands are folded upon their
knees in token of weariness and their eyes
are darkened for the errors of men go up
before them as dark vapours.
Strange figures advance from a cave.
They are not as tall as man. One does not
seem to stand quite apart from another.
Their faces are phosphorescent, with darker
streaks. They peer at me and their eyes
seem to ask me something. They do not
speak. [p. 522]

In the "Siren" section of Ulysses, the discordant
singing of the living-dead barflies recalls middle
earth imagery and it becomes a lietmotif of Joyce's
music of invisibility. Bloom muses:

Low in dark middle earth. Embedded ore.
Naminedamine. All gone. All fallen. . . .
[p. 257]
. . . .
But wait. But hear. Chords dark.
Lugugugubrious. Low. In a cave of the dark
middle earth. Embedded ore. Lumpmusic.
The voice of dark age, of unlove,
earth's fatique made grave approach, and
painful, come from afar, from hoary mountains, called on good men and true.
[p. 283]

In "Hades," middle earth varies as Bloom mourns over
the omaphalos, the grave of Parnell, mythologized by
the half-hearted Irish as sacred ground. This
omaphalos and the nationalistic sentiments
surrounding it are debunked in "Circe" when freshly
buried Paddy Dignam appears from his coalhole-grave
and immediately jumps back in:

He worms his way through a coalhole, his
brown habit trailing its tether over rat-
tling pebbles. After him toddles an obese
grandfather rat on fungus turtle paws under
a grey carapace. Dignam's voice, muffled,
is heard baying under ground: 'Dignam's
dead and gone below.'
He executes a daredevil salmon leap in
the air and is engulfed in the coalhole.
. . . [p. 474]

A great admirer of Parnell, Joyce is parodying the alleged sentimentality inherent in Irish Nationalism, the need expressed by the Dubliners to passively worship heroes (whom they inevitably betray) rather than to actively develop a conscience.

The theme of middle earth culminates in the Wake. If Dostoevsky could explore the convoluted "underground of my heart," Joyce could do variations on his variations. HCE's confession becomes a discordant hymn or dirge of interpenetrating volcanic passions and desires from the "ding idself" and the many false selves that exist there. Shem the "coalprince," Finn MacCool and HCE end up as a composite figure of the Irish when they await rebirth from the nightmare of history. Shem is described as an "unseen blusher in an obsene coalhole, the cubilibum or your secret sigh, dweller in the downandoutermost where voice only of the dead may come. . . ." [p. 194] Then too, HCE, as Hibernian, "hibernating Massa Ewacka," leads a "demidetached life" as a symbol for the sleeping Irishman. [p. 79] Finn set the prec dent, for the English Pale drove him "to the underground." [p. 128] In the "coalcellar," "my invisibly lying place," the Wakean anti-hero must separate "i, from my multiple me's." [p. 410] But as Yawn disintegrates and the coalhole of his mind gradually emerges, the tremendous confusion and paralysis of the "gratefully oppressed" is "dully expressed" to an "invisible" fairy watcher from Finn's ancient party. The fairy presence seats himself on a knoll, brags of his singing, and proceeds to talk to the Four Old Men when he is interrupted by wild singing and nationalistic chants and battle cries reverberating from the mound. And these cries echo the drunken desire both for vengeance and for masochistic self-punishment as well:

--The snare drum! Ley you lug til the ground. The dead giant manalive! They're playing thimbles and bodkins. Clan of the Gael! Hop! Whu's within?
--Dovegail and finshark, they are ring to rescune!
--Zinzin. Zinzin.
--Crum abu! Cromwell to victory!
--We'll gore them and geah them and gun them and gloat on them.
--Zinzin.

> --O, widows and orphans, it's the
> yeomen! Redshanks for ever! Up Lancs.
> --The cry of the roedeer it is! The
> white hind. Their slots, linklink, the
> hound bunthorning! Send us and peace!
> Title! Title!
> --Christ in our irish times! Christ on
> the airs independence! Christ hold the
> freedman's chareman! Christ light the dully
> expressed!
> --Slog slagt and slaughter! Rape the
> daughter! Choke the pope!
> --Aure! Cloudy father! Unsure!
> Nongood!
> --Zinzin!
> --Sold! I am sold! Brinabride! My
> ersther! My sidster! Brinabride, goodbye!
> Brinabride; I sold! [p. 500]

Deep in the coalhole of the Irish mind is that masochistic desire for punishment that has resulted as a by-product of imperialism and its devaluation of a people who now would sell out their women. A battle scenario of the Protestants versus the Catholics of Ireland emerges from the unconscious landscape, and Joyce reveals a national psyche filled with splits, with the fissures of confused allegiances. The Wakean anti-hero must transcend all of this ballyhoo and return from the coalhole not as an IRA gunman, or fighting Orangeman, but as a liberated Bloom or an incubating Stephen. The image of the coalhole is transformed by Joyce, much as it is by Ellison and Wright, from a nationalistic image to a psychic symbol by means of a portmanteau word: "astroglodynamonologos," a word which Robert Boyle has broken down as follows:

> "astro" - star
> "troglodyte" - cave dweller
> "dynamo" - source of power
> "monologos" - lonely speaker
> "logos" - the Word.[101]

He argues that Aristotelian Shem must go deeper than Buck Mulligan into the coalholes of sensuality and sluggish matter in order to reach an artistic conscience that can transubstantiate matter into the divine life of art.[102] The image of the lonely

artist as cave dweller recalls the painful attempts
at honesty by Dostoevsky's narrator in <u>Notes From</u>
<u>Underground</u> who confesses:

> It seems that all this human business really
> consists only in man's proving to himself
> every minute that he is a man and not a cog,
> proving it even it if costs him his own
> skin, proving it even if he has to become a
> troglodite. [103]

This portmanteau word also reveals that the
artist must probe the inner recesses of the human
psyche in order to release and articulate repressed
energy, both benign and sadistic, rather than dam it
up as the mother and the priest would do. In the
coalhole resides the "ding idself," and intwined with
it, the inner music Stephen hears, the "hot red
light" Jack experiences, and the black glistening
coal. Ellison explains it all:

> The final act of <u>Invisible Man</u> is not
> that of a concealment in darkness in the
> Anglo-Saxon connotation of the word, but
> that of a voice issuing its little wisdom
> out of the substance of its own inwardness--
> after having undergone a transformation from
> ranter to writer.
> . . . .
> And in keeping with the reverse English
> of the plot, and with the Negro American
> conception of blackness, his movement verti-
> cally downward (not into a 'sewer,' Freud
> notwithstanding, but into a coal cellar, a
> source of heat, light, power, and through
> association with the character's motivation
> self-perception) is a process of rising to
> an understanding of his human condition.
> [<u>SA</u>, p. 57]

74

First you were Nomad, next you were Namar,
now you're Numah and its soon you'll be
Nomon. [FW, p. 374]

Douglass came North to escape and find work
in the shipyards; a big' fellow in a sailor's
suit who, like me, had taken another name.
What had his true name been? Whatever it
was, it was as Douglass that he defined himself. And not as a boatwright as he'd
expected, but as an orator. Perhaps the
sense of magic lay in the unexpected transformation. 'You start Saul, and end up
Paul,' my grandfather had often said. 'When
you're a youngun, you Saul, but let life
whup your head a bit and you starts to
trying to be Paul - though you still Sauls
around on the side.' [IM, p. 372]

CHAPTER II

Paradoxically, behind the frequent, compassion-
ate, or vicious diatribes against parental figures in
the fiction of Joyce, Ellison, and Wright there
emerges a central, although only partially articu-
lated, complaint. Each writer laments the near
non-existence of a viable patriarchal family structure which, through the exertion of positive forms of
authority, might allow their various fictional heroes
to internalize a conscience during the adolescent
years. And would-be authority figures are often
deflated, not because they possess that quality, but
because they use improper authority to suppress
instead of to nuture the young, because they
jealously horde power rather than willingly transfer
it gradually to the next generation. That both the
Ireland and the America depicted in the fictional
worlds of these writers are largely devoid of
nurturing, confident fathers, authority figures, or
of competent mothers who might create a sense of
basic trust in their children appears to serve as
a root cause for the ordeals of many of these
writers' heroes, and as a leaven for the schizoid
tendencies often evinced by their protagonists.

But the blame cannot be placed on families, on
teachers, on college administrators, or on ministers
alone, for these fictional societies, from cradle to
grave, reveal at nearly every stage a rejective,
schizogenic inclination which not only reinforces
feelings of rejection experienced by these heroes in
early childhood and adolescence, but also insures
that throughout life further unwarranted rejection
will result. Familial rejection becomes a kind of
psychological epicenter of shock waves that will
ripple throughout all the institutions of the highly
individualistic, competitive societies depicted by
this Irishman and by these two Americans in the
church, in the college, in industry, or in political
parties and movements. And for Ellison and Wright,
the black character's pronounced experience of invisibility, of being an outsider, tends to display in
greater relief the inhumanity of the schizogenic
society as a whole.

Wright was fascinated by the cross-cultural
pathology of family life in America. Sensing the

loss of genuine fatherhood in <u>White Man, Listen!</u>, he would go so far as to somewhat ambivalently recall the hierarchical order of medieval Europe, an order which validated the patriarchal family:

But another and deeper dilemma rose out of the white man's break with the feudal order, a dilemma more acidly corroding than even that of slavery, one which colored and toned every moment of his life, creating an anxiety that was never to leave him. The advent of machine production altered his relationship to the earth, to his family, to his fellow man, and even to himself. Under feudalism the family had been the unit of production, the nexus of emotional relations, a symbol of the moral order of the universe. The father was the head of the family, the king the father of the state, and God the ruler of man. The eternal and temporal orders of existence coalesced and formed one vivid, timeless moment of meaning, justification, and redemption. Man and earth and heaven formed a unit. [p. xxii]

The loss of this moral center resulting from the new servile relationship of men to machines had a spinoff in America later on. For men developed "a riven consciousness," they tried to

cling to the emotional basis of life that the feudal order gave them, while living and striving in a world whose every turn of wheel, throb of engine, and conquest of space deny its validity. [p. xxii]

Yet for Wright the feudal order was a "feudal dragon" that had to be slain by the oppressed masses who fell outside its orderly rhythms. [p. xiii] But the death of this dragon, the loss of its authority over men, created a new dragon, a new awakening:

But man refuses to behave; having once awakened from the feudal dream and tasted of the sweet fruits of sensuality, speculation, wonder, curiosity, freedom of movement, he will accept nothing less. Stimulated by the pinch of circumstance, he acts irrationally;

> he won't let well enough alone; he sulks; he
> broods; he dreams; he revolts. . . .
> [p. xiii]

The loss of a system of authority, biased as it was,
then, created new monsters. Behind Wright's protest
is a subtle, apparently unacknowledged conclusion:
There can be two kinds of repression in family and
state, one malignant, the other benign and positive.
If feudalism largely fell short of instilling positive forms of repression, the 20th century for
Wright appeared virtually divested of any but the
more primitive and degenerate forms of authority.

For Ellison, the collapse of feudalism was to be
applauded. It created the novel form:

> the novel developed during a period which
> marked the breakup of traditional societies,
> of kingship, and so on; and by the 1950's,
> the great masters of the nineteenth century
> had fashioned it into a most sensitive and
> brilliant form for revealing new possibili-
> ties of human freedom, for depicting the
> effects of new technologies upon per-
> sonality, and for chartering the effects
> wrought by new horizons of expectation upon
> the total society. [1]

Yet, despite the creation of new possibilities and
the promise of equality predicated by the demise of
feudal order, both writers seemed to lament the near
absence both in American families and in institutions
of benign patriarchs (be they fathers or father-
figures) who ideally would not restrict the world of
possibility, but instead provide the rites of passage
and the inculcation of a conscience that would
prepare their various heroes for the adventure of
life. Both Ellison and Wright revealed that new,
more debased forms of paternalism, of 20th century
feudalism, had perverted the natural growth of men
and women toward autonomy in the fatherless world of
America. The radical separation of the world of
work from the home, the attempted emasculation of the
black male in an oppressive milieu, the thrust to
relegate the working class to a cog-like brotherhood
with the machines of farm and factory, the usurpation
of the father's authority by wife, church or by the
fraternal, fatherless orders that emerge in the

fiction of these writers, orders that have slain the dragon of feudalism and parcelled out its lifeless pieces, all have contributed to the cross-cultural demise of genuine fatherhood in the America of these writers.

And out of this chaos arose defensive matriarchal families, battlefields of the sexes, prompting the male protagonists of these writers to often reject their parents and to further mitigate the possibility of mature heterosexual love in later life. Cold, confused mothers skirmish with hypermasculine, insecure men while the masquerade of viable family life is played and replayed throughout much of this fiction. Sinister fathers and father surrogates clutter their works: Richard's sadistic father, Bledsoe, Brother Jack, Brockway, Emerson, Norton, and the bosses of Wright's farms and factories. Incompetent mothers and mother-figures attempt to dominate crippled males in an effort to create some order and familial cohesion: Richard's puritanical grandmother; Bigger's mother; Cross Damon's mother, from whom he learned "dread;" Jack's incestuous mother-lovers; Aunt Mackie in "A Coupla' Scalped Indians"; and Trueblood's hatchet-swinging wife, Kate. But the attempt to stabilize the family through the expression of female domination complicates the chaos, and intensifies the self-destructive familial and social battles of the sexes. For Wright, Ellison and their mentor Joyce, true fatherhood could emerge only when biological fathers were superceded, when the sham of paternalism inherent in usurping institutions and in the diseased logic of political and social oppression could be exposed. And Ellison's and Wright's observations of a nearly fatherless America dovetailed also with observations of writers of the American Renaissance concerning the corruption of institutions and the crippling effect institutions have on individual autonomy.

But it was Stephen Dedalus' project of restoring the "fallen father" by a kind of Apostolic succession through Stephen's identification with select heroes instead of with his own father that must have exerted the most analogies to their own similar projects. Stephen Dedalus hears a "worldly voice," from his ambivalent conscience that bids "him raise up his father's fallen state." [P, p. 333] Stephen has just reflected upon the fraternal nature of male

comradeship at Clongowes school, an order which seems
to deter the formation of conscience:

> This spirit of quarrelsome comradeship which
> he had observed lately in his rival had not
> seduced Stephen from his habits of quiet
> obedience. He mistrusted the turbulence and
> doubted the sincerity of such comradeship
> which seemed to him a sorry anticipation of
> manhood.
> . . . he had heard about him the constant
> voices of his father and of his masters,
> urging him to be a gentleman above all
> things and urging him to be a good catholic
> above all things. The voices had now come
> to be hollowsounding in his ears. [P, p.
> 332-33]

What constituted an authentic father-son
relationship? What constituted the proper relationship between men and institutions? What was the
genuine "politics" of human relations in the family
and in the state? Such questions guided these three
writers in their analogous quests for a vision and
definition of genuine human freedom, of successful
family relations and of workable parental authority.

In two letters to Alessandro Francini, Joyce
angerly confessed:

> My political faith can be expressed in a
> word: Monarchies, constitutional or
> unconstitutional, disgust me. Kings are
> mountebanks. Republics are slippers for
> everyone's feet. Temporal power is gone and
> good riddance.[2]

Later he wrote:

> As an artist I am against every state. Of
> course I must recognize it, since indeed in
> all my dealings I come into contact with its
> institutions. The state is concentric, man
> is eccentric. Thence arises an eternal
> struggle.[3]

Yet, it would be wrong to assume that Joyce was
opposed to a proper authority. Ellmann summarizes

Joyce's battle with the usurpations of conscience in Ireland:

> . . . secular power and spiritual power egg on their adherents to persecute others and to abase themselves. Imperialism, which can be religious as well as profane, is in either aspect missionary for hatred although it pretends, through father-figures such as king, priest, fatherland, to proffer paternal love. In the church militant, as in Caesarism, the Marquis de Sade and the Freugerr von Sacher-Masoch are conjoined. Their ultimate expression is Nobodaddy, as Blake called the tyrant god, and Nobodaddy may only be overcome by imaginative sympathy. [4]

Indeed, Joyce appears to have opposed illegitimate authority, that bogus authority that would prevent the orderly transference of power from the adult to the adolescent, as opposed to authority which judges the young because it has earned the right to judge, that nurtures and reassures the adolescent, that is secure enough not to recoil into a defensive and rejective paternalism. For as Joyce probed Irish masculinity, it may well have been the demise of legitimate concepts of authority that finally proved most distasteful and threatening to him. The result of such a demise was devastating: The Joycean hero's emerging selfhood is not recognized as valid; the hero regresses into perpetual adolescence, into the kind of eternal boyhood epitomized by Mr. Dedalus, an admitted "pal" rather than a genuine father for young Stephen. Jack the Bear, much as Stephen, looks beyond the family for nurturing authority but only encounters a series of paternalistic father surrogates who are even more distant than his biological father. In a study on the abuses of authority, Richard Sennett describes this phenomena. He reveals that the metaphor of the boss, the teacher, and the preacher as fatherly figures is basically a distorted metaphor, for, unlike an ideal father-figure, these individuals are often too distant to offer recognition or to encourage emulation in modern bureaucratically oriented society. [5] Stephen and Jack the Bear walk through this exahusted bureaucracy.

In 12 Million Black Voices Wright spoke of the
persistence of feudalism in Southern plantations, a
feudalism which bred a perverse parent-child depen-
dency between the "Lords of the Land" and the black
serfs:

> Although our association partakes of an odd
> sort of father-child relationship, it is
> devoid of that affinity of blood that
> restrains the impulse to cruelty, empty of
> that sense of intimate understanding born of
> long proximity of human lives. [p. 49]

For Joyce, Ellison, and Wright such a oblique and
confused paternalism could be found in nearly all the
institutions they examined: in the industrial shop,
in the union, in the school, in the paternalism of
the white culture, in the priesthood, in political
mass movements, and in the family itself.

The near demise of masculine integrity encouraged
by overt, imperial institutions also led to a tragic
conclusion in Joyce's fiction. For the expectations
of dominating forces, be they church or state, could
become internalized in the Irishman. In "The
Wandering Rocks" section of Ulysses, usurpation
becomes highly successful, for the Centenary
Celebration of Robert Emmet's execution has been can-
celled by some docile Irish in order to both
celebrate the visit of King Edward VII and to mourn
the death of Pope Leo XIII. Such an act recalls the
"confused" loyalties in Dubliners when Martin
Cunningham praises the Jesuit priesthood for its lack
of corruption and Pope Leo XIII as "one of the lights
of the age." [p. 142] Such ambivalent loyalty
reveals, then, an internalization of the value system
of the oppressor or usurping force, and a similar
state of unmind reverberates in Wright's Lawd Today
when the men ridicule Africa, the black women in
America, and nearly all aspects of black life; and in
The Long Dream when Fish realizes that Gladys accepts
the white value system along with its definition of
her as an "inferior." Mixed loyalty reaches its
extreme in Ellison's portrait of Supercargo
("superego"), whose name puns his internalized white
racist precepts concerning the need to control the
"primitive" impulses of blacks.

In a discussion of the plight of Jews in Nazi
concentration camps, Gordon Allport notes that such

an internalization of the superego of the oppressor can become the last ego defense in any oppressed group:

. . .identification with one's oppressors was a form of adjustment that came only when all other methods of ego defense had failed. At first prisoners tried to keep their self-respect intact, to feel inward contempt for their persecutors, to try by stealth and cunning to preserve their lives and their health. But after two or three years of extreme suffering many of them found that their efforts to please the guards led to a mental surrender. They imitated the guards, wore bits of their clothing (symbolic power), turned against new prisoners, became anti-Semites, and in general took over the dark mentality of the oppressor.[6]

Such tragic usurpation of human autonomy stimulated by the debased paternalism of British rule cut deeply into the Irish as well. O'Farrell notes how English rule "fossilized" Ireland, how it prevented the creation of autonomous Irish institutions that could foster a genuine, national identity. The vestiges of Irish identity could not be totally annulled, however, and Ireland regressed defensively. O'Farrell explains:

Failing to destroy that identity, it provoked a reaction in which the Irish clung stubbornly to the only identity they knew, while the years, and centuries passed. Thus, eventually, Counter Reformation Ireland, a historical and religious relic, out of time but very much in place, confronted modern, secular, industrial Britain. Much that was of spiritual and human value had been retained.
Nevertheless, for Ireland whatever was British had become suspect, tainted, not least that modern, social and economic progress characteristic of the oppressor nation. But not only did English rule arrest the internal development of Irish self-awareness, preserving it in a premodern condition, it also gave that self-

awareness a savage directional twist--
towards England, creating the Irish-English
relationship into an Irish obsession.[7]

The Irish became the victims of a vast double-bind.
They retrenched into an outmoded and half-heartedly
accepted Irishness while at the same time they looked
to a more advanced England and Continent for reciprocity and validation of their worth as a nation.
This confused state is apparent in young Stephen
Dedalus when he oscillates between a desire to "raise
up Ireland's fallen language and tradition" and a
counter impulse to transcend Irish nationalism. The
ruling principle of the English was often neither
strong repudiation of Irish traditions and language
nor active concern for its subjects. Rather, the
English practiced neglect of their colony more often
than not, a neglect which became an ingredient in
Irish invisibility, in the ultimate devaluation of
the Irishman's sense of worth, a neglect that Ellison
and Wright found so analogous to white American
ambivalence over black America.

In the fictional worlds of these writers, genuine
male and female plenitude has nearly atrophied. For
Ellison, only the grandfather, Trueblood, the brown
girl singer, Wheatstraw, the singer at Tod's funeral,
Brother Tarp, and Susie Gresham retain vestiges of
self-confidence and autonomy, vestiges derived in
part from their African and American folk heritages.
The folk heritage retained by these characters was
disintegrating in the urban centers of America; the
family was splintering, according to Ellison and
Wright. Indeed, the cultural uprooting and migration
of all new arrivals to America often hastened the
decay of the patriarchal family, however, and Ellison
and Wright drew comparisons between the traumas both
of black families and of the families of European
transplants on American soil.

The whole issue of psychological disturbances
among blacks, the Irish, and among oppressed people
in general is a delicate one that must be discussed
with proper qualifications. If an affluent, objective suburbanite were to walk down a crowded, poor
ghetto street in New York City or Belfast today, this
observer might very well take note of several people
who reveal symptoms of "abnormal" behavior. He might
be tempted to conclude that poor blacks or poor Irish

84

are generally more prone to escapism and role
playing, that they are more filled with repressed
anger, aggression, paranoia and discontent than their
wealthier counterparts. These "abnormal" symptoms
are ubiquitous in international ghetto life, but such
symptoms should not necessarily be regarded as
indigenous or somehow innate in ghetto dwellers. For
these reponses may often be perfectly normal reactions to dehumanized, oppressed conditions that
anyone in such a situation might exhibit. If this
same objective suburbanite were to study a sampling
of the family structure in ghettoes, he might also
conclude that poor, urban American black and Irish
Catholic families reveal greater incidences of inter-
familial violence, oedipal fixations, incest,
divorce, fragmentation and the like than families in
wealthier circumstances. This observation sometimes
proves to be true, but the miracle is that family
life can survive at all in ghetto conditions. In
many cases our observer might even discover that some
ghetto families are more intact, that parents in
these families deal with children more competently,
that ghetto family life may sometimes be more
enriching and structured than much of the disintegrating family life in affluent suburbs.[8] In our
discussion of the paralysis inherent in the ghetto
families depicted by these writers, then, it should
never be inferred that blacks or Irish Catholics
either as individuals or as families are in some ways
less equipped to strive for social order and cohesion. On the contrary, it should be clear after
countless sociological studies that oppression itself
often forces psychological adaptations to the ghetto
environment that allow groups such as poor urban
blacks and Irish Catholics to survive in a hostile
environment. Then too, writers such as Joyce and
Ellison may tend to describe extremes in the behavior
of their characters and in the family life of their
cultures so that the emotional damage can be
dramatized.

For Ellison, especially, American families in
general were under assault. For the fallen father
haunts the ghetto and the affluent white world as
well in Invisible Man, and Ellison's depiction of
fatherhood recalls Leslie Fiedler's comment:

. . . for marriage also means an acceptance
of the status of a father: an abandonment

85

of the quest to deliver the captive mother
and an assumption of the role of the ogre
who holds her in captivity. There is no
authentic American who would not rather be
Jack than the Giant, which is to say, who
would not choose to be 'one of the boys' to
the very end. The ideal American postulates
himself as the fatherless man, the eternal
son of the mother.[9]

Joyce's descriptions of the fallen fathers of
Dublin may well have exerted their impact on the
imaginations of Wright and Ellison as they, too,
lamented the demise of the family in their own
fiction; and it is to the Joycean family that we now
turn in an attempt to trace possible lines of
literary influence.

As Barbara Tomasi has carefully noted in her
discussion of the fraternal theme in Joyce's fiction
"on June 16th, 1904, there is no father, no ruler, no
Parnell, and his loss engenders a vision of sexually
inadequate and mutilated Ireland."[10] Indeed, from
<u>Dubliners</u> through <u>Finnegans Wake</u> the "unsubstantial
father," himself scarred by church and state and the
women of Ireland, must retaliate by warring against
his own children. As Mark Troy has noted, the
apostrophe is missing in <u>Finnegans Wake</u> because Finn,
like Osiris, has been figuratively castrated,
deprived of his manhood, the apostrophe as penis.[11]
Such psychic castration is a lietmotif in Joyce's
fiction. Little wonder that the priests and fathers
in <u>Dubliners</u> are paralysed. The memory of Father
Flynn in "The Sisters" evokes for the boy-hero the
feeling of "paralysis" when this nameless hero gazes
at the dead priest's flat:

Every night as I gazed up at the window I
said softly to myself the word paralysis.
It had always sounded strangely in my ears,
like the word gnomon in the Euclid and the
word simony in the Catechism. But now it
sounded to me like the name of some malefi-
cent and sinful being. It filled me with
fear, and yet I longed to be nearer to it
and to look upon its deadly work.[12]

It is no coincidence that echoes of the word
"paralysis" appear repeatedly in much the same context in the fiction of Ellison and Wright. From
fallen priests, Dubliners leads us to fallen fathers:
the green-eyed pervert in "An Encounter," who would
beat the young boys for having sweethearts; Eveline's
predatory father, who chases children with a
blackthorn stick, who prevents his daughter's love
affairs, and who, long ago, put on his wife's bonnet
at the symbolic Hill of Howth to make his children
laugh during a picnic; Little Chandler (an embodiment
of the Irish cultural inferiority complex along with
Jimmy Doyle in "After the Race"), who reveals a "row
of childish white teeth," who symbolizes the Irish
bureaucrat employed under "the feudal arch of the
Kings Inns," and who raises children conscious of
their father's helplessness before their mother; the
stout drinkers of "Ivy Day in the Committee Room,"
who praise Edward VII and unwittingly debase the
memory of Parnell; and Tom Kernan, a "confused"
Protestant in "Grace," who has submitted through
marriage with a shrew to the "pale" of the Catholic
Church and who has fallen down the stairs and bitten
his tongue to add confused speech to his confused
marriage. [D, pp. 80, 81, 171] Join with these
fallen fathers Farrington of "Counterparts," who
beats his son to compensate for his own failings and
humiliations suffered during an abortive day; or
weak-blooded Freddy Malins or bitched Gabriel Conroy
in "The Dead." The hopeless movement of Gabriel's
grandfather's horse around the statue of William the
Conqueror and Gabriel's own failure in love with
Gretta epiphanize the emasculation of Joyce's
Dubliners, for Gabriel representatively struggles
with half-acknowledged humiliations visited upon him
from political domination and the Dublin matriarchy.

The fallen father and emasculated male haunt
Stephen's thoughts in Stephen Hero and A Portrait as
well, and Stephen's reflections reach an epiphany
when he discovers the word "foetus" etched on his
father's student desk:

But the word and the vision appeared before
his eyes as he walked back aross the
quadrangle and towards the college gate. It
shocked him to find in the outer world a
trace or what he had deemed till then a
brutish and individual malady of his own
mind. [P, p. 340]

For Stephen realizes that he is not so unlike his father, that he, too, is "all in all," a potential fallen father, the bearer of a fetal conscience. To prevent this future plight, Stephen must search for a Daedalus, a Thoth, a Shakespeare, an artistic father to inculcate in him an artistic conscience, to free him from Dublin's paralysis through Apostolic succession. And Joyce will increasingly view his own fiction as a kind of intellectual shock-therapy applied hopefully to the fallen family, a therapy that assumes a cure.

The dearth of fathers preoccupies much of Dublin's youth, who, like Stephen, resemble "Japthet in search of a father." Indeed, Baby Boardman cannot say the word "papa"; Boody Dedalus, Stephen's sister, wishes Simon Dedalus dead; and Gerty McDowell, whose own father drank himself to death, resembles Stephen in her sentimental yet genuine need for a father.

And the laments and rage of the Wakean dreamer reverberate on similar frequencies, when the hopeless attempts to restore genuine authority are thwarted by ubiquitous parricidal wishes from the unconscious, wishes which fuel the nightmare of history.

The composite picture of fatherhood emerging from Joyce's fiction, then, is a vision of male insecurity, of drunkeness, of hypermasculine attempts at the domination/degradation of the women of Ireland, a mockery of paternity.

Ellmann's criticism often implies that Joyce either preferred the collapse of the oedipal configuration, that Joyce denied its validity altogether, or that he applauded the father's fall. However, Ellmann partially misses the pathos of Joyce's fictional family, and he underestimates Joyce's desire to restore in Stephen a semblance of viable oedipal identification with father surrogates lifted from the historical litter of artistic and political heroes. Ellmann argues:

> Joyce disagreed, then, with Jones and Freud about the oedipal situation, probably because he found little trace of it in himself. He preferred the filial Greeks to the parricidal (and matricidal) ones, Telemachus and Ulysses (for Ulysses also is a son in the book) to Oedipus and Orestes.[13]

Barbara Tomasi comes closer to the main source of the paralysis of many Joycean fictional families: the failure of the proper working out of the oedipal family drama. She concludes:

> The father is not the enemy, then; Simon Dedalus is a minor and pathetic figure in the novel, but he sings of Ireland's troubles, brought down on her by the real enemy, the fraternity.[14]

This fraternal structure of Irish and American society as seen through the eyes of these writers will be developed later, but now the emotional consequences of these fatherless worlds needs to be examined.

A central image pattern found both in A Portrait and in Invisible Man helps isolate one of the major consequences--feelings of inadequacy which express themselves in Stephen's or Jack's often unconscious fears either of actual or of subliminal castration.

Richard Wasson's study of sight imagery in A Portrait and in Ulysses reveals that blindness or weak, often distorted vision can symbolize castration anxiety for Joyce as for Freud. The threat to the sight of Stephen and of other Joycean male characters results directly from their fearing the power of the phallic eyes of mothers and lovers in the "petticoat" regime from the Dublin family to the Dublin brothel.[15] Although Wasson does not stress colonialism as a major cause for the family dislocation leading to the appearance of these castrating females in Joyce's fiction, he does argue that the image patterns evoking subliminal castration anxiety are most pronounced in Dante Riordan's admonition to young Stephen that he "apologize" for his adolescent sexual fantasies of marriage to Protestant Eileen Vance:[16]

> "--O, Stephen will apologize.
> Dante said:
> O, if not, the eagles will come and pull out
>   his eyes.
>
> Pull out his eyes,
> Apologize,

```
"Apologize,
Pull out his eyes.

Apologize,
Pull out his eyes,
Pull out his eyes,
Apologize." [P, p. 246]
```

"Dante's curse" haunts this novel. Veiled in its ambiguities lurks her divided, confused nationalism, for despite her Republican sympathies (she hit an Irishman with her umbrella for taking his hat off when a band played "God Save the Queen"), she nonetheless, confusedly serves the forces of imperialism and the "hangman god" as they have coursed through history from ancient Rome. Her allegiance to the "eagles of Rome," the mentality of imperial dominance, symbolically aligns the Irish matriarchy with a most severe implementation of those Roman eagles: The colonization of Ireland. Wasson argues: "The punishing eagles of Rome fly at the command of female furies, not father images."[17] The word "apologize" curiously echoes throughout the fiction of Joyce and Ellison. In both cases it often signals guilt resulting from submission to the oppressor or to one's inauthentic selves. In fact, the word is punned in the Wake as "apoloquise." [p. 414]

Castration anxiety is also evoked in Stephen during the meal when Stephen remembers how Eileen put her "long white hands" over his eyes.[18] This playful blinding by Eileen's phallic fingers associates with Stephen's memories of Clongowes where he earlier "felt his body small and weak amid the throng of players and his eyes weak and watery." [P, p. 278] For Wasson, Joyce links Stephen's weak eyes with feminine, red, watery eyes, eyes which are punished as "a sexually offending organ," eyes which would begin the adolescent encounter with the bodies of women.[19] He notes Freud's discussion of hysterical blindness where Freud symbolically equates the eyes with the penis, and blindness with castration.[20] Stephen's "visual lust" will develop defensively into the theme of sexual voyeurism. It begins as he hides under the table to look at women's legs. For Stephen, looking implies sexual curiosity that can evoke castration anxiety in this icy, puritanical matriarchy.[21]

Ellison's use of eye imagery as a subliminal index of castration anxiety appears to have been partly influenced by sight imagery in A Portrait. In the battle royal episode of Invisible Man, the parody of Joycean imagery begins to emerge along with Ellison's American variations on Dante's curse. The similarity of the white stripper to Stephen's vision of the bird girl has been noted by several critics. When Stephen reflects on his vision, he closes his eyes and feels "the strange light of some new world." [P, p. 435] Like Stephen, Jack can only look: "Had the price of looking been blindness, I would have looked." [IM, p. 19] Ironically, that price is similar to the one the white Southerners are suggesting to the young men through this perverted rite. For as George Kent notes, this ritual is designed to implant in the young men the reality of castration for any actual sexual contact between black men and white women.[22] Jack recalls the ambivalent emotions of attraction and repulsion he experienced toward the stripper, and goes on: "I had a notion that of all in the room she saw only me with her impersonal eyes." [p. 19] Jack, like Stephen, experiences this woman as a maternal surrogate. He reestablishes the narcissism of the child. The ritual continues and castration imagery associated with the eyes becomes more threatening for Jack when he enters the ring, much as in a primitive initiation rite, blind-folded. When "confused" Jack wonders if he should violate the false humility he will speak of in his speech, he is slugged in the eye and goes down.

Reminiscent of the manner of Joyce, Ellison offers us a substructure of unconscious meanings in this episode and those to come. As with Stephen, Jack's awakening sexual desire is entwined with his need for mother-love. Nonetheless, such awakening passions for Stephen and for Jack are mixed with threats that evoke castration anxiety expressed through eye imagery. Jack's reddened eye is the first symbolic wound of the novel. It will be followed by other wounds.

Sight imagery continues when Jack recalls the statue of the college Founder,

. . . the cold Father symbol, his hands outstretched in the breathtaking gesture of

91

lifting a veil that flutters in hard,
metallic folds above the face of a kneeling
slave; and I am standing puzzled, unable to
decide whether the veil is really being
lifted, or lowered more firmly in place;
whether I am witnessing a revelation or a
more efficient blinding. And as I gaze,
there is a rustle of wings and I see a flock
of starlings flighting before me and when I
look again, the bronze face, whose empty
eyes look upon a world I have never seen,
runs with liquid chalk--creating another
ambiguity to puzzle my groping mind. . . .
[p. 36]

Like the vacant eyes of Joyce's priests, the
Founder's eyes are "empty." [p. 36]

For we recall from A Portrait that it is not only
the Irish husband or lover who has been symbolically
castrated by the matriarchy, but also the priests
have come under the knife. Wasson discusses the
imagery of priestly vision in A Portrait:

God is in both punishing and redeeming roles
conceived in female imagery, and the church
becomes an instrument by which the will of
women makes itself felt. Priests, the male
servants of the church, bear the marks of
the fury; their eyes are described as
"nocolored," "pale," "loveless," "devoid of
spark." [23]

Interestingly enough, the Founder, who knew only his
mother, and the "empty" eyes of the statue are reinforced by the "eyes blind like those of robots" of
the students. [IM, p. 36]

Subliminal castration anxiety reemerges in the
Trueblood section. Jack, in a "confused" fashion,
introduces Norton to tabooed Jim Trueblood. Jim
suffers an unhealed wound on his face. The conver-
sation between Trueblood and Norton reveals humorous
misunderstandings. Envious Norton asks Trueblood,
"you feel no inner turmoil, no need to cast out the
offending eye?" Trueblood answers: "My eyes is all
right too. And when I feels po'ly in my gut I takes
a little soda and it goes away." [p. 51] The fact
is that Trueblood is in better tune with human

sexuality than his inquisitor. Norton has repressed his own sexuality which includes his lingering incestuous desires for his dead daughter. In this section Ellison provides similar subliminal castration imagery such as that found in Joyce's works, but he goes well beyond the Joycean skills he so admired. Like Dante, Kate has learned her concepts of sin, her guilty vocabulary and her propriety from the preacher. When she calls Matty Lou's unborn baby a "black bomination" (which according to Kate's logic would "bawl yo wicked sin befo the eyes of God"), Trueblood laments, "She musta learned them words from the preacher." [p. 66] Indeed Trueblood, along with Wheatstraw and finally Jack, is one of the only whole characters in the novel. Trueblood is unable to feel any abhorrence at his sexuality, at his "dream sin." He accepts Matty Lou's pregnancy as unfortunate, but irreversible; whereas Kate, with the help of Aunt Cloe, would abort the child and, in the logic of the novel, commit the real sin. The imagery of eyes and castration reveal that Kate, like Dante, is a phallic castrator. Rather than accept the powers of darkness, of the bodily desires, she would repress those desires and link them with the demonic.

This whole episode is ironic, for Trueblood, who appears to have been symbolically castrated by his wife, is actually never broken. He retains his manhood and dignity. Norton, however, is lacking. When he listens to Trueblood, Norton holds a symbolic "unlit cigar," while Trueblood bites "into a plug of chewing tabacco." [p. 53] Jack, who rejects Trueblood as he will later reject Peter Wheatstraw, sees "a red mist" before his eyes when he listens to Trueblood's almost guiltless recounting. [p. 58] When Kate discovers the coitus of Trueblood and Matty Lou, she tries to stop it, but dreaming Trueblood can't stop, and he later recalls:

"There was only one way I can figger that I can get out--that was with a knife, and if you'all ever seen them geld them young boar pigs in the fall, you know I knowed that that was too much to keep from sinnin'." [p. 59]

He rejects self-castration just as he later rejects abortion. But Christian Kate would do the castration herself. When Kate stands over him like an enraged

Medusa from a terrible nightmare, Trueblood looks
into Kate's eyes and later remembers: "Lawd, them
eyes." [p. 61]   This terrifying image of Kate,
hatchet in hand, recalls Stephen's vision of his dead
mother in "Circe," whose image is superimposed with
the hangman god. "Paralysed" Trueblood feels like a
jay bird that has been stung to death and goes "way
back a distance into my head, behind my eyes," but in
his inner being he can find no guilt to equal Kate's
accusations. When Kate, curiously likened to "a
switch engine," throws the axe, Trueblood opens and
closes his eyes and feels like a dog with its tail
"tucked between" its legs running in circles. [p.
66ff] Trueblood is threatened, but like the dog, not
broken. And like Perseus facing his Medusa without a
reflective shield, he feels the effects of symbolic
castration when he stands "stark stone still."   Yet
he refuses to let her steal his manhood and his place
as father, as patriarch. He sings the blues that
well up from his authentic self:

> "Finally, one night, way early in the
> mornin'. I looks up and sees the stars and
> I starts singing'.   I don't mean to, I
> didn't think 'bout it, just start singing.
> I don't know what it was, some kinda church
> song, I guess." [p. 65-66][24]

He makes up his mind to resist bad faith, to stand up
to Kate's religious affectation, ". . . I ain't
nobody but myself," and he later asserts to Kate,
"I'm a man and a man don't leave his family." [p.
66] When she challenges his resolution again, he
stands firm, "I'm still a man." [p. 67]

Subliminal imagery continues.   Kate buys some
"eyeglasses. . . what she been needin' for so long."
Perhaps she will respect the folk wisdom and strength
of her husband and see through her condemnation of
his act, and act which, as Bluestein has noted, would
be a normal occurrence in some African families where
incest assumes entirely different connotations.[25]
Norton's eyes remain "unseeing," however, and he
stares blankly while Trueblood's children sing
"London Bridges Fallin' Down." [p. 68]

Ellison has used several Joycean motifs to
construct the Trueblood episode: the collusion of
the matriarch with the clergy to usurp the father's

authority; castration anxiety linked to possible harm to the eyes that itself emanates from the phallic eyes and postures of Kate; the contrast between sex tainted with guilt and the hope for a measure of sexual freedom; the states of "paralysis" and "confusion;" and the contrast between authentic selfhood and the identity for the "other" that Kate tries to emulate. But Ellison's parody goes far beyond its Joycean echoes to become one of the most complex treatments of human sexuality and male resoluteness in world literature.

With its incestuous overtones, Trueblood's dream draws from Joycean motifs but goes well beyond any slavish adherence to them. For Trueblood, much like Stephen and Bloom, dreams a sexual quest for the oral, pregenitial good mother, a figure dimly recalled from earliest infancy, a figure which appears inimical to ultimate repression. In recounting his dream, Trueblood recalls that it was his Ma that went with him to Mr. Broadnax's dream house. Therefore, the white woman Trueblood penetrates in his dream may be a surrogate for the mother, much as his daughter serves as a surrogate for a younger Kate. For Trueblood's "dream sin" amounts to a uterine return of his entire body, not merely of his penis, as his dream-self wanders through the uterine canal:

"I git aloose from the woman now and I'm runnin' for the clock. At first I couldn't get the door open, it had some kinda crinkly stuff like steel wool on the facing. But I gits it open and gits inside and it's hot and dark in there. I goes up a dark tunnel, up near where the machinery is making all the noise and heat. It's like the power plant they got up to the school. It's burnin' hot as iffen the house was caught on fire, and I starts to runnin', tryin' to get out. I runs and runs till I should be tired but ain't tired but feelin' more rested as I runs, and runnin' so good it's like flying' and I'm flying' and sailin' and floatin' right up over the town. Only I'm still in the tunnel. Then way up ahead I sees a bright light like a jack-o-lantern over a graveyard. It gets brighter and brighter and I know I got to catch up with it or

else. Then all at once I was right up with
it and it burst like a great big electric
light in my eyes and scalded me all over.
Only it wasn't a scald, but like I was
drownin' in a lake where the water was hot
on the top and had cold numbin' currents
down under it." [p. 58]

Indeed, food, "sweatmeat," helps to trigger
Trueblood's oral fantasy, and any phallic level in
the dream, except for the disguised hymen as
"jack-o-lantern," seems nearly absent. In his "oral"
quest appear suggestions of Bloom's similar
unconscious fantasies. Both retain their manhood,
their stubborn consciences. both are able to negotiate the deeper layers of the psyche, and the
Trueblood episode comes more and more to resemble
both Bloom's acknowledged cravings for his daughter
Milly and his attraction to Gaea Tellus, the pregeni-
tal, oral mother, Molly Bloom.

And Trueblood, like Bloom, is a central
character. For Trueblood has discovered a freedom.
In the Prologue a "confused," dreaming Jack asks the
black mistress of the dead slave master "What is
this freedom you love so well?" She has told him
that freedom lies not in hating, but "it's in
loving." [pp. 10-11] She was able to love the
masked humanity of her white master and receive his
"gift" of humanity, her sons, but she hated his
false-self, his social self that he revealed through
dominance. Trueblood, much like Jew-Greek Bloom with
Catholic Molly, is able to discover, if only in
fantasy, a universal experience which only inciden-
tally involves a white woman but fundamentally
initiates Trueblood into his authentic sexuality and
selfhood. Perhaps this is why Jack must learn race
consciousness as he masks his inner self with social
values. That love transcends artificial human
barriers appears to be Ellison's assertion. It was
so for Joyce, as well.

In the Golden Day episode, subliminal castration
imagery reveals a strange variation. When Norton,
sporting a wound on his head, closes his eyes, he is
more terrifying to Jack than when those eyes were
open:

He was like a formless white death, suddenly
appeared before me, a death which had been

there all the time and which now revealed itself in the madness of the Golden Day. [pp. 84-85]

Norton resembles Joyce's weakeyed priests, those servants of the hangman god in A Portrait who have surrended their manhood to a thirsty diety. Norton is "trustee of consciousness," as Vet ironically puts it, or more accurately "To some, you are the great white father. To others the lyncher of souls, but for all, you are a confusion come even into the Golden Day." [pp. 88, 91-92] Like Joyce's priests, Norton reveals a sexless, petrified paternalism, and, like those priests again, he would block the growth of his "children." Jack senses the paternalistic relationship when he fantasizes his apology to Norton:

I wanted to stop the car and talk with Mr. Norton, to beg his pardon for what he had seen, to plead and show him tears, unashamed tears like those of a child before his parent. . . . [p. 97]

Homer Barbee's blindness also aligns him with the weakeyed priests in A Portrait, and his name recalls Joyce's Barbe, the bearded father. Homer sermonizes on the religion of the fatherless Founder as he casts him into a composite from various hero myths. Barbee continually makes the Founder's life representative of the lives of all black people and in so doing he molds the audience into a mythic frame:

"You awakened when he awakened, rejoiced when he rejoiced at their leaving without further harm; arising when he arose; seeing with his eyes the prints of their milling footsteps and the cartridges dropped in the dust about the imprint of his fallen body; yes, and the cold dustencrusted, but not quite fatal blood. And you hurried with him full of doubt to the cabin designated by the stranger, where he met that seemingly demented black man. . . ."[p. 119]

And then:

"His is a form of greatness worthy of your imitation. I say to you, pattern yourselves upon him. Aspire, each of you to some day follow in his footsteps." [p. 131]

The student who sits next to Jack accepts the vicariousness and paternalism of Barbee's speech when the student's eyes resemble "a distorting cataract of tears." [p. 121] Ironically, Barbee's sermon is hardly a call for freedom; it is a plea for subservience to myth, to heroics that are inauthentic, larger than life. When Jack listens to the histrionic rhetoric, a Joycean brand of juxtaposition occurs which humorously undercuts Barbee's message during a sterile silence, "As Barbee paused the silence was so complete that I could hear the power engines far across the campus throbbing in the night like an excited pulse." [p. 129] As if to epiphanize his paternalism, Barbee crumples to the stage; his glasses fall off and his blind eyes are revealed. Bledsoe offers Joycean-like "apologies" to the nervous audience.

One of the few authentic moments Jack observes in the chapel occurs when the students express their emotions after the Barbee performance.

Dr. Bledsoe walked to the edge of the platform and lifted his arms. I closed my eyes as I heard the deep moaning sound that issued from him, and the rising crescendo of the student body joining in. This time it was music sincerely felt, not rendered for the guests, but for themselves; a song of hope and exaltation. [pp.131-32]

Here the students submit by closing their eyes in the face of the true call to freedom. They recall Susie Gresham's closed eyes before the sermon. For Susie, like Trueblood, reveals an authenticity of self that survives regardless of the expectations and limitations imposed by racism, expectations symbolized earlier by the moon which hovers over the campus to observe the students who appear "as though on exhibit even in the dark," to that sphere, "a white man's bloodshot eye." [pp. 107-108]

Jack, much like Stephen, will finally learn not to collude with paternalistic forces be they from the camp of the oppressed or of the oppressor. As Jack walks across the College, eye imagery continues. He cautiously listens to a group of old women while they enthusiastically discuss Barbee's speech: "One used a cane which from time to time she tapped hollowly upon the walk like a blind man." [p. 134] And when Jack meets Bledsoe after the sermon, he notices that Bledsoe's eyes, which seem to emerge from the half shadow, are "burning." [p. 134] And he is introduced to paternalism gone mad when Bledsoe calls him "boy," nigger," and "son," while he tries to initiate Jack into debased authority that conspires with the white power structure, much as Joyce's priests collude with British expectations. [p. 135] Indeed, Jack feels that he is at a perverse fraternity initiation when Bledsoe attempts to coerce Jack into playing the submissive Negro to Norton.

> "This is a power set-up, son, and I'm at the controls. You think about that. When you buck against me, you're bucking against power, rich white folk's power, the nation's power--which means government power. " ....
> "But I've made my place in it and I'll have every Negro in the country hanging on tree limbs by morning if it means staying where I am." [pp. 140-41]

As we might expect, Bledsoe's "power" motif echoes the priest's hope that Stephen Dedalus might join the priesthood.

> "To receive that call, Stephen," said the priest, "is the greatest honour that the Almightly God can bestow on a man. No King or emperor on this earth has the power of the priest of God. No angel or archangel in heaven, no saint, not even the Blessed Virgin herself has the power of a priest of God: the power of the keys, the power to bind and to loose from sin, the power of exorcism, the power to cast out from the creatures of God the evil spirits that have power over them, the power, the authority, to make the great God of Heaven come down upon the altar and take the form of bread and wine. What an awful power, Stephen!" [P, p. 418]

Bledsoe's paternalism temporarily triumphs over Jack's will, and, reminiscent of Stephen who must justify his broken glasses to the Dean, Jack suffers a "distorted vision."

The subliminal castration imagery continues when Jack is interviewed by Emerson's nameless son. And the son's advice becomes more ironic, for Totem and Taboo appears on the son's desk adjacent to exotic birds trapped in bamboo cages. Like the rebellious homosexual sons in Freud's Primal Horde, this son seems to have undergone the terror of a psychological emasculation. He advises Jack:

> "Ambition is a wonderful force," he said, "but sometimes it can be blinding. . . . On the other hand it can make you successful--like my father. . . ." A new edge came into his voice and he frowned and looked down at his hands, which were trembling. "The only trouble with ambition is that it sometimes blinds one to realities. . . ." [IM, p. 181]

The twitching of Emerson's son's face recalls the facial imagery of wounds (Jack's cut eye, Trueblood's cut face, Norton's laceration), and it indicates deeper mutilation, for this homosexual "Huckleberry," who bears no name but that of his father, has been unable to reach an independent manhood. The nameless son tells Jack: "Identity! My God! Who has any identity any more anyway?" [p. 184] When he warns Jack not to meet with Emerson, he snatches off his own glasses and shuts his eyes. He then confesses to Jack that he is the entrepreneur's son: "My father, yes, though I would have preferred it otherwise." He also links Bledsoe with his own father when he looks at Jack with "a burning eye." "He's like my. . .he ought to be horsewhipped." [pp. 186-87] Like Baby Boardman, this American son cannot say the word. Admidst the nightmarish screams of the caged birds, he reminds Jack not to "blind himself" to reality, and confesses of his monster father,

> "You're free of him now. I'm still his prisoner. I'm still his prisoner. You have been freed, don't you understand? I've still my battle." He seemed near tears. [p. 189]

The episode ends with the Parker melody about "poor Robin." Jack realizes that he himself may be Robin with a "shaved tail"; that he is not unlike the exotic birds in the cage of America, or in the cages that Barbee and Bledsoe nervously make with their hands. Jack's solution to his possible entrapment? ". . . I decided that I would go back and kill Bledsoe. Yes, I thought, I owe it to the race and to myself. I'll kill him." Jack, like Stephen who never reacts so violently, finds himself in a world of fallen fathers and fallen father-figures. This theme crosses racial lines in the novel. Emerson's son's rage at his father is not so different from Jack's astonishment at the debased authority of Bledsoe, an authority epiphanized by images: Bledsoe's fishbowl with its miniature feudal castle, and the pillared President's home. When we recall that one of the veterans at the Golden Day curses his father's memory; that the boys in Jack's marijuana dream in the Prologue would rend their white father to pieces; that Jack has few memories of his own bland father, the memory of whose voice fills Jack, as do the shouts of Ras, with an "emptiness," we further understand the depth of the Joycean influence as well as Ellison's originality. Vet's Joycean advice seems to be the only way out:

> "Now is the time for offering fatherly advice," he said, "but I'll have to spare you that since I guess I'm nobody's father except my own. Perhaps that's the advice to give you. Be your own father, young man. And remember, the world is possibility if only you'll discover it." [p. 154]

And if College is a "kind of mother and father," as Emerson's son puts it, nonetheless, Jack's grandfather, Trueblood, Wheatstraw and the Vet will serve as true fatherly initiators for Jack, much as Bloom serves as a marginal initiator for Stephen. [p. 180]

Jack's struggle for a conscience, the threat to sight, and other familiar themes continue when Jack enters the industrial hell of Liberty Paints. Here, a 20th century analogue to slavery, the industrial "plantation," is exposed. The boss is Sparland, a name which, like Supercargo, recalls the terminology of the British Imperial Navy. This industrial master

is in trouble, for the Union, another version of the
fraternal secret society, has formed. Masters
proliferate when another small time tyrant, Kimbro,
known as the "colonel," the "slave driver," the
"Yankee cracker," and the "northern redneck," sends
Jack to mix black dope to whiten the symbolic paint.
[pp. 194, 196] When Jack asks the purpose of the
dope, Kimbro snaps "you must do as you're told."
[p. 196] Jack does, and he commits his first grandfather act when he subversively caps the paint mixed
with remover after his Joycean "hesitating." He is
then transferred into a modern Inferno "three levels
underground" to work for "Mister" Lucius Brockway.
In this underground slapstick plantation, the
machines comically imitate the motions of men, while
men imitate machines. After Jack returns from the
fraternal and exclusive Union meeting, subliminal
castration imagery reappears when Jack looks at
Brockway "through a kind of mist." [pp. 195ff]
Jack, much as Stephen who wishes no harm to the
peasant that Mulrennan speaks of in the final "diary"
of A Portrait, acquiesces to Brockway: "You were
trained to accept the foolishness of such old men as
this. . . ." And when he tells furious Brockway that
he has not joined the Union, after being falsely
accused of doing so, "a black blur" irritates his
young eyes. Jack curses Brockway as the slapstick
continues, and Brockway bites him as they stuggle.
[p. 221]

Mock submission turns to real castration during
the ensuing explosion, however, when "a blinding
flash" puts Jack into the company hospital where his
identity and name nearly dissolve. [p. 225] And as
memories from a more authentic folk identity flash
through his mind, he closes his blurring eyes. Then
he experiences the electric shocks which recall his
"initiatory" ordeal on the rug at the battle royal.
Through "a white mist" he squints at the blazing eyes
of the dreamlike monster Doctor whose questions:
"Who was Buckeye the Rabbit?" and "Boy, who was Brer
Rabbit?" ironically recall "an old identity." [p.
236] Like Trueblood, who watched a noiseless, moving
mouth in his dream, Jack finds himself in a dreamy
mechanical womb ("a machine my mother") as he drifts
through layers of false values and the maya of clock
time and space only to hit on a more fundamental
self, an inner music. [p. 235] He, like Trueblood
again, cannot be mentally castrated by the shock

machine, despite a voice's suggestion "Why not
castration doctor?" No castrated Samson, Jack lives
out the advice of the slave mother in the Prologue as
he contemplates his possible destruction of the
machine. He will seek freedom by avoiding destruction in a passage that echoes Stephen's confrontation
with the hum of the mechanical in Ulysses: "Whoever
else I was I had no desire to destroy myself even if
it destroyed the machine; I wanted freedom, not
destruction." [p. 237] He then has another epiphany
that further echoes Stephen's search for the freedom
that results from an authentic sense of self. "When
I discover who I am, I'll be free." [p. 237] For
Jack, as for Stephen, the mechanizers of
consciousness and the machine environment they have
created are ominous. Stephen muses in Aelous:

> The whirr of flapping leathern bands and hum
> of dynamos from the powerhouse urged Stephen
> to be on. Beingless beings. Stop! Throb
> always without you and the throb always
> within. Your heart you sing of. I between
> them. Where? Between two roaring worlds
> where they swirl, I. Shatter them, one and
> both. But stun myself too in the blow.
> [p. 242]

Freedom for Stephen and for Jack will result in
the subjective act of destroying the false selves
that veneer human innerness rather than in disturbing
the universe. Stephen and Jack will not play their
cultural versions of the "dozens"; they will resist
the masks that result in the destruction of transit
with their fundamental self; they will avoid external
violence that would block the genuine violence
necessary to achieve a measure of conscience and
freedom. As the Vet told Jack on the bus, "there's
always an element of crime in freedom." [p. 153]
Jack will not commit the existential crime of slaying
his social roles, those fabrications of the fraternal
or maternal forces of dominance which try to set the
limits on possibility. He will name himself and
escape the white fog of conformity. Like Trueblood,
Jack finds himself compensated for his plunge into
the unconscious, for his epiphany of forgotten layers
of the self. But unlike Trueblood, he will articulate why such compensation is made. When Jack leaves
the factory hospital the implications of his electric
rebirth become manifest:

. . . I had been talking beyond myself, had
used words and expressed attitudes not my
own. . . . I was in the grip of some alien
personality lodged deep within me. Like the
servant about whom I'd read in psychology
class who, during a trance, had recited
pages of Greek philosophy which she had
overheard one day while she worked. It was
as though I were acting out a scene from
some crazy movie. Or, perhaps, I was
catching up with myself and had put into
words feelings which I had hitherto
suppressed. Or was it, I thought, starting
up the walk, that I was no longer afraid? I
stopped, looking at the buildings down the
bright street slanting with sun and shade.
I was not longer afraid. Not of important
men, not of trustees and such; for knowing
now that there was nothing which I could
expect from them, there was no reason to be
afraid. [p. 244]

Like Stephen, again, Jack has begun his fortunate
fall: "And I felt that I would fall, had fallen,
moved now against a current sweeping swiftly against
me." [p. 244] Stephen, likewise, begins his downward fall into the coalhole of existence after his
vision of the bird girl, a vision which sparks
rebirth: "To live, to err, to fall, to recreate life
out of life!" [p. 434] And Jack, like Stephen, is
about is about to begin his transformation from
ranter to writer in Ellison's portrait of the artist
as a young bear, to tap that inner "hot red light"
underneath the ice of false selves.

The struggle to form a conscience, to stop
apologizing, to separate authenticity from these
false selves that would confuse and petrify human
innerness, concerns chapter after chapter of these
cyclic novels. Variations on the theme continue when
Jack undergoes another epiphany. When he bites into
a delicious, warm yam, he feels a new freedom quite
antithetical to the presumptions of Bledsoeism:

I walked along, munching the yam, just as
suddenly overcome by an intense feeling of
freedom--simply because I was eating while
walking along the street. It was exhil-

arating. I no longer had to worry about
who saw me or about what was proper. To
hell with all that, and as sweet as the yam
actually was, it became like nectar with the
thought. If only someone who had known me
at school or at home would come along and
see me now. How shocked they'd be! I'd
push them into a side street and smear their
faces with the peel. What a group of people
we were, I thought. Why, you could cause us
the   greatest   humiliation   simply   by
confronting us with something we liked.
[p. 258]

His recognition of and pride in his roots, "I yam
what I am," parody Finnegans Wake and Shaun's similar
realization of the value of underground tuber. For
during Shaun's inquest, he is asked to define his
relation to the primal father. Now reduced to
exhausted Yawn, he answers "I am yam" in an attempt
to prove that he is of Irish lineage, that he is of
direct descent both from the primal father of
Ireland and from the Totem God. [pp. 481-82] Such
certainty of lineage is questionable among the
culturally mixed Irish, and Yawn's assertion is a
nervous one. Clearly, Jack's freedom in eating yams
mocks Bledsoe's desire to imitate the habits and
expectations of the decadent whites who would define
him. Yet Jack's experience with the yam sensation is
a nervous one as well, for this nostalgia for happy,
freer childhood days, this new pride in his rural
background, can become a trap in itself, a
sentimental escape into ethnicity:

Continue on the yam level and life would be
sweet-though somewhat yellowish. Yet the
freedom to eat yams on the street was far
less than I had expected upon coming to the
city. An unpleasant taste bloomed in my
mouth now as I bit the end of the yam and
threw it into the street; it had been frost-
bitten. [p. 261]

Conscience must be made, not ready made. The days of
childhood when one had not yet been yoked into a
role, when the self was freer to explore the world
without blinders, are a base for a mature conscience
and not ends in themselves. The self must be forged.

Yam-like nostalgia threatens to keep Jack in a
passive, dependent state when the sight of Primus
Provo and Provo's wife helps spark the childhood
memory Jack's mother at a frozen clothesline. And
much as the yam has a bitter spot, so too, the
vision of the Provos, for the sight of the breast
pump nauseates Jack, much as the matronly Mary Rambo
"threatens" Jack's "infant eyes" with the sight of
her fleshy body on the street. Jack is still not
fully weaned. And the dependence on food that
underlies the yam fantasy continues with maternal
undertones when Jack reacts to the odor of cabbage in
Mary's kitchen, an odor which reminds him of the
"leaner years" of his childhood. He realizes that he
has set up a parent-child relationship. Indeed, he
is a kind of "motherfouler." He asks himself, "What
kind of man was I becoming?" when he realizes his
dependence on her maternal protection. It is during
his attempt to apologize" for failing to pay her all
the rent, that he grows taller: "Suddenly I felt an
urge to go look at her, perhaps I had never really
seen her. I had been acting like a child, not a
man." [p. 289ff]

The use of the cabbage odor to wake nostalgic
memories of childhood, whether pleasant or
unpleasant, invites speculation on another Joycean
echo. For the odor recalls Stephen's acceptance of
the smell of rotten cabbages in A Portrait, a smell
which he links to the disorder of his father's
poverty-stricken home. Stephen's mature tolerance of
the smell parallels his ability to accept Mr. Dedalus
despite the man's failings. And it is this smell
that sways Stephen to reject the role of priest,
later on.

The episode at the Chthonian continues to suggest
the theme of incest, and reveals how this particular
incest desire we are investigating in the fiction of
both Joyce and Ellison hampers the formation of
conscience and maintains the alleged fraternal structure of Irish and American life. Jack's entry into
the splendid rooms, which so glaringly contrast with
the modest boarding house, wakes a false sense of
freedom in Jack, and, on the subliminal level, he
enters into his unconscious, for elements of
Trueblood's dream are again interwoven. And here, as
throughout Invisible Man, the use of slang phrases
such as "mamma," "daddyo," "son," "Mac," "baby,"

"motherfouler," and "boy" reveal the desire of "adults" to relate to others in child-parent configurations. Such regressive and maternal-paternal urges are ubiquitous in this eerie, chthonic underground of the mind.

When Jack is driven to the Chthonian over the "mid-country peace" of the snow-covered city, he knows that this seemingly calm psychological landscape is a facade. For in a zoo nearby the caged animals sleep and appear peaceful only because of their bars; and a nearby "reservoir of dark water," another symbol of the repressed psyche, is ominously buried under a blanket of snow. [p. 272] The owl door knocker seems to guard the entrance to this Circean unconscious place, and when Jack enters the elevator, he cannot tell whether he is going up or down. Then, like Trueblood, Jack is greeted by a "hard, handsome face," by a maternal and masculine white woman who gives him the feeling that there is "only she and I." [pp. 293ff] Reminiscent of Hemingway's Jake Barnes, Jack experiences deja vu; he wonders if he is reenacting a "scene in the movies," from a book, or "from some recurrent but deeply buried dream." The distortion of time and space that characterize Trueblood's unconscious explorations continues when Jack looks at the lighted dial of a radio that, like the vaginal clock in Trueblood's dream, seems to emit no sound. The several musical instruments, which serve to decorate the music room, add latent phallic ingredients to the unconscious interior decoration of the Chthonian, as well: "An Irish harp, a Hunter's horn, a clarinet and a wooden flute were suspended by the neck from the wall on pink and blue ribbons." The color symbolism and the useless instruments serve as a schematic of the repressed desires of these would-be carousers. The music of the inner self is absent in this part of the Chthonian underground, and absence of music seems to indicate a denial of the energy of the inner self by the Brotherhood. This sterile silence differs substantially from the blaring music that will echo through Jack's underground in Harlem. Brother Jack escorts the invisible man into yet another room "in which one entire wall was hung in Italian-red draperies that fell in rich folds from the ceiling." Amid "pale" beige upholstery of the blond wood chairs, Jack sees many "attractive young women," but he avoids "giving them more than a glance," for the latent sexual and pre-sexual level of his descent becomes more apparent. [p. 294]

Emma serves her maternal bourbon to an aroused Jack, and he experiences a twitching of a leg muscle. Oral imagery continues when Brother Jack argues that "The people always throw up their leaders." Emma, whose name puns "ma," and recalls the Emma of A Portrait, counters, "nonesense, they chew them up and spit them out. Their leaders are made not born. Then they're destroyed." [p. 295] America, too, is "an old sow that eats her farrow." Pseudo-liberal Emma, with her penetrating eyes, might harbor her own subliminal desire for devouring as well, for she says "not quite softly enough" to Brother Jack, "But don't you think he should be a little blacker?" [pp. 297ff]

The immaturity of the Brotherhood, its sibling and incestuous impulses, are finally epiphanized as a drunk blurts out a Freudian slip through the door, "St. Louis mammieeee--with her diamond riiiings." Laughter overwhelms Jack when he, perhaps intuitively if not intellectually, understands the perpetual adolescence of the Brotherhood. Jack tries to be one of the "boys" and laugh it all off, but his laughter reveals a lack of insight; his eyes fill with tears. [pp. 305ff]

The struggle to forge a conscience continues. When Jack looks at the photograph of the fighter before giving his arena speech, the imagery of the battle royal is recalled. Again Jack will give a speech; again the boxing imagery and the suggestion of blindness recall the blindfolds worn by the boys at the smoker. Jack remembers that his father had told him long ago how this fighter died in a home for the blind. When Jack continues to betray and surpress his "grandfather self," that "oldness" that "waits inside him," Jack assumes his new heroic mask as black leader for the Brotherhood. Yet the "oldness" drives him during his dispossession speech, and he seeks vengeance for Provo's "cataracted eye" in a confused mental counterpoint. [p. 326ff] Visual distortion occurs when Jack is blinded by the spotlight, a light which recalls the image of the threatening moon shining over the college campus.

His reaction to his role as representative of the people recalls Joyce's satire on the hero-martyr men-

tality of his Dubliners. Jack acts out the people's
anger in a ritual performance that usurps the
audience's thinking while it substitutes theatrics
for action. Predictably, "a curtain" of darkness
seems to separate Jack from the enthused audience,
and sight imagery becomes obsessive when he
metaphorically describes the dispossessed of America
as "a nation of one-eyed mice" with "pillaged eyes."
The image of the "cataracted eye" of Primus Provo's
dream book is recalled, and when Jack labels the
audience his "new family" in the "fraternal land,"
"red spots" appear on Jack's "streaming" eyes. [p.
338] He is "unable to see," and decides that he will
need to wear dark glasses when he speaks again. But
despite his chauvinism, Jack's speech makes him feel
"more human," a feeling he "confesses" to the
audience. For Jack's need to create what his former
teacher, Woodridge, called, in a deliberate Joycean
parody, the "unformed features of his own face"
asserts itself to counterpoint the psychology of
mass movements. Ellison and Joyce agree that all men
are capable of dispossesing others. And it is this
drive in all men that can only be neutralized through
existential exegesis rather than through the rituals
of mass movements. The racist Brothers sense that
counterpoint, and regard it as a threat. Later, Jack
reflects on his college teacher Woodridge, who
argued: "Why waste time creating a conscience for
something that doesn't exist? For you see, blood and
skin do not think!", and concludes that Woodridge
also has not exactly hit the meaning of what being
"more human" really implies:

> But no, it wasn't Woodridge. "More human"
> . . . Did I mean that I had become less of
> what I was, less a Negro, or that I was less
> a being apart; less an exile from down home,
> the South?. . . But all this is negative.
> To become less--in order to become more?
> Perhaps that was it, but in what way more
> human? Even Woodridge hadn't spoken of such
> things. It was a mystery once more, as at
> the eviction I had uttered words that had
> possessed me. [p. 346]

How to reach humanity, how to keep the inner self
alive in the face of potential physical and emotional
castration, how to truly see, this is the riddle Jack
must unravel. And he will discover that onto the

wisdom of Woodridge or of Trueblood must be added the complex and self-conscious inner journey into the depths of the unconscious where hope and tragedy intertwine in the heart of darkness shared by all men. Jack reflects, "For the first time lying there in the dark, I could glimpse the possibility of being more than a member of a race. It was no dream, the possibility existed." [p. 346]   Jack is awakening from the nightmare of history.

With the introduction of Jack's alter-ego, Tod, a new chord is sounded in the theme of psychic and physical castration that will be more thoroughly explored in Chapter III. For Tod comes to serve as a Frazerian scapegoat king during Tod's ritual slaying. For now, we need to mention that hatless Tod is Jack's age; he has an "Afro-Anglo-Saxon" face, a face which recalls Joyce's description of Shem noted earlier as a "Europasianized Afferyank." [IM, p. 324]   Tod's face bears a wound inflicted by a black nationalist. Tod, whose eyes look "inward," is visited with all of the "confusion" being a black person in America can bring. [p. 358] His hatred of black nationalism is justified by his fear of its consequences: a racial war which could decimate Harlem, and a definition of blacks that would limit them solely to alleged racial patterns of behavior and to self-exclusion from Western culture. Tod's awareness of the sincerity of Ras' position (after all Tod respects Marcus Garvey), his fear of rejection by an America that cannot stop defining what a black person is to be, force his movement outside of history. For Tod swings ideologically like a human pendulum from black nationalism to the often hypocritical call by whites for equality and integration. "It'll run you crazy if you let it," he confesses to Jack, and, as we shall discover, Tod's movement outside of daylight history does not remove him from unconscious politics, for his life ends in a ritual martyrdom he compulsively invites.   [p. 367]   Jack will die a little because of Tod's Frazerian death, and that death will urge Jack to articulate the mental archetypes that Tod's death exhume.

Castration imagery continues to subliminally manifest itself with Brother Tarp's psychosomatic limp resulting from his memory of the chain link. Tarp gives Jack the link as a father passes down a watch to a son, and Jack prefers this gift over his grandfather's Hamilton watch that was left to Jack's brother. For Jack would move out of clock time and into the around-the-beat tempo of the music of invisibility. And this subliminal imagery, in the legs again, continues when the "committee" decides that Jack must pull out of Harlem to address the woman question. Jack feels "weak" in the legs. [p. 396]

His humiliating affair with a nameless white woman, who prefers his alleged phallic powers to those of her milktoast husband Hubert, leads to dreamy incestuous overtones that recall the linkage of Stephen Dedalus' "lovers" with mother surrogates. When the woman (nameless because she, too, is an inauthentic "broad") offers him milk or wine, he finds "the idea of milk strongly repulsive." And when he enters her room, he is taken by an image that appears symbolic, that of "an abstract fish of polished brass mounted on a piece of ebony." Is Jack to be a sacrifical fish to this woman's vaginal sea? Combined with the offer of wine, he certainly may be her next victim, for sex is seen through Ellison's mythical perspective as soft murder. The "poignancy of his love for her," combined with the strange man at the door, set up a perverse love triangle and recall Trueblood's fears of Mr. Broadnax. And her "soundless lips" echo the earlier dream, while her offer of milk, symbolically the offer of the maternal breast to her latest "boy," reveals the incest motif once again. [p. 401ff]

Jack's confrontation with Brother Jack after Tod's death reveals the next variation on the father-son pattern with still more castration imagery. After Jack calls Brother Jack "great white father" and "Marse Jack," Brother Jack's eye drops into a glass of water causing him to squint with "Cyclopean irritation." [p. 462ff] In this Homeric-Joycean take-off, we may wonder why Ellison choses to parody here at all. The answer is revealing, for in Homer the Cyclops have rejected the authority of Zeus. They exist with no social sense, no conscience. The demise of fatherhood has led to a fraternal order on the isle of the Cyclops much as it has led to those in Dublin and Harlem, as we shall see in detail in Chapter IV. Joyce's Michael Cusak, the citizen who Bloom symbolically blinds in "Cyclops," and Ellison's Brother Jack have institutionalized and usurped

proper authority. And Jack has unwittingly forsaken
his family for this fascist order of sons. But Jack
threatens the Brotherhood because he wishes to
restore autonomy to men, to free them from the
lynchers of consciousness, from all fraternal orders:
the Nortons, the Bledsoes, the Sparlands, and the
Brotherhood. Jack sees "the spots fading" from his
own eyes. He has the Joycean experience of "waking
from a dream," the nightmare of history. [p. 465]
Like Trueblood, he cannot be spiritually unmanned.
His sight is getting clearer. He is articulating the
ultimate weakness of the Brotherhood, its impotence,
its neurotic need to neutralize genuine authority.

Yet he must become nearly blind to really see
into the confusion of American life, to comprehend
the dream of his grandfather. He puts on dark
glasses and assumes the mask of another fraternal
figure: Rinehart, the ultimate "Poppa-stopper" and
"motherfouler" of the ghetto. Rinehart plays on
superstitions. Like perverse, weakeyed, Joycean
priests, he offers hope through the numbers game and
through religious opiates. When Jack is mistaken for
Rinehart, Jack feels as if he "had enlisted in a
fraternity in which I was recognized at a glance--not
by features, but by clothes, by uniform, by gait."
[p. 474] Rinehart, the primal "daddyo" of the
ghetto, offers the illusion of fatherhood and
authority to men and lovers, an illusion based on a
near total lack of identity, on chaos, on the loss of
cultural continuity. Echoing Joycean ambiguity, Jack
contemplates:

You could actually make yourself anew. The
notion was frightening, for now the world
seemed to flow before my eyes. All boundaries down, freedom was not only the
recognition of necessity, it was the
recognition of possibility. And sitting
there trembling I caught a brief glimpse of
the possibilities posed by Rinehart's
multiple personalities and turned away. It
was too vast and confusing to contemplate.
[p. 488]

The near fatherless world of Ellison's Harlem ghetto
becomes as "confused" as Joyce's Dublin, where
multiple "mes" multiply, as conscience is burlesqued
and found ineluctable in the Joycean-Conradian-like
"nowhere" of Rinehart's world.

The near fatherless condition is improvised upon
again when Jack visits Hambro. Hambro relates
Brother Jack's notions of "sacrifice" to Jack, of the
need to hold back ethnic groups so that dispossessed
whites may become the pioneers of reinfranchisement
among the poor. When Hambro talks, his children are
already preparing their own sacrifice. Sensing their
father's inadequacy, they sing nursery rhymes much as
do the Wakean children in the "Nightletter" section
of Finnegans Wake, rhymes that predict the father's
fall: "Hickory Dickory Dock" and "Humpty Dumpty."
[p. 488ff] Jack humorously leaves his white hat at
Hambro's to emphasize that Hambro is a kind of
Rinehart, another exploiter of black masses.

On leaving Hambro's sacrificial home, Jack has a
crucial epiphany. He is able to recognize the pattern, the theme of the improvisations that have been
his life, the redundant lietmotif of his false
selves. He begins to see that his experiences style
an inner drive to define himself, to create a
conscience.

And now all past humiliations became
precious parts of my experience, and for the
first time, leaning against that stone wall
in the sweltering night, I began to accept
my past and, as I accepted it, I felt
memories welling up within me. It was as
though I'd learned suddenly to look around
corners; images of past humiliations
flickered through my head and I saw that
they were more than separate experiences.
They were me; they defined me. I was my
experiences and my experiences were me, and
no blind man, no matter how powerful they
became, even if they conquered the world,
could take that, or change one single itch,
taunt, laugh, cry, scar, ache, rage, or pain
of it. They were blind, bat blind, moving
only by the echoed sounds of their own
voices. . . . And now I looked around a
corner of my mind and saw Jack and Norton
and Emerson merge into one single white
figure. They were very much the same, each
attempting to force his picture of reality
upon me and neither giving a hoot in hell
for how things looked to me. I was simply a
material, a natural resource to be used. I

had switched from the arrogant absurdity of
Norton and Emerson to that of Jack and the
Brotherhood, and it all came out the same--
except I now recognized my invisibility.
[pp. 496-497]

Jack decides to apply his grandfather's advice to
the Brotherhood. He will "yes" them to death; he
will subvert Brother Jack by gaining Emma, Brother
Jack's mistress; he will give Brother Jack fake lists
of new Brotherhood conscripts; he will create a
confrontation between the ghetto and the Brotherhood:
"If I couldn't help them see the reality of our lives
I would help them ignore it until it exploded in
their faces." [p. 500] His strategy of taking Emma
from Jack fails; he is lured instead by Sibyl as the
"confused" interracial love theme reaches its
slapstick conclusion in the novel.

Much as Stephen's dreamy visit to the Dublin
prostitutes, who line the streets and halls of
Nighttown "arrayed as for some rite," creates an
interface between Frazer's description of sacred
prostitution and modern prostitution, Jack's
encounter with Sibyl is "a very revolting ritual."
She calls him "Brother Taboo" and cries incestuously,
"come to mamma beautiful." Jack regards her seduc-
tion as a Swiftean "modest proposal." Is he a child
to be eaten by the mother surrogate after he bakes in
the "oven" of her apartment? [p. 505ff] And like the
Joycean lover, Sibyl reveals the fetish in the form
of a "bird's feather." Indeed, her concept of
sexuality is a kind of phallic revenge. She tells
Jack that her ineffectual husband George is "blind
'sa mole in a hole 'n doesn't know a thing about it."
Then she plays the role of masochistic child: She
taunts her new "daddy" to beat her while she lies
"aggressively receptive." Jack feels like a strange
Aeneas as well as a stereotyped stud, and he imagines
the episode to be "a new birth of a nation." Sibyl
feels "so free" with Jack, for she is able to use him
both in the incestuous father-daughter and mother-son
relationships. She is able to thingify him and vent
all her repressed fantasies. When they walk down the
street, Sibyl reverses roles. "Don't go up, boo
'ful, Sibyl'll tuck you in." At this final, dreamy
reversal Jack closes his eyes "and they sailed red
behind my lids." [p. 513ff] Like Trueblood, Jack

feels "drowned in the river," in the uterine river of incest, no doubt, the near victim of a "phallic" mother-surrogate. [p. 521]

In the Harlem riot, Jack's run with Dupre, another folk character, reveals an alternative to the fraternal nightmare of history and still more variations on the imagery of sight. Jack responds to Dupre's independence, to Dupre's ability to organize the looting of essential goods, and to his burning of a rotten tenement building. Dupre does not want followers. He tells his friends: "don't think I'm your papa!" He's cagey enough to remain anonymous; his friends are not to speak his name. Of Dupre Jack concludes: "He was a type of man nothing in my life had taught me to see, to understand, or respect, a man outside the scheme." [p. 535] Yet as the tenement is prepared for the torch, Jack notices that "The men worked in silence now; like moles deep in the earth." Blind moles? Perhaps, because Jack realizes the danger of losing his identity in mass action:

> I went into the crowd, walking slowly, smoothly into the dark crowd, the whole sur- face of my skin alert, my back chilled, looking, listening to those moving with a heaving and sweating and a burr of talk around me and aware that now that I wanted to see them, needed to see them, I could not; feeling them, a dark mass in motion on a dark night, a black river ripping through a black land; and Ras or Tarp could move beside me and I wouldn't know. I was one with the mass, moving down the littered street over the puddles of oil and milk, my personality blasted. [p. 537]

Jack begins to realize his utility to the Brotherhood. He has been used to create a riot. He must reject the "yessing" of his grandfather's advice and look for a variant message in the cryptic death bed speech to fit the times.

Jack feels sadly responsible for the riot. His conscience nudges him into the awareness that from now on his actions must not be reactions. The riot has been part of the nightmare of history rather than a reprisal against the Brotherhood, a "blue dream" from which he awakens into a new realization of conscience.

The disturbing appearance of the obese black woman, who swills down gulps of beer on the abandoned milk cart when she sings of Joe Louis' betrayal by the referee (reminiscent of Joyce's Dante Riordian's exuberence at Parnell's betrayal), reveals to Jack the "holiday" release inherent in the abortive riot. [p. 524] Her waste of milk, along with her drunkeness, contrast with the wiser acts of Dupre, Scofield and company. Jack has a nervous reaction to this oral, maternal figure and her squandering of nurturing milk: "The big woman left me unnerved. Milk and beer--I felt sad, watching the wagon careen dangerously as they went around a corner." [pp. 532-33] The woman seems cut off from any folk wisdom, from any survival instincts. She merely enjoys the violence and endulges in the carnival-riot.

The riot works a catharsis on Jack, and he discovers that his dark glasses, his "Rineharts," are broken. He has removed yet another blindfold. And when he puts Tarp's leg chain over his fingers, he feels a new "sense of self," of "relief." He will tell Ras and his followers that they are being used; he will "awaken them and me." He pleads, "Can't you see it? They want you guilty of your own murder, your own sacrifice." [p. 545ff] Jack has reached a self free of illusions, and he discovers that those he would advise must go through a similar process before he can move them to inaction:

But even as I spoke I knew it was not good. I had no words and no eloquence, and when Ras thundered, "Hang him!" I stood there facing them, and it seemed unreal. I faced them knowing that the madman in a foreign costume was real and yet unreal, knowing that he wanted my life, that he held me responsible for all the nights and days and all the suffering and for all that which I was incapable of controlling, and I no hero, but short and dark with only a certain eloquence and a bottomless capacity for being a fool to mark me from the rest; saw them, recognized them at last as those whom I had failed and of whom I was now, just now, a

116

leader, though leading them, running ahead of them, only in the stipping away of my illusionment. [p. 546]

Joycean "confusion" echoes again when Jack's epiphany continues: Jack contemplates the "absurdity of the whole night and of the simple yet confoundingly complex arrangement of hope and desire, fear and hate, that had brought me here running." But Jack will run no more, for he has learned

> who I was and where I was and knowing too that I had no longer to run for or from the Jacks and the Emersons and the Bledsoes and Nortons, but only from the confusion, impatience, and refusal to recognize the beautiful absurdity of their American identity and mine. [p. 546]

He discovers that "it is better to live out one's absurdity than to die for that of others, whether for Ras' or Jack's." [p. 547] Jack has become a rugged individualist of the folk tradition. More forcefully than Stephen, who strikes the chandelier in the underworld of Nighttown, Jack acts: he spears Ras through the cheeks.

Later, in a dream scenario reminiscent of <u>A Portrait</u> where Stephen faces visions of debased monster parent-images, Jack fantasizes his own literal castration by all the father-figures who have threatened his own birth of conscience throughout the novel. Yet, like Trueblood, Jack remains a man "In spite of the dream, I was whole." [p. 558] In fact, Jack recalls Trueblood's "paralyzed" jaybird and links it to himself. Similar to the bird's unaffected eyes, Jack's eyes still can see without distortion.

For Ellison as for Joyce, the imagery of sight reveals a complex, symbolic matrix. As the emblem of the soul's quest for freedom and authenticity of self, eyes replace the penis as the true organ of genuine potency. No Oedipus, Jack confesses "I'm invisible, not blind." Jack has initiated himself in one long rite of passage filled with perverse twists of the knife. He is finally free of Mary, of his need for false roles:

117

I couldn't return to Mary's, or to the campus or to the Brotherhood, or home. I could only move ahead or stay here, underground. So I would stay here until I was chased out. Here, at least, I could try to think things out in peace, or, if not in peace, in quiet. I would take up residence underground. The end was in the beginning. [p. 558]

Unlike one-eyed Brother Jack, Jack looks inward to his authentic self in order to form an internalized conscience freed from the role playing that would annihilate all traces of that inner self. Freedom lies in the recognition of the existential uniqueness of self, and, paradoxically, as in Oriental religion, in the brotherhood of man, in the cooperation of diverse individuals toward the maintenance of the half-applied dreams of the Founding Fathers of America for equality:

I'm not blaming anyone for this state of affairs, mind you; nor merely crying _mea culpa_. The fact is that you carry part of your sickness within you, at least I do as an invisible man. I carried my sickness and though for a long time I tried to place it in the outside world the attempt to write it down shows me that at least half of it lay within me. It came upon me slowly, like the strange disease that effects those black men whom you see turning slowly from black to albino, their pigment disappearing as under the radiation of some cruel, invisible ray. You go along for years knowing something is wrong, then suddenly you discover that you're as transparent as air. At first you tell yourself that it's all a dirty joke, or that it's due to the "political situation." But deep down you come to suspect that you're yourself to blame, and you stand naked and shivering before the millions of eyes who look through you unseeingly. That is the real soul-sickness. . . . [p. 562]

Jack's great epiphany, as Stephen's, lies in his existential insights on the need to forge a conscience, on the need to escape from debased maternal and paternal surrogates, on the need to flee

from the fraternities that would extend adolescence
and debased authority into perpetuity, on the need to
truly "see." Joyce certainly was a powerful
influence for Ellison, and the ordeals of Stephen and
Jack are remarkably similar. And finally, both
heroes discover with Norman O. Brown ". . . the true,
the only contrary of patriarchy is not matriarchy but
fraternity." [26]

120

In our society it is not unusual for a Negro
to experience a sensation that he does not
exist in the real world at all. He seems
rather to exist in the nightmarish fantasy
of the white American mind as a phantom that
the white mind seeks unceasingly, by means
both crude and subtle, to lay.

Ralph Ellison
[SA, p. 304]

It is a peculiar sensation, this double
consciousness, this sense of always looking
at oneself through the eyes of others, of
measuring one's soul by the tape of a world
that looks in amused contempt and pity. One
ever feels his two-ness--an American, a
Negro; two souls, two thoughts, two unrecon-
ciled strivings; two warring ideals in one
dark body, whose dogged strength alone keeps
it from being torn asunder. [1]

W. E. B. Dubois
The Souls of Black Folk

The primary proposition of Existentialism--
that existence which is defined as the
immediate living experience of the individual, takes priority over essence, that is,
the rational abstractions reflecting the
laws, properties and relations of objective
reality--militates against orderly thought.
The Existentialists hold that it is far more
important and imperative for the person to
exert his will, chose among possible courses
of action, and commit himself for better or
worse to an enterprise than to gear ideas
and projects into the environing conditions

of action.   Otherwise, the   individual is
false to his authentic self.[2]

George Novak
Existentialism and Marxism

. . . he drank to the undoing of his foes, a
race of mighty valorous heroes, rulers of   the
waves, who sit on thrones of alabaster silent
as the deathless gods. [U, p. 325]

CHAPTER III

Another shared theme of the Joyce-Ellison connection involves their scathing satires on the values of Protestant Europe, values that invade and paralyse their respective fictional worlds, that create the modern city and urban spin-offs such as overt chattel slavery and the "softer" institution-alized dehumanization of the working class on farms, factories, and in political parties. Indeed, the Ireland of Joyce and the America of Ellison operate under half-articulated, internalized, philosophical, economic, and religious systems that are rejective, schizogenic, as it were, in nature. If many of Joyce's Dubliners unwittingly mimic survivals of the world views of Locke, Hume, Descartes and, ironically, Luther; if these Dubliners tend to equate human sub-jectivity with 17th and 18th century mechanical models of human perception; if they perceive Dublin as one vast, cogridden, clanking machine; if they, in short, unwittingly internalize the lingering values of Protestant Europe with its world-as-machine metaphor, so, too, do such perceptions inform the mentality of many of the characters in Ellison's wasteland. For Ellison appears to have been pro-foundly influenced by Stephen Dedalus' struggle against the robot city of Dublin, against its multi-tude of Irish Frankensteins, and against the tendency Stephen notices finally in himself to regress to robot behavior where his subjective response to the world might yield to a mechanical, reified percep-tion. Automatons, human dolls clutter these already cluttered novels; their fictional worlds come to resemble a giant robot, or a poorly adjusted watch. Stephen's struggle against the robot in himself and against the ennui of Dublin, then, exerted its influence on Jack the Bear's analogous battle against the "iron man" of his final nightmare, against the "mechanizers of consciousness" and their deadened, ticking world.

For Joyce, as for Ellison, the mechanized, schizogenic social order that would deny the individ-uality and subjectivity of its members and reduce them to standardized roles was clearly an offshoot of 17th and 18th century empirical philosophies and of

123

the materialism of Social Calvinism that began to
crystalize after Luther's vision of the world as a
privy. The world-as-machine, world-as-excrement-
commodity metaphors could for them, as for Blake
before them, only produce the infectuous "dark
Satanic mills." And the near certainty of David Hume
that the demoted self is really a complicated mechanism (in modern terms, a stimulis-response machine)
devoid of any essence, genuine uniqueness, or dialectic with the outer world becomes a well-formed myth
in the encrusted minds of many characters in Ulysses
and Invisible Man. It is against such philosophical
and religious survivals that Stephen and Jack
struggle for transcendence. For them, the elusive,
subjective "self," the "human," must be more than a
series of social roles, more than the product of
social conditioning, more than the pulse of the
clock-universe, more indeed than a passive Lockeian
camera that records and innacurately encodes the
surfaces of the world.

Joyce was well aware that his exhausted Dublin
was limping through the motions of an effete, 18th
century empirical tradition. As Hugh Kenner tells
us, Joyce was satirizing the Humeian-Lockeian
suggestion that the mind is a kind of stimulus-
response machine, that any dialectical interface the
mind may have with the world "out there" exists
largely between its inaccurate encoding of the
sights, smells, sounds of that world into an
autonomous, metalanguage that dafty disconnects the
associative, linguistic mental realm from the "real
world"--the res extensa, as Descartes, in a slightly
different philosophical mood, would put it.[3]

Descartes, however, was unwilling to ride the
empirical mental train to Locke's or Hume's destina-
tions. In the Frenchman's system, a dialectic,
threatened albeit, must exist between res cogitans
and res extensa. For Descartes, the self was not
reducible to mechanical, quantitative processes; the
human mind, unreliable as it often was in its
linguistic selections of the res extensa, was,
nonetheless, an entity, a self, not Hume's stimulus-
response machine in miniature, or Locke's camera
model. Yet Descartes had his doubts about this
peculiar dialectic; for it might collapse; the human
self might be swallowed up by its contact with the
ennui of the music of the spheres, with the blank,

indifferent res extensa, the ennui so well described as being not only attached to the material world, but to the alienating, lonely city that was so capable of annihilating the delicate res cogitans. In Discourse on Method, Descartes characterizes the modern city as a profoundly lonely place:

. . . in the midst of a great crowd of busy people, more concerned with their own business than curious about that of others, without lacking any of the conveniences offered by the most populous cities, I have been able to live as solitary and withdrawn as I would be in the most remote of deserts.[4]

To understand the ultimate origins of this city and its society whose principles and unconscious defenses have been imposed upon and often imitated by the Catholic Irish and by black Americans, it is necessary to place the Protestant Ethic once again on the psychoanalytic couch, for the modern city is essentially the child of the Reformation.

Joel Kovel's brilliant linkage of the unconscious defenses of the Protestant mind with racism and other forms of social exclusion must be summarized if we are to understand many of the pyschological implications of dominance and the resultant paralysis of Joyce's Dubliners and of Ellison's black and white characters. Kovel spends the bulk of his psychoanalytical study x-raying the unconscious defenses of what he labels "dominative" and "aversive" racists. He argues that the superego of both groups often remains primitive throughout their lives because dominance facillitates the continuance of infantile defense mechanisms employed, initially, by the emergent ego. We need to imagine the period of infancy when the child is both moving toward autonomy, a separation from the mother, and at the same time resisting the looming autonomy and the separation-anxiety that he begins to experience. The child of two solves this problem of anxiety through a form of defensive splitting. For to overcome the pain of separation from the mother, according to Kovel, the child defensively splits his person, segregates it, as it were, into bad and good parts.[5] The child does this because of a dimly intuited

125

guilt. If the child is becoming separate, his unconscious logic argues, the mother must have rejected him: He must be bad. In order to rid himself of guilt, then, the child eventually projects it onto a "bad" part of the self, ultimately onto his feces. Kovel explains:

> In the act of defecation, the person gives a part of himself to the world. True, feces are formed of those substances the body must reject, and are eminently dispensable. But at first the baby has no reason to believe this piece of objective knowledge: what comes from the body belonged to the body; it should be considered as part of the body, and so of the self. In the first stage of knowledge, whatever is known is loved. Therefore, in the beginning (and so, at bottom throughout life), excrement is loved.[6]

It is at this point that Protestant culture provides the child with some insidious and ready-made solutions to this ambivalence over feces, solutions that involve sublimations of feces into symbols. For Protestant culture offers the child rituals of purification which involve the "thingification" of the oppressed and an unconscious identification of the oppressed with feces, dirt, and with that ultimate sublimation, feces-property. Building upon Norman O. Brown's controversial critique of the "excremental vision" of the West, Kovel unravels the paralysis of the "obsessive-compulsive" personality, a paralysis that surfaces in the dominant type of Western man:

> . . . in the modern West, reality has been restructured according to the symbolism of the excremental vision of infancy. In both the historical and infantile systems, a universe is radically split along lines of goodness and badness; . . . what is good is pure, clean and white, and what is bad is impure, dirty, smelly and black. Both systems are dominated by the fantasy of dirt: the body is dirty; what comes out of the body is especially dirty; the material world corresponds to what comes out of the body, and hence it is also especially dirty.

Not the whole world is dirty, but only those
more concrete, sensuous aspects that are
symbolically close to the concrete, sensing
body. If something in the world can be made
clean and pure, and if it can be made cold
and non-sensuous as well, then it will meet
the criterion of goodness. What is good in
the world is identified with what is good in
the person--not his body, but his mind.[7]

Kovel notes that this irrational dualism helps to
form the Protestant world view, its value judgments
on the nature of "good" and "evil." But the original
love-hate the child experiences toward his feces continues to attach itself to his sublimations. Hence,
when an adult, he may both unconsciously love and
hate his material possessions, his money, and those
classes he oppresses, for in Western culture individuals have projected the pain of separation onto the
feces which are, because of the unconscious survival
of infantile narcissism, really loved as part and
product of the child's body. So the infantile
longing for union, the regressive desire to recapture
that golden age prior to separation, continues in the
unconscious of the adult and fuels the ambivalence of
the adult over feces and its sublimated symbols--the
oppressed, money and possessions. Kovel goes on:

And it is because of the basic human
intolerance of separation--that is, through
man's eternal desire for reunion with the
source of his being--that we cannot even
give up that which we hate and are disgusted
by, but seek to return abstracted portions
of it into the self. Insofar as this is
done, then self-hate and self-disgust--that
is to say, guilt--becomes permanently
established within the personality and spurs
it onward to further abstract differentia-
tions. And it is this primitive and
universal fantasy that the West has mobi-
lized in its culture, and turned to the
generation of material power--an endlessly
transformed guilt.[8]

For Kovel, blacks are the most obvious target of the
ambivalence, but we need to add that oppression also
finds ways of linking its white outcasts--the Irish,
the Jews, for example, to feces and the darkness of
the unknown id.

So the Protestant superego must "clean up" the world when it becomes the puppet of its unresolved infantile fantasies. Kovel explores the unconscious, excremental base of Calvinism, its need to disguise its unconscious linkage of feces with possessions and the oppressed through sublimation, that splitting process which tries to continually desexualize its excremental symbols. The Protestant god is projected as a god in love with the purity of spirit, but opposed to the body and to the material world. To win the favor of this god, men

> could not enjoy the filthy world, but could attempt to bring order to it, to clean it up as much as could be humanly possible. The logical outcome was clear: make, produce, work over the given world, control both it and the body, and you will have virtue, you will be revealed as part of the elect and will receive heavenly reward. Here on earth, however, virtue-moral perfection--was the sole reward. The sensuous enjoyment of reality was confined to pure activity--the cold efficiency of work for itself, gain for itself. What is gained cannot be enjoyed; it should not even be seen, but must instead by progressively abstracted until the only things that "matter" are money and moral purity--the former being the abstraction of a deadened filthy world, and the latter, the abstracted quality of a deadened, clean self. To be sure, there was no satisfaction intended by this system. All that "counted" was movement, striving for an endless goal that became ever more remote precisely through the process of striving.[9]

The joylessness of material gain in the West, the need to create the illusion of moral purity to overcome the guilt generated by acquisition, caused the deadening process of splitting and abstracting to become genuinely demonic.

Descartes' res extensa had been in the making long before he concluded that the world of objects was a dead, alien, fallen garden. The abstracted world of objects posited by Calvinism, or by Luther's visions of an excremental devil and the world as a privy, then, had become an unconsciously derived

symbol of the dead, alien excrement, well before
Descartes, as Alfred North Whitehead first observed.

The guilt generated by these unrepressed
infantile urges was manifest in the anal-sadistic
"mystique of production," according to Kovel,

> by which the world is reduced to abstract
> form and then worked over aggressively.
> What we allow ourselves to see of the pro-
> duct is considered "saved," created by order
> out of chaos, manufactured, and worthy of
> inclusion. But our products are also things
> that have been killed.[10]

The reduction of people and of the material world to
dead excrement had begun. Anal-sadism had triumphed.
And many whites would transfer this ambivalence over
things onto their dealings with the oppressed.

For Kovel, the religion of money and property,
reinforced in America by the God-like pronouncements
in the doctrine of Manifest Destiny, prevented the
superego of the dominant white culture from devel-
oping out of its primitive base. The greater the
illusion of white purity, the stronger the revenge of
the id. Norton in Invisible Man is Ellison's symbol
for this unstable superego. For Norton, an aversive
racist reminiscent of Kurtz in Conrad's Heart of
Darkness, mentally disintegrates after his dim
recognition that he, like Trueblood, harbors compulsive, incestuous desires for his own dead
daughter. And, again, like Kurtz, Norton must "save"
blacks by educating them while at the same time
preserving their alleged menial/fecal status.

Conversely, the final acceptance by Shem and Jack
of the excremental coalhole, with its subterranean
symbolism that thinly denotes the labyrinthine
entrails of the body; the "commode" pun in the Wake,
which reveals that civilization has an excremental
base; Joyce's gypsie-like flaunting of private
property when he slummed from apartment to apartment
throughout Europe; his linkage of chapters in Ulysses
with organs and orifices of the human body; Peter
Wheatstraw's advice that "shit, grit and motherwit"
might be needed to survive in the "bear's den" of
Harlem; Joyce's raucous satire in the Wake of the
"angelsexonism" of the British; all of this points to

a perhaps half-articulated acknowledgement by both writers that Western abstraction, the "thingification" of the oppressed of the world, the attempted reduction of the oppressed to excrement and property, had led to a cultural failure. For Jack and Shem it is time to get back to the coalhole, or, in psychoanalytical terms, back to the intuition that the splitting process must be exposed and resisted.

The American heart of darkness logically bred not only chattel slavery, but the softer forms of alienated labor people endure in our cities today. For the ultimate application of the compulsive marketplace mentality first resulted in the absurdity of the slave trade. Kovel explains:

> In the institution of slavery the abstractification and splitting of the world extended not simply to nature, to manufactured commodities, nor even to labor, but to human beings--and from this extremity, to an entire civilization organized about slavery. Humans were made into things, into abstract equivalents of bodily filth to be regained by the white Western self.[11]

And when slavery became impractical, the dehumanization impulse had to find a new mode of operation. It aimed its energies at dehumanizing the working class, the industrial "slaves." Ellison's clear articulation of this linkage allows him to frame Liberty Paints, metaphorically, with a Southern plantation. And, as with Joyce, it allows him to designate racism as only the tip of the iceberg of the Protestant Ethic, of the West's attempted fecal reduction of the world of objects and of the bodies and minds of the cities' working millions.

Frank McConnell has demonstrated that motion pictures are in reality a kind of language of this deadened Cartesian space. Because of its concrete mise en scene, film, more so than the novel or poetry, he argues, is better able to represent the cluttered, deadened space of the crowded city, or the alien landscape of the American West, or the threatening, indifferent void of outer space.[12] He mentions Alexandre Astruc's assertion that

> A Descartes of today would already have shut himself up in his bedroom with a 16mm camera

and some film and would be writing his
philosophy on film: for his <u>Discours de la
Methode</u> would today be of such a kind that
only the cinema could express it
satisfactorily.[13]

It is in this Cartesian, filmic space that so
many of Joyce's human cogs grind out their lives.
McConnell compares the dangerous space of Hitchcock
films, where objects and other people threaten the
freedom of heroes and heroines, threaten their
ability to communicate and thus bridge the loneliness
and ennui of their lives, to the filmic space of
Joyce's <u>Ulysses</u> which also depicts "a vision of the
space surrounding us as threatening, dangerous for
language."[14] And in Hitchcock films, or in <u>Ulysses</u>
or in <u>Invisible Man</u> as well, it is language--people
talking to people in meaningful dialogue (or in the
case of writer-ranter Jack the Bear, a person largely
talking to oneself and to the invisible and hopefully
agreeing public which reads novels) that can affirm
a human dialectic and identity against the <u>res
extensa</u>, and against the roles individuals are asked
to accept in order to fit into the modern city.
McConnell explains this concept of language in filmic
terms:

> . . . if each mind is indeed alone, if each
> mind constructs its own reality out of the
> originating abyss of its doubt and raw
> sensations, then what guarantee have we that
> there are other minds--that each of us is
> not a unique myth of self-consciousness,
> projecting our own shapes on a absolutely
> alien universe, devoid even of brothers or
> lovers? Language is the fragile net
> connecting humans to each other, the one
> ambiguous contract which seems to ally my
> pain and my joy to yours, even though
> language itself is a bundle of misunder-
> standings, mistranslations, badly decoded or
> undecoded messages.[15]

Both Joyce and Ellison, along with a host of
other contemporaries, hybridized the novel form with
techniques and themes from the cinema, then, in order
to depict this threatening Cartesian space the modern

world has created. Indeed, the space delineated by both writers is often a slapstick space akin to the movies, that dangerous space of Chaplin films, for example, that might destroy the hero. The obvious linkages of Bloom and Peter Wheatstraw to Chaplin, to the baggy pants vagrant of silent films, are, therefore, deliberate. For Chaplin's comic struggles to free himself from the attacks of Murphy beds, from the revenge of automobiles, from the entrails of the machines of mass production, and from a surrender to any of the innumerable, dehumanized roles and stereotyped behavior other inhabitants of the slapstick world have embraced in order to fit in and "harmonize" with the modern city typifies the struggles of Stephen Dedalus, Bloom, Peter Wheatstraw, and Jack the Bear. Referring to City Lights, McConnell describes Chaplin's representative art:

> Chaplin's greatness is simply, to have incorporated within his film personality a crucial, archetypal aspect of all film personality: that struggle of the human to show itself within the mechanical. . . . Slapstick is the purest structural version of this struggle, the manifestation of the mechanical opening of City Lights--trying to survive among the marmoreal, mythicized versions of the self with which tradition has surrounded and nearly strangled us.[16]

Henri Bergson's famous definition of the comic as the struggle of human will both against the material world and against the ubiquitous mechanical roles describes ordeals that inform the slapstick of Chaplin, Bloom, Stephen, Jack, Wheatstraw, Norton, and countless other characters. But it is not only the resistence against the possible victory of Cartesian space or mechanical roles over the threatened self that point to the filmic quality of the fiction of Joyce and Ellison, but also the struggle of Stephen and Jack the Bear, especially, against the ontology of film form itself. Several critics have noted how the camera mocks the human, how the cinema reduces the human image to an equality with the surrounding objects on the film frame, to a two-dimensional partnership. As a result, according to McConnell, the successful film performer, like the jazz artist, through Cagney-like presence, through mime or verbal force must "elucidate a myth of personality out of the mechanism," out of the mechanical reproductive technology that is film.[17] Calling film "a mechanical, artificial means for reproducing human existence, which strives, in spite of its artificiality to return that existence to the status of natural phenomena," McConnell contrasts the dynamics of stage and film acting:

> The stage actor's craft, whatever else it may be, is the art of assimilating himself to a predetermined dramatic role--to an abstract, demonic potency of action--and of behaving in such a way that potency becomes realized in his physical presence on the stage. The film performer, on the other hand, is burdened with the necessity of realizing his role--which is to say, his physical presence--through a medium which resists the full reality of that presence.[18]

Chaplin's art dovetails with the art of Joyce and Ellison, finally, because each art is Romantic, each presents heroes who attempt to maintain a human self, a subjectivity, amid the mechanical nets implicit in the myth of Cartesian space.

If Joyce and Ellison depict the Chaplinesque struggles of their threatened heroes, they also assess the human casualties who succumb both to the defeat of the mind by space and to the pressure to conform to mechanized roles and stereotypes. We have argued that Ellison's concept of "invisibility" stems in part from Joyce's documentation of the brain-washing of characters with negative Irish stereotypes resulting from England's colonial experiment, a brainwashing that has too often been willingly embraced by the oppressed Irish, by the "gratefully oppressed." What is not generally known is that both writer's describe many of their human casualties in terms and images which clearly anticipate or conform to psychological descriptions of schizophrenia, a mental illness we might well characterize as the epidemic of post-Cartesian man struggling through the crazy movie of modern times.

Joyce was fascinated by early case histories of schizophrenia and multiple personalities. In fact, several of his "doubliners" in <u>Finnegans Wake</u> are linked by puns to famous case histories of psychotic patients treated by William James, Morton Prince and others. Morris Beja explains:

> The theme of the dissociation of personality was of central importance to Joyce's concerns and techniques throughout his career, from Stephen's theory of dualism which would symbolize "the twin extremities of spirit and nature" . . . through Stoom-Blephen to <u>Finnegans Wake</u>. By the time he wrote the <u>Wake</u>, Joyce clearly knew about case histories of multiple personality which provided fascinating correlation for some of his most deeply felt assumptions and convictions about human character.[19]

Beja notes the various puns in the <u>Wake</u> derived from the names of patients afflicted with schizophrenia: Patience Worth, Christine Beauchamp, Reverend Ansel Bourne, and Doris Fischer. He cites Shaun's accusation that Shem is "a dividual chaos, perilous, potent, common to all flesh. . . dorian grayer in its dud hud."[20] For Joyce, much as for clinical psychologists, the ego can become hopelessly splintered; human personality can be described, on the unconscious level at least, as a confused tangle of selves, of imposed and rejected roles, an "invaded" ego that exists without a center. The ego, like Humpty Dumpty, can become a shattered egg in a schizogenic society.

Ellison appears to have noted this theme of "dividual chaos" in Joyce's fiction. And he seems to have improvised upon it, combining it with his own reflections on American identity and with further observations derived from the fiction of Melville and continental writers such as Flaubert, Dostoevski, Sartre, Camus, and Malraux when he developed his version of the confused state of modern man in search of a self.

Joyce's Dublin, Ellison's Harlem: these cultural failures are epiphanies of the deadened space and "confused" inhabitants of the post-Cartesian city. And the deep fears of the potentially schizoid characters who populate so much of modern fiction, from Dostoevsky's underground man to that character's derivatives: Stephen Dedalus, Bloom, Shem-Shaun, Jack, Rinehart, fears of the invasion by urban ennui of their inner, subjective cores of the self, reveal a disasterous culmination of Descartes' concern over the possible defeat of the mind by space. Indeed, the drift of the world-as-machine metaphor: its over-evaluation of the necessity of individual conformity to social roles, its reduction of the human self into a ticking, mechanical microcosm, results for Joyce and for Ellison in the rampant schizoid "confusion" of the mechanizers of conscious-ness and of their would-be victims, in a "dividual chaos."

In a Langian approach to Invisible Man, E. M. Kist has argued that the schizoid experience of invisibility, of not having one's individuality or uniqueness confirmed by the attention and praise of others, of being forced into inauthentic social roles, leads to a derealization by "rejected" individuals of both the self and the outer world.[21] Kist links the main cause of such defensive behavior in Invisible Man to the "schizogenic" society "which tears the speaker apart, dismembers, and symbolically emasculates him."[22] According to Kist, Invisible Man is

> not psychoanalytic in the traditional sense, but it confirms more recent developments in psychoanalytic theory which understand the individual not soley in terms of past rela-tions with the nuclear family, but in his social context.[23]

He refers to Laing's concept of the "false- self system" and reveals how Jack tries and discards several inauthentic roles throughout Invisible Man. The Laingian description of the penetration, the impingement of these false-self systems into the remnants of many of his patient's inner selves, is relevant here:

> The heightened sense of always being seen, or at any rate of being always potentially seeable, may be principally referable to the body, but the preoccupation with being seeable may be condensed with the idea of the mental self being penetrable, and vulnerable, as when the individual feels

that one can look right through him into his
"mind" or "soul." Such "plateglass"
feelings are usually spoken about in terms
of metaphor or simile, but in psychotic conditions the gaze or scrutiny of the other
can be experienced as an actual penetration
into the core of the "inner" self.[24]

Such fears of invasion haunt Jack, as well,
especially in his final dream of castration.

Joyce's and Ellison's use of the complex cinema
metaphor to expose the inauthentic role playing, the
"dividual chaos," and the spectatorial detachment of
the victims of the schizogenic society is the key
link in the Joyce-Ellison connection that will concern us now. Joyce's attempts to blend the novel
form with themes and techniques usually associated
with film; his Bergsonian fascination with likening
ordinary consciousness with the cinematograph; his
nervous fusion of the perception of various characters with the mechanical, two-dimensional, reified
recording of the camera eye; his metaphorical treatment of Dublin as a surreal Hollywood set stocked
with inauthentic players; and his anxiety that the
robot, slapstick city might triumph over the human
essence, all of these concerns appear to have deeply
influenced Ellison's creation of the filmic scenarios
of the modern city in Invisible Man and his description of the often reified, cinematic consciousness of
Jack, who, like Stephen Dedalus, is in constant
danger of becoming one more automaton, one more
burned out "object" in the res extensa of the modern
city.

Alan Spiegel has linked the style of many of
Stephen's interior monologues in Ulysses with
cinematic form. He argues that Stephen's visual
perception of the objective world is analogous to
that of a camera eye which passively records visual
images and flattens perspective.[25] Using the following
passages from "Telemachus" to prove his case, he
notes that Stephen's eyes do not select one object
out of a visual field as the eyes normally would,
but, like the camera eye, they record everything from
the "fraying edge" of the coat sleeve to "the ring of
the bay":

Stephen, an elbow rested on the jagged
granite, leaned his palm against his brow

136

and gazed at the fraying edge of his shiny
black coatsleeve. Pain, that was not yet
the pain of life, fretted his heart.
Silently, in a dream she had come to him
after her death, her wasted body within its
loose brown grave-clothes giving off an
odour of wax and rosewood, her breath, that
had bent upon him, mute, reproachful, a
faint odour of wetted ashes. Across the
threadbare cuff edge he saw the sea hailed as
a great sweet mother by the wellfed voice
beside him. The ring of the bay and skyline
held a dull green mass of liquid. A bowl of
white china had stood beside her deathbed
holding the green sluggish bile which she
had torn up from her rotting liver by fits
of loud groaning vomiting. [p. 5]

Spiegel explains:

The camera, unlike the human eye, is an
instrument of precision: it is, in a manner
of speaking, like an eye that has been
severed from a brain . . . a dumb eye. Once
it has been placed in position the camera
must see everything that can be seen within
its frame. It cannot pick or choose like
the human eye however unconsciously the eye
may perform this function; nor can it be
fascinated, or unattentive or obsessive or
absent-minded (as often happens when a
preoccupied observer stares unseeingly). It
can only see whatever is to be seen; the
accidental as well as the necessary, the
ephemeral as well as the essential, the cuf-
fedge as well as the sea, both held and
coordinated, without distinction, in a
single field of vision. [26]

Joyce appears to have likened Stephen's eyes to
the cold camera eye in order to reveal the alienation
that Stephen experiences from the empirical world.
For Stephen, the realm of objects is coldly indifferent and "other." Spiegel realizes that Stephen
often mythologizes his field of vision to make order
out of the chaos of his "fragmented visual field,"
but he goes on to show that Stephen does not grasp
any essence in objects:

Joyce's rendering makes it clear that the only <u>objective</u> connection between the seen objects in Stephen's oval of vision and the personal objects in Stephen's mind are based almost entirely upon material, mechanistic, and essentially non-human similarities; "the ring of the bay" is associated by its shape with the "bowl of china," just as the "green mass of liquid" is associated by its texture and tonality with the "green sluggish bile." Thus Stephen goes from one object to another not by any comprehensive grasp of or participation in the object's "being" or "essence," but simply by a primarily visual apprehension of its graphic and material surface. [27]

Spiegel further notes that elaboration of space in <u>Ulysses</u> is often "cinematic" revealing a fragmented space containing many "closeups" which wrench the object from the visual field. And such fragmentation belies the artist's skepticism about knowledge of the empirical world since perception renders an incomplete, disparate fragmented view of reality.[28] The standardized cityscape and "langscape" of Dublin, then, exert so much pressure on Stephen that he begins to mechanize his consciousness, to attune his mental perception to the robot city or often to tune the city out entirely, and to perceive gray, dirty Dublin in two-dimensional, derealized film scenarios. His consciousness begins to simulate a Lockeian camera.

That Locke metaphorically described human perception as analogous to the operation of a camera was no doubt understood by Joyce. Locke supposed that

the understanding is not much unlike a (camera or) closet wholly shut from light, with only some little openings left, to let in eternal visible resemblances or ideas of things without. Would the pictures coming into such a dark room but stay there, and lie so orderly as to be found upon occasion, it would very much resemble the understanding of man.[29]

Colin Turbayne explains the passivity involved in the 18th century view of the camera model for human perception:

> By this extended application, Locke was describing the <u>dioptrics, as it were, of the mind in perception</u>. He and his colleagues proceeded to represent the facts about the mind in the idioms appropriate to cameras. Just as there are images on the back of the camera, so there are <u>ideas in the mind</u>. Just as there are <u>obscure and confused, clear and distinct</u> ideas. Just as we inspect the images on the screen, so we <u>introspect ideas</u> in the mind. Just as images are reflected light, so there are <u>ideas of reflection</u>. These idioms, some of <u>which are still</u> fashionable, refer to central concepts in seventeenth- and eighteenth-century epistemology.[30]

According to the Lockeian model, however, the mind is not totally passive in perceptual acts. Locke writes: "As the mind is wholly passive in the perception of all its simple ideas, so it exerts several acts of its own."[31] For Locke the mind actively combines, separates and abstracts, and compares the data it receives from the senses. When Stephen mulls over both the "ineluctable modality of the visible" and Berkeley's idealism in "Proteus," he pretends to view the beach through a stereoscopic camera:

> Coloured on a flat: yes, that's right. Flat I see, then think distance, near, far, flat I see, east, back. Ah, see now. Falls back suddenly, frozen in stereoscope. Click does the trick. You find my words dark. Darkness is in our souls, do you not think? [p. 48]

While Stephen ponders the imposition of perspective by the mind, he flattens his visual field into two dimensions like a camera lens and then mentally pulls that field into the illusion of perspective by imitating the stereoscopic camera. In "Circe" Stephen recalls these reified optics:

> Must get glasses. Broke them yesterday. Sixteen years ago. Distance. The eye sees

all flat. . . . Brain thinks. Near: far.
Ineluctable modality of the visible. [p.
560]

If Stephen's perception reveals a possible
surrender to the reductive mechanism of a still
camera, Bloom's perception more accurately mimics a
motion picture as Harry Levin observed:

> Bloom's mind is neither a tabula rasa nor a
> photographic plate, but a motion picture,
> which has been ingeniously cut and carefully
> edited to emphasize the closeups and fade-
> outs of emotion, the angles of observation
> and the flashbacks of reminiscence.[32]

And the reified perception often characteristic of
Stephen and Bloom recalls Bergson's linkage of
rational, non-intuitive perception with the early
cinematographs of his day. For Bergson, the rational
faculties of human intellect apprehend reality as a
series of dead objects to be manipulated. Likewise,
the analogous camera does not see the continuity of
processes. Rather, the intellect slices up this
continuity into separate "snapshots." In Creative
Evolution Bergson describes the "cinemagraphical"
nature of rational thought:

> It is because the film of the cinematograph
> unrolls, bringing in turn the different
> photographs of the scene to continue each
> other, that each actor of the scene recovers
> his mobility; he strings all his successive
> attitudes on the invisible movement of the
> film. The process then consists in
> extracting from all the movements peculiar
> to all the figures an impersonal movement
> abstract and simple, movement in general, so
> to speak: we put this into the apparatus,
> and we reconstitute the individuality of
> each particular movement by combining this
> nameless movement with the personal
> attitudes. Such is the contrivance of the
> cinematograph. And such is also that of our
> knowledge. Instead of attaching ouselves to
> the inner becoming of things, we place our-
> selves outside them in order to recompose
> their becoming artificially. We take

snapshots, as it were, of the passing reality, and, as these are characteristic of the reality, we have only to string them on a becoming, abstract, uniform and invisible, situated at the back of the apparatus of knowledge, in order to imitate what there is that is characteristic in this becoming itself. Perception, intellection, language so proceeded in general. Whether we would think becoming, or express it, or even perceive it, we hardly do anything else than set going a kind of cinematograph inside us. We may therefore sum up what we have been saying in the conclusion that the <u>mechanism</u> <u>of our ordinary knowledge is of a cinematographical kind</u>.[33]

Stephen's need to transcend reified perception appears more pressing than the need of more compatible, gadget-loving Bloom. In fact, Spiegel describes Stephen Dedalus as one of the "great spectator heroes of modern fiction," a voyeuristic "non-participant" who "refuses to engage in any part of the living spectacle that passes before his eyes."[34] Paradoxically, he perceives mechanically to escape a robot existence.

In Ellison's Invisible Man, Jack is also a spectator-hero, for his eyes often submit to the one-eyed, schizoid perception of the camera in order to put some distance between himself and the landscape of nightmare. Jack's visual alienation begins at the battle royal:

They were yelling for us to break it up and Tatlock spun me half around with a blow, and as a joggled camera sweeps in a reeling scene, I saw the howling red face crouching tense beneath the cloud of blue-gray smoke. [pp. 24-25]

During the chapel service Jack perceptually swaps a camera lens for a reversed telescope.

I looked out at the scene now from far back in my despair, seeing the platform and its actors as through a reversed telescope; small doll-like figures moving through some meaningless ritual. [p. 115]

The world is a movie set, Jack, the camera, for his constant use of the word "scene" to describe events recalls the Joycean cinema. At the Chthonian Jack is greeted at the door by a cold, mechanical, female cog toward whom he feels some strange closeness; but his perception pushes him in the opposite direction.

> Then I was past, disturbed not so much by the close contact, as by the sense that I had somehow been through it all before. I couldn't decide if it were from watching some similar scene in the movies, from books I'd read, or from some recurrent but deeply buried dream. Whatever, it was like entering a scene which, because of some devious circumstance, I had hitherto watched only from a distance. [p. 293]

During his dispossession speech at the Brotherhood meeting, he equates his perception to a roving camera:

> And I seemed to move in close, like the lens of a camera focusing into the scene and feeling the heat and excitement and the pounding of voice and applause against my diaphram, my eyes flying from face to face, swiftly, fleetingly, searching for someone I could recognize, for someone from the old life, and seeing the faces become vaguer and vaguer the farther they receded from the platform. [p. 332]

Yet Jack's Hollywood exuberence is undercut. He feels alone; the audience becomes an indifferent "other" forcing his isolation.

> Someone pulled on my coat sleeve--my turn had come. I went toward the microphone where Brother Jack himself waited, entering the spot of light that surrounded me like a seamless cage of stainless steel. I halted. The light was so strong that I could no longer see the audience, the bowl of human faces. It was as though a semi-transparent curtain had dropped between us, but through which they could see me--for they were applauding without themselves being seen. I

felt the hard, mechanical isolation of the
hospital machine and I didn't like it. [pp.
332-33]

Jack himself has become a cinematic spectacle. He is
in danger of losing his authenticity if he acts out
the heroic role, and his reaction to the experience
of seeing an earlier photo of himself reveals this
perceptual ontology as well. For as Jack fears that
he will forget his name, recently granted by the
Brotherhood, he perceives his own image as alien.
His legs look like independent objects he cannot
control, objects that have transported him in the
arena "of their own volition." For after looking at
a faded photo of a former boxer who was blinded in
that arena years before, Jack links his own experience at the arena to that of seeing one's adolescent
photograph where one appears to his older self as
strangely alien and unreal.

> I seemed aware of it all from a point deep
> within me, yet there was a disturbing
> vagueness about what I saw, a disturbing,
> unformed quality, as when you see yourself
> in a photo exposed during adolescence: the
> expression empty, the grin without
> character, the ears too large, the pimples,
> "courage bumps," too many and too well
> defined. [pp. 326-27]

For Jack, the murder of Tod Clifton becomes a
slow-motion cinematic experience, a "scene" that he
cannot erase from his mental cinema when the remem-
brance is rewound and re-played over and over again:

> I saw a flight of pigeons whirl out of the
> trees and it all happened in the swift
> interval of their circling, very abruptly in
> the noise of the traffic--yet seeming to
> unfold in my mind like a slow-motion movie
> run off with the sound track dead. [p. 425]

Noting the technique of filmic slow motion that Joyce
appears to parody in Ulysses: the anatomized
descriptions of the dog's frame-by-frame movement in
"Proteus," the time-motion parodies of "Ithaca," and
the green-eyed pervert's circular motion in "An
Encounter," Spiegel notes that

143

the tendency in the most extreme forms of anatomization, as in the most extreme forms of all aspects of the cinematographic manner, is not only to separate the phenomenal world from the mind of man but also, in so doing, to reduce this world to an inhospitable machine, a dehumanized exteriority.[35]

Joyce's use of anatomization does not always reach this extreme, but Jack's schizoid, slow-motion perception of Tod's death does reify the event and place Jack in greater jeopardy than Stephen of submitting to the camera model of consciousness. The influence of Joyce's reified optics on Ellison's style and themes, then, is certainly a possibility.

As with the Frankenstein film medium, much of Joyce's and Ellison's fiction reveals a deep anxiety that human perception, consciousness, might be susceptible to a reduction to the kind of atomic necessitarianism explored by Descartes, Locke, Hume and the many philosophical precursors of modern day cybernetics. Is consciousness reducible to mechanical reflex behavior? Are characters in danger of becoming budding, neo-Gothic Frankensteins? Is the dialectic between man and the material world, between res cogitans and res extensa, susceptible to collapse in the urban nightmare? Are men and objects devoid of essence? Are men devoid of a self? Indeed, a central anxiety in this fiction revolves around the hero's encounter with the mechanical dragons, both internal and external, with his own internal robot and with his social order. Much as Chaplin, these heroes may wind up in the guts of the machine, while they mentally bleed nuts and bolts in the slapstick space of Dublin or Harlem. Ellmann summarizes this ontological conflict that is never resolved in Ulysses.

> Throughout the book Stephen deals with two philosophical problems: the first is whether the world has an objective existence, as maintained by Aristotle, or whether, as Hume considered, "Nothing exists but subjective states, organized by the brute force of association. There is no self, no external world."

144

In "Proteus," Ellmann argues, Stephen sides with Aristotle, but in "Scylla and Charybdis" Stephen is less convinced and begins to swing in the direction of Hume. In "Circe," however, "neither the world nor self seems so solid afterwards as it did before being melted down in Bella Cohen's brothel."[36] Stephen's belief in an authentic, transcendent self is threatened by the slapstick city as well as by his own philosophical dialectics. And in their cinematic struggles to assert that self amid the clutter and danger of the Cartesian city and amid the mechanical false selves that their milieus encourage and validate, the heroes of much of this fiction, then, resemble not only Frankenstein's monster but the struggling heroes of slapstick comedy.

Ellison's depiction of novelistic equivalents of slapstick may be partially derived from his reading of Joyce. Certainly, Joyce was intrigued by slapstick. He referred to Mack Sennett, Charlie Chaplin, Mae West, and films such as The Kid, Modern Times, and The Perils of Pauleen in the Wake, which itself reveals a slapstick space of dreamy "langscapes" that threaten to inundate with guilt and disorientation.[37] And in Ulysses the perilous sea of matter, of slapstick space, replaces Homer's "wine dark sea." Much as Stephen reaches his lowest point of resistance to this Dublin tide at the end of "Circe," so Jack nearly drowns in the sea of matter during the symbolic hospital scene where a surreal, industrial incest mythology is revealed when the electronic labotomy machine becomes a kind of vagina dentate. His "industrial rebirth," which luckily is abortive, reveals a near total defeat of his self by the material world. This scene appears to be the genesis for the ordeal of Alex in Anthony Burgess's A Clockwork Orange where a frontal labotomy actually succeeds, and where the recurrent Beethoven's Fifth Symphony is likewise played and replayed in the struggling hero's imagination.

The murderous space of the city which is the backdrop of slapstick comedy and which Decartes first recorded on paper in Discourse on Method as a lonely res extensa informs the fiction of Joyce and Ellison much as it informs de Sica's or Fellini's 20th century Rome, Goddard's Paris, Bergman's Stockholm, Ruttmann's Berlin, Eliot's cinematic, "unreal city," Ellison's Harlem, or Wright's Chicago. Loneliness is the dominant emotion. Nearly everyone is isolated in a dreamy prison of self. Jack glimpses this ennui: "How many days could you walk the street of the big city without encountering anyone who knew you, and how many nights?" [IM, p. 321] Language, the property of consciousness, of the res cogitans, language, which separates men from the material other, becomes garbled, clichéd noise that does not lead to any bridging of the gap that separates each imprisoned ego. Jack will wind up listening to blaring jazz melodies in the coalhole in an attempt to humanize the empty void. No one will really communicate amid the noise of Ulysses, and unconscious scripts will reveal "rote words in rite order" in the mental "langscape" of the Wake. Speech itself, which should separate the self from the material world and join the self with others, becomes false and scripted by the roles characters mimic from society and fiction.

The slapstick theme in Ulysses especially, then, may have certainly influenced Ellison's descriptions of Harlem. For example, in "Hades" Chaplinesque Bloom finds the Dublin cemetery to be a "treacherous place," as Mr. Kernan nervously observes at the Dignam funeral. When Bloom contemplates the printing press, he warns in his cinematic, truncated style:

Hynes here too: account of the funeral probably. Thumping thump. This morning the remains of the late Mr. Patrick Dignam. Machines. Smash a man to atoms if they got him caught. Rule the world today. His machineries are pegging away too. Like these, got out of hand: fermenting. Working away, tearing away. And that old rat tearing to get in. [p. 118]

In "Lestrygonians" Bloom reaches a nadir in the Cartesian city:

His smile faded as he walked, a heavy cloud hiding the sun slowly, shadowing Trinity's surly front. Trams passed one another, ingoing, outgoing, clanging. Useless words. Things go on the same; day after day: squads of police marching out, back: trams in, out. Those two loonies mooching about. Dignam carted off. Mina

Purefoy's swollen belly on a bed groaning to have a child tugged out of her. One born every second somewhere. Other dying every second. Since I fed the birds five minutes. Three hundred kicked the bucket. Other three hundred born, washing the blood off, all are washed in the blood of the lamb, howling maaaaaa.

Cityful passing away, other cityful coming, passing away too: other coming on, passing on. Houses, lines of houses, streets, miles of pavements, pileup bricks, stones. Changing hands. This owner, that. Landlord never dies they say. Other steps into his shoes when he gets his notice to quit. They buy the place up with gold and still they have all the gold. Swindle it somewhere. Piled up in cities, worn away age after age. Pyramids in sand. Built on bread and onions. Slaves. Chinese wall. Babylon. Big stones left. Round towers. Rest rubble, sprawling suburbs, jerrybuilt, Kerwan's mushroom houses, built of breeze. Shelter for the night.

No one is anything. This is the very worst hour of the day. Vitality. Dull, gloomy: hate this hour. Feel as if I had been eaten and spewed. [p. 164]

And the slapstick "coalhole" image haunts Bloom in "Hades" when he contemplates the graves of Parnell and of Dignam:

Mr. Bloom walked unheeded along his grove by saddened angels, crosses, broken pillars, family vaults, stone hopes praying with upcast eyes, old Ireland's hearts and hands. More sensible to spend the money on some charity for the living. Prayer for the repose of the soul of. Does anybody really? Plant him and have done with him. Like down a coalshoot. [p. 113]

In "The Wandering Rocks" the image recurs when Lenehan points the manhole out to McCoy where Tom Rochford extricated a man who nearly suffocated from sewer gas. This "act of a hero" finds its way into hallucinatory "Circe" when Paddy Dignam "worms down through a coalhole" followed by "an obscene grandfather rat." [pp. 232-33] Tom Rochford dives into the coalhole and is "engulfed" while Bloom walks on down the hallucinatory street. [p. 476]

Slapstick scenes continue on the streets of Dublin where Bloom and his fellow Dubliners must dodge trams, street machines, running newsboys, and bicycles. Bloom is almost run down several times, and he wisely cautions: "Our lives are in peril tonight. Beware of the steamroller." [p. 662]

As a cinema-novel hybrid, Ulysses reveals one of the great themes of cinema ontology which makes this slapstick world more poignant: the struggle of the human personality, the subjective self, to manifest itself within the mechanical film medium. McConnell examines this theme in numerous novels and films as he reiterates the tendency of the film image to flatten objects and actors, or human subjects onto the "democratic," two dimensional screen, the tendency to equate objects with people.[38] The ability of the film projector to animate and emphasize through close-ups the "equality" of ordinary objects reduces the human subject to a competition with objects, which, for McConnell, Stanley Cavell and other critics concerned with the ontology of film, creates the unique, stacatto style of film acting, a style that emphasizes the ongoing struggle of the actor to prevent his being upstaged by the would-be alien material world. The actor finds himself nearly embalmed by celluloid, a ghost in the frame. The tendency of the cinema to animate dead objects and deaden living actors serves to eiphanize the modern consciousness for both Joyce and Ellison. Recall Bloom's cinematic animation of the printing press in "Aelous."

Slit. The nethermost deck of the first machine jogged forwards it flyboard with slit the first batch of quirefolded papers. Slit. Almost human the way it slit to call attention. Doing its level best to speak. That door too slit creaking, asking to be shut. Everything speaks in its own way. Slit. [p. 121]

In the theatrical films of Joyce's day, the use of the close-up was also a means of emphasizing the importance of objects within the plot. Eisenstein developed the use of the close-up to a fine art and gave objects "active" roles. In Potemkin, we recall the maggot infested meat and the tight close-ups of the almost living ship's machinery. And much as in film, objects tend to upstage characters in Ulysses and Invisible Man, and they are often used pars pro toto as metonyms to signify the characters they become associated with: Molly's dirty draws, Bloom's soap, Stephen's lost key and ashplant, Mrs. Dedalus' bowl of bile, Mulligan's razor and mirror.[39] Indeed such objects bear as much importance to the reader as do the characters themselves. Invisible Man reveals a similar series of metonyms, of objects that recall the Joycean importance given to similar material emblems: Brother Jack's glass eye; Tarp's leg chain; Tod's Sambo dolls; Barbee's bullet head; Rinehart's glasses, Cadillacs and electric guitars; Jack's briefcase; Mary's cabbage; the grandfather's Hamilton watch; Ras' horse and spear; the pun "restroom" for Wrestrum; and more. Characters are in danger of becoming as dead as the objects that represent them, so it is doubly reassuring when Jack burns the contents of his briefcase in the coalhole. Other characters in Ellison's America do not transcend the mechanical quite so successfully, and this theme carries over into Ellison's "And Hickman Arrives" where the boy photographer, when asked why he has snapped a shot of the crowd standing beneath Hickman's outstretched arm, replies that the picture revealed "good composition. . . I thought their faces would make a scale of grays between the whiteness of the marble and the blackness of the shadows." [p. 696]

Much as Ulysses, then, Invisible Man is, in many respects, a hybrid cross between film and novel forms. For both share a powerful 19th and 20th century theme of scores of Gothic and neo-Gothic novels, horror films, and cartoons--the Frankenstein myth, the nervous suspicion that the human can be synthesized in the laboratory with the aid of a little electricity; that human consciousness can be reduced to a complex mechanical operation, an operation that even Mary Shelley, with her creature of poignant humanity, would find ludicrous. For many of the characters who people the fiction we are examining are so many advanced Frankensteins devoid of that monster's human urges, so many soulless horrors. As McConnell explained, the technology of the cinema is one further realization of the myth, one step closer to the materialistic triumph of technology, to the effacement of humanity. For the projector can mechanically reproduce the speech, the song, and the dance of characters embalmed on celluloid.

Joyce's obsessive concern with the collapse of the human/object dialectic, then, seems to have been recapitulated in the fiction of Ellison. Ellison may well have spotted the theme as early as Dubliners, for in this novel robot characters reminiscent also of Dickensian mechanical men from novels such as Hard Times crowd the pages. In "Two Gallants" Corley's head is likened to "a ball on a pivot"; in "Counterparts" Farrington perceives "Humpty Dumpty" Alleyne as a "manikin," while Alleyne's fist is described as "the knob of an electric machine"; and in "Ivy Day in the Committee Room" old Jack's mouth chews "mechanically." [D, pp. 66, 102, 142, 145] Spiegel has noted that many of these depthless, cinema-cartoon characters reveal an "obsessional tic," a repetitive, machine motion.[40] For the girl in "Araby" turns her bracelot obsessively; Mr. O'Connor rolls and unrolls his cigarette in "Ivy Day in the Committee Room"; the green-eyed pervert in "An Encounter" walks in circles, a movement which is imitated by the boy who "wanders aimlessly." [D, p. 91] Ellison's description of Homer Barbee's "bullet head set on a short neck" seems to arise from this Joycean-Dickensian imagery. [IM, p. 115] Related imagery appears throughout Joyce's fiction when many of these Irish Frankensteins pay return visits in A Portrait and Ulysses. Most interesting are Bloom's many mechanical ruminations. In "Hades" he muses macabre when he finds a similarity between the parts of the human body and the parts of machines:

Your heart perhaps but what price the fellow in the six feet by two with his toes in the daisies? No touching that. Seat of the affections. Broken heart. A pump after all, pumping thousands of gallons of blood every day. One fine day it gets bunged up and there you are. Lots of them living around here: lungs, hearts, livers. Old rusty pumps: damn the thing else. [p. 105]

Bloom's guarded love of gadgets, and his tendency to constantly draw analogies between machines and living creatures can be likened to the Wakean dreamer who compares Shaun's skull to a magic lantern, HCE's mind to a radio transmitter or camera ("Hired in Cameras Extra"), the speech of Dublin's dreaming to "rite words in rote order."

If Irish Frankensteins walk the streets, the shops, the homes, the brothels and the pubs of Joyce's Dublin, so too does the robot threaten to triumph over most of Ellison's characters. Recall Vet's outburst concerning Jack, "He's invisible, a walking personification of the Negative, the most perfect achievement of your dreams, sir! The mechanical man!" [IM, p. 92] The dialectical struggle of the human to assert itself within the mechanical is again in danger of collapse when modified Frankenstein imagery informs the battle royal scene where Jack fights "automatically." [p. 24] And when he gropes on the electric rug, he notices that he can "contain the electricity." [p. 27] Ellison's blooming, neo-Gothic Frankenstein then "speaks automatically" when he delivers his speech at the smoker while he confidentially praises the Protestant Ethic. [p. 30] In the hospital scene, Jack, much as his Gothic predecessor, again is able to absorb the electric shock that threatens to blank out his inner self through an electronic labotomy.[41]

Tony Tanner reveals how nearly everyone Jack encounters in the novel tries to mechanize his consciousness by programming him with his particular view of the world.[42] Norton would make Jack into a "cog" of the social machine. And in the "cold steel civilization" that threatens to annihilate the self, many have become nearly that. The students at the college are likened to "blind robots"; Norton sprawls like "a lifeless machine" in the Golden Day; Trueblood, who like Jack can contain electricity, is described as a "cotton picking machine"; Emerson's son reminds Jack of an "alarm clock without control"; Brockway spouts a blue-collar version of Norton's dream when he informs Jack "we're the machines inside machines"; Jack tells Wrestrum over the phone "I'm a cog in a machine. We here in the Brotherhood work as a unit. . . ." (a philosophy Jack soon outgrows); and Hambro's scientific detachment and his reduction of the members of the Brotherhood to pawns reminds Jack of the hospital machine:

151

        I sat forward in my chair, suddenly
conscious of the unreality of the conver-
sation. "But who is to judge? Jack? The
Committee?"
        "We judge through cultivating scien-
tific objectivity," he said with a voice
that had a smile in it, and suddenly I saw
the hospital machine, felt as though locked
in again.
        "Don't kid yourself," I said. "The
only scientific objectivity is a machine."
[pp. 493]

        Invisible Man becomes a series of cinematic
tableaus; many of its depthless characters merge with
their mechanical backdrops. Robots yield to dolls
and dummies. Tod's symbolic Sambo dolls reveal with
their two faces that the human still lives within the
mechanized, animated stereotypes that America would
impose on blacks. But some dummies are without human
potential. Jack perceives Sibyl, a "broad" straight
from Hollywood "B" movies, as a "dummy" when the
Harlem riot commences. And we recall Jack's description of the "hurrying people" on Wall Street "who
walked as though they had been wound up."

        But Jack matures, and he satirically describes
history itself as a vast machine, for Hambro's desire
to slow down the black cause reminds Jack of Hambro's
earlier logic of white power as a brake on the
struggle for equality of opportunity: "You mean the
brakes must be put on the old wheel of history," I
said. "Or is it the little wheels within the wheel?"
[pp. 492-93] For Jack, Hambro is one of the little
wheels who operates within the mechanistic reduction
of history to a political machine. That historical
models are created to cover over the human urge to
seek naked power is evident in Hambro's euphemisms.
Bledsoe, however, defies euphemism in the presence of
Jack.

        "Power is confident, self-assuring, self-
starting and self-stopping, self-warming and
self-justifying. When you have it, you know
it. Let the Negroes snicker and the
crackers laugh! Those are the facts, son.
The only ones I even pretend to please are
big white folk, and even those I control

more than they control me. This is a power
set-up son, and I'm at the controls. You
think about that. When you buck against me,
you're bucking against power, rich white
folks power, the nation's power--which means
government power!" [p. 140]

As Laing has described clinically, the imposition
of false-self systems on individuals can finally
mechanize consciousness, robotoze the self and ultimately possess and annihilate the subjective
experience of an inner self. To avoid this schizoid
annihilation, Jack must reject the strange "iron man"
in his dream of castration, his own Bledsoe-urges to
deaden and oversimplify life through reductive perceptual models of human existence and through
inauthentic masks, false selves. Jack runs the risk
of experiencing the psychic collapse suffered,
profitably, by Rinehart, who, as Marcus Klein notes,
is also associated with mechanical imagery: "He is a
master of the latest inventions: he drives a
Cadillac and at his religious meetings, he uses an
electric guitar."[43] But before Jack can confidently
assert a dialectic between the mechanical environment
and his own innerness, he will feel the machine in
his guts, and like Bloom and Stephen, view and reify
the world as through the lens of a camera, or, as a
voyeuristic cinephile, experience Harlem as a movie
set filled with actors.

The complex theme of role-playing had been
developed by Joyce throughout his fiction. Everywhere in Joyce's Dublin characters mimic and "feel"
themselves into roles from Greek mythology to the
postures of Edwardian novelese to negative, ethnic
stereotypes from the silver screen. The nature of
oppression only aggravates such role playing, for in
an oppressed milieu, where a measure of human autonomy and a wide selection of assertive roles cannot
be guaranteed, fantasy roles and endless role playing
may be used to fill the emotional vacuum leading
often to a dangerous flirtation with "dividual
chaos." Indeed, Joyce linked the dreamy Dubliners to
ante-bellum blacks on American plantations as
"dreamonaire," or dreamy Ireland, becomes "our sweet
plantation" and Dublin or "Dreamcountry" is likened
to a forest full of "darkies" by Kev: "In the lazily
eye of his lapis, . . . Vieus Von DVbLin, 'twas one
of dozedeams a darkies ding in dewood). . ." [FW,

153

pp. 280, 293] For Joyce, Dublin is "a phantom city, phaked of philim pholk, bowed and sould for a four of hundreds of manhood. . ." [FW, p. 264]

Various characters in Ellison's fiction also exist in the dreamy Hollywood of role playing, and, much as Joyce's Dubliners, they too have been robbed of their identity through the legacy of four hundred years of oppression. Ellison's description of Harlem in Shadow and Act reveals a schizoid epidemic.

Hence the most surreal fantasies are acted out upon the streets of Harlem; a man ducks in and out of traffic shouting and throwing imaginary grenades that actually exploded during World War I; a boy participates in the rape-robbery of his mother; a man beating his wife in a park uses boxing "science" and observes Marquess of Queensberry rules (no rabbit punching, no blows beneath the belt); two men hold a third while a lesbian slashes him to death with a razor blade; boy gansters wielding homemade pistols (which in the South of their origin are but toy symbols of adolescent yearning for manhood) shoot down their young rivals. Life becomes a masquerade, exotic costumes are worn every day. Those who cannot afford to hire a horse wear riding habbits; others who could not afford a hunting trip or who seldom attend sporting events carry shooting sticks.
For this is a world in which the major energy of the imagination goes not into creating works of art, but to overcome the frustrations of social discrimination. Not quite citizens and yet Americans, full of the tensions of modern man but regarded as primitive, Negro Americans are in a desperate search for identity. Rejecting the second-class citizenship assigned them, they feel alienated and their whole lives become a search for answers to the questions; Who am I, What am I, Why am I, and Where? Significantly, in Harlem the reply to the greeting, "How are you?" is very often "Oh man, I'm nowhere'--. . ." [p. 297]

In the "nowhere" of Joyce's Dublin and of Ellison's Harlem, characters must role-play by assuming several masks in order, hopefully, to discover some viable identity. Life for the oppressed is often comparable to the fantasy sets of theater and cinema, and these real-life sets exhibit a perverted masked dance where only unreality is real. The above description of Harlem recalls Jack's observations of theatrics in the Men's House:

> Yes, and that older group with similar aspirations, the "fundamentalists," the "actors" who sought to achieve the status of brokers through imagination alone, a group of janitors and messengers who spent most of their wages on clothing such as was fashionable among Wall Street brokers, with their Brooks Brothers suits and bowler hats, English umbrellas, black calfskin shoes and yellow gloves; with their passionate argument as to what was the correct tie to wear with what shirt, what shade of grey was correct for spats and what would the Prince of Wales wear at a certain seasonal event; should field glasses be slung from the right or from the left shoulder; who never read the financial pages though they purchased the Wall Street Journal religiously and carried it beneath the left elbow, pressed firm against the body and grasped in the left hand--always manicured and gloved, fair weather or foul,--with an easy precision (Oh, they had style) while the other hand-whipped a tightly rolled umbrella back and forth at a calculated angle; with their homburgs and Chesterfields, their polo coats and Tyrolean hats worn strictly as fashion demanded. [IM, pp. 250-51]

Jack is also susceptible to the life of fantasy and the dreamy cinema. After he leaves a film, the dream consciousness asserts itself:

> In the evening I went out to a movie, a picture of frontier life with heroic Indian fighting and struggles against flood, storm and forest fire, with the out-numbered settlers winning each engagement; an epic of wagon trains rolling ever westward. I

forgot myself (although there was no one
like me taking part in the adventures) and
left the dark room in a lighter mood. But
that night I dreamed of my grandfather and
awoke depressed. I walked out of the
building with a queer feeling that I was
playing a part in some scheme which I did
not understand. [p. 167]

Joyce and Ellison further reveal that the
mechanization of modern life, the spiralling
industrialization of the cities, has created a
superimposed "slavery" and a reification of the human
that rivals the attempts of slave owners to reduce
their black purchases to chattel. As we have mentioned, each writer exposes the existence of human
cogs in the industrial nightmare of the West, cogs
who must be standardized into a limited variety of
personality types ammenable to the mindless throb of
the city. "Metaracism," as Joel Kovel has called it,
threatens the characters of these novels, cross-
culturally, much as overt oppression threatens
blacks. When Jack gazes at the flurry of activity on
Wall Street, he notes this insidious phenomena:

The streets were full of hurrying people who
walked as though they had been wound up and
were directed by some unseen control. Many
of the men carried dispatch cases and brief-
cases and I gripped mine with a sense of
importance. And here and there I saw
Negroes who hurried along with leather
pouches strapped to their wrists. They
reminded me fleetingly of prisoners carrying
their leg irons as they escaped from a chain
gang. Yet they seemed aware of some self-
importance, and I wished to stop one and ask
him why he was chained to his pouch. Maybe
they got paid well for this, maybe they were
chained to money. Perhaps the man with run-
down heels ahead of me was chained to a
million dollars. [IM, pp. 161-62]

Following the lead of Melville, Conrad, Joyce and the
many critics of the urban jungle, Ellison attempts to
expose the dreamy industrial consciousness resulting
from this new form of soft slavery, mankind's latest
nightmare.

The causes of this complex dream consciousness, a mentality that may become most severe among oppressed groups, have been the subject of much speculation. Certainly, in a culture where fatherhood is devalued, role playing replaces genuine emulation, and role playing also substitutes for viable, allowable roles. Frantz Fanon has studied this particular consciousness extensively among the oppressed of the Antilles. He argues that when no significant social rites of passage are formed for the young, the young can only play ad infinitum.

It is said that the Negro loves to jabber; in my own case, when I think of the word jabber I see a gay group of children calling and shouting for the sake of calling and shouting--children in the midst of play, to the degree to which play can be considered an initiation into life. The Negro loves to jabber, and from this theory it is not a long road that leads to a new proposition: "The Negro is just a child."[44]

Speaking of the "pathology" of Black ghetto life in Martinique, Fanon elaborates on the role playing that results in the colonial, Hegelian nightmare.

The Martinicans are greedy for security. They want to compel the acceptance of their fiction. They want to be recognized in their quest for manhood. They want to make an appearance. Each of them is an isolated, sterile, salient atom with sharply defined rites of passage, each one them is. Each of them wants to be, to emerge. Everything that an Antillean does is done for The Other.[45]

In an oppressed culture where people are "invisible" because the dominant culture ("The Other") will not recognize their unique accomplishments or even permit accomplishment, it is difficult, as Hegel suggested, for a stable consciousness to be born. The oppressed must either seek recognition in a power structure they have created and sealed off, or, if this fails, they may lapse into role playing on theatrical or filmic sets, theatrical Dublin, dreamy Harlem.

Roles are assumed in defensive ways in the
fiction of these writers, as well. Often the hero
will wear the masks of power derived from mythic
figures such as Daedalus, Osiris, Icarus, Christ,
Sigfried, Thoth, God (in "King of the Bingo Game,"
and in Wright's "The Man Who Lived Underground,"
Native Son and The Outsider), or African chieftain in
the case of Ras, who, armed with spear, seems to walk
off the silver screen. The incessant role-playing
that emerges throughout these novels allows a release
from feelings of powerlessness and inferiority. The
worlds of these writers resemble the antics of a vast
Golden Day. Indeed, Bloom has an unconscious
compulsion to assume masks, and he is closer in his
fantasy life to the other Dubliners than is Stephen.
The need to assume the mask of power to compensate
for the feelings of impotency that inevitably result
among the oppressed occupies many of Bloom's paranoid
fantasies in "Circe." Bloom has double or even
"quadruple" lives in "Doublin." He is depicted as
benevolent ruler and hero of his nation, who ends the
repression of priest and king in some idealistic and
muddled way. He then becomes a Jewish law-giver,
then God, then a great lover who causes women to
commit suicide. His fantasy life allows him to act
out aggression too, and he becomes an oppressor. He
liquidates MacIntosh and other enemies with a glance;
he condones the slave trade; and he appears as
Napoleon. The failure of society to provide rites
of passage complicates the hope for the formation of
a self free from these theatrics which aggravate the
schizoid state. As we have seen, Joyce and Ellison
realized that oppression often weakens the father and
prohibits successful oedipal identification.
Stephen's discovery of the word "Foetus" carved on
his father's schoolboy desk in A Portrait reveals to
a sickened Stephen the symbolic state of Irish
conscience. This unformed or fetal state of the
personality informs Invisible Man, as well.

Throughout Invisible Man the protagonist
experiences regressions to childhood and to an
unformed identity. Such regressions reinforce the
idea that for the oppressed the dream is the real.
After the retreat from the Golden Day, the protagonist looks to Norton as a great white father-image,
and he feels that his marginal sense of identity is
disintegrating. During Barbee's sermon, the state of
the preborn ego is alluded to again when the

protagonist listens to the wail of an old woman, "Somewhere in the audience an old woman's voice began a plaintive wail; the birth of a sad, unformulated song that died stillborn in a sob." [pp. 129-30] After Bledsoe lashes out at him, the protagonist again feels unborn, "For three years I had thought of myself as a man and here with a few words he's made me feel as helpless as an infant." [p. 142] Following the explosion in the paint factory, Jack cannot remember his name. The fetal theme continues.

> I lay experiencing the vague processes of my
> body. I seemed to have lost all sense of
> proportion. Where did my body end and the
> crystal and white world begin? [p. 233]

All of this, then, is implied in the dream consciousness of the oppressed, and it is from this nightmare of history that the narrator must awake.

Like so many of Dostoevsky's role playing specters, characters in the fiction of Joyce and Ellison live out dream roles, often in the form of the ethnic stereotypes that the schizogenic social order has created. This theme of dream consciousness becomes more varied and complex, and it appears to be partially derived from Joyce's extended metaphor of the nightmare of history.

Norris' observations on the complexity of dreaming in the Wake also help to explain the ordeals of Ellison's heroes.

> The confusion of the reader of Finnegans Wake is
> a fitting response to a kind of terror implicit
> in the world of the dream, a terror confronted by
> Alice in Through the Looking Glass when Tweedle-
> dee suggests that she is merely a sort of thing
> in the Red Knight's dream.[46]

For it is often difficult to determine whether Wakean characters are to be understood as characters or merely as dream projections from the dreamer of the Wake. Jack's sense of the unreality of his consciousness, a component of his invisibility, results partly from this nervous Wakean phenomena. In the Prologue to Invisible Man, Jack angerly reflects, "You wonder whether you aren't simply a phantom in other people's minds. Say a figure in a nightmare which the sleeper tries with all his strength to destroy." [pp. 3-4] And in a calmer mood he reveals, "I remember that I am invisible and walk softly so as not to awaken the sleeping ones. Sometimes it is best not to awaken them; there are few things in the world as dangerous as sleepwalkers." [p. 5]

The view of the self as "all in all," as a superimposition of "multiple me's," as Joyce puts it in the Wake, along with Malraux's Baron Clappique and Melville's confidence man, all appear to be possible literary cousins of the character of Rinehart, who serves as the epiphany of the nightmare. Rinehart, with his Hollywood glasses, has no innerness. He is a mad carousel of black stereotypes, flashy dress, and jive talk. He lives the ultimate inauthenticity, the lowest on the Kierkegaardian scale of human worth. For Kierkegaard, defining oneself through dress, a habit of Rinehart and of several of Joyce's Dubliners, is indicative of the ultimate form of escape from one's humanity.[47] Kenner has discussed the imagery of clothing in Joyce's fiction. He argues that "no other novelist is so preoccupied with clothes."[48] For characters in Joyce's fiction, he argues, are often only described externally by the clothes they wear: "All is appearance, all," in the protean facade of Dublin.[49]

Jack is endangered. He, too, might become another Rinehart. Only his tentative attachment to his grandfather self prevents his disintegration into Ellison's version of the "dividual chaos," into a surrender of authenticity to negative ethnic stereotypes. Rinehart recalls many of Laing's patients who have assumed so many false selves that their inner core of self has atrophied. Laing noted that the task of therapy for such individuals "comes to be to make contact with the original 'self' of the individual, which or who, we must believe is still a possibility, if not an actuality, and can still be nursed back to a feasible life."[50] Rinehart and the confidence men before him can be understood as functioning schizoids who exploit and "fit into" a rootless culture. No wonder, then, that life for Ellison's characters often resembles a "feverish dream," an eerie deja vu. In an encounter with Emma, the volatile dream-film consciousness emerges again:

Then I was past, disturbed not so much by the close contact, as by the sense that I had somehow been through it all before. I couldn't decide if it were from watching some similar scene in the movies, from books I'd read, or from some recurrent but deeply buried dream. [p. 293]

All a dream, a landscape of nightmare. Harlem becomes a perverse slapstick scenario; the Brotherhood resembles a vaudeville performance. When Jack runs from the commotion of the Provo's dispossession, he tries to avoid being tailed, ". . . I stepped into the street with a nonchalance I copied from characters I had seen in the movies." [p. 279] Later when he meets Brother Jack, he notes that the Brother resembles an actor:

So he's heard my speech; well, I'll hear what he has to say, I thought, seeing him start toward me with his rapid, rolling, bouncy, heel and toey step. It was as though he had taught himself to walk that way and I had a feeling that somehow he was acting a part; that something about him wasn't exactly real--an idea which I dismissed immediately, since there was a quality of unreality over the whole afternoon. [p. 282]

When Jack symbolically and unwittingly "eats cheese," the cheese cake that Brother Jack offers him, this political actor cites Jack's theatrical prowess as allegedly revealed in the dispossession speech, "Then you're very talented. You are a natural." [p. 283] While Jack attends a Brotherhood committee meeting, he is unable to classify these new faces into familiar types from this southern background. He marvels at the apparent concord of the black and white membership concerning causes and issues, but somehow Jack knows that these people are not so different from people in his southern exposure. He reflects, "They seemed familiar but were just as different as Brother Jack and the other whites were from all the white men I had known. They were transformed, like familiar people seen in a dream." [p. 293] Jack will later articulate that Northern dream as a disguised counterpart to the Southern nightmare.

And when he and Wrestrum become embroiled over Jack's alleged assertion of ego, Jack describes the argument with the "clown" Wrestrum: ". . . we sounded like characters in a razor slinging vaudeville skit." Jack feels lost and unreal during this disagreement. He ponders, "Where the hell am I?" [p. 393] To become captured by a role that one must play in such a fraternity can only lead to a derealized self, to a sense of being "nowhere." The Brotherhood is merely one more means of controlling blacks; its liberal facade peels off at the Chthonian where Jack is stereotyped once again. The North and South differ only in climate.

Ubiquitous racial stereotypes are a constant net in the fiction of Ellison and Joyce. Eldridge Cleaver's explanation of the dreamy splitting process that creates such stereotypes and which locks the dominant culture into its own roles is a classic description of the perverse process that creates a debilitating mind/body split among the races in America (and by inference in every oppressed society). A similar split can be seen as the cause of much of the paralysis of Joyce' Dublin where the qualities of the mind have been assumed by the oppressor and the qualities of the body have been assumed by the oppressed. Cleaver argues that in America the white male tends to project his sexuality and physicality onto the black male, while the white retains mental and intellectual qualities and becomes half-developed, a creature of the mind. Just as this process occurs with the black male, it also occurs with the black female.

Cleaver explains:

In order to project an image of Ultrafemininity, the woman of the elite repudiates and abdicates the Domestic Function of the female (which is, in the female, the counterpart of the function of Brute Power in the male). To enhance her image and to increase her femininity, the domestic component of her nature is projected onto the women in the classes beneath her, and the femininity of the woman below is correspondingly decreased. In effect, a switch is made: the woman of the elite absorbs into her being the femininity of the

woman below her, and then extirpates her
domestic component; the woman below absorbs
the elite woman's castoff domestic component
and relinquishes her own femininity. The
elite woman thus becomes Ultrafeminine while
the woman below becomes Subfeminine. For
the purposes of social imagery, the woman
below becomes an Amazon.[51]

The Irish woman often has problems analogous to
those of the black woman. Seen through the eyes of
Joyce, she often accepts her label of clay and
refuses to tolerate the mind in herself and in her
men. Hence, she often becomes a source of paralysis
and passivity. Joyce's women may be sexual and
alluring, but they rarely escape the Irish peat. In
the face of this stagnant female force, Stephen must
deliver his non serviam. Ellison's, Eliotic white
women are defined, or perhaps overdefined, by this
split, as well. Sibyl, Emma, and the nameless woman,
are, paradoxically, physical sex objects and,
simultaneously, cold, ethereal, Ultrafeminine
creatures who parody genuine sexuality.

Concerning the black male Cleaver argues:

The chip on the Supermasculine Menial's
shoulder is the fact that he has been robbed
of his mind. In an uncannily effective
manner, the society in which he lives has
assumed in its very structure that he, minus
a mind, is the embodiment of Brute Power.
The bias and reflex of the society are
against the cultivation or even the functioning of the mind, and it is born in upon
him from all sides that the society is
actually deaf, dumb, and blind to his mind.
The products of his mind, unless they are
very closely associated with his social
function of Brute Power, are resented and
held in contempt by society as a whole. The
further away from Brute Power his mental
productions stand, the more emphatically
will they be rejected and scorned by
society, and treated as upstart invasions of
the realm of the Omnipotent Administrator
[the white man]. His thoughts count for
nothing. He doesn't run, regulate, control

or administer anything. Indeed, he is himself regulated, manipulated, and controlled by the Omnipotent Administrators. The struggle of his life is for the emancipation of his mind, to receive recognition for the products of his mind, and official recognition of the fact that he has a mind.[52]

Cross-culturally, this body/mind split causes both the dominant groups and their respective victims to become cemented into stereotyped and confused roles. These groups act out dreamy parts invented by those who perversely attempt to create an order based on dominance. All exist in the nightmare of history, derealized by their respective invisibilities.

The perception of his own invisibility is lost to Norton who attempts to relegate the body stereotype to his student benefactors. He only entraps himself in the Omnipotent role and loses transit with his authentic self. Spouting his debased Emersonian philosophy, Norton tells Jack,

> So you see, young man, you are involved in my life quite intimately, even though you've never seen me before. You are bound to a great dream and to a beautiful monument. If you become a good farmer, a chef, a preacher, doctor, singer, mechanic--whatever you become, and even if you fail, you are my fate. And you must write me and tell me the outcome. [IM, p. 34]

In the Epilogue Jack encounters Norton years later when the old man walks the streets of New York in search of "Centre Street," a symbolic search for the center of his being. For Norton the college was "a great dream become reality," and old Norton will never wake from the dream. [p. 38] He fails to see that what has happened at the college and in America is the fulfillment of a nightmare.

Vet understands the masquerade fostered by oppression, and he warns Jack that Norton's sadistic dream is creating Jack's identity. And Jack will live in the convolutions of Norton's representative dream throughout the main action of the novel, when Jack assumes one mask after another, when he

constantly reacts to experience, when he lives under
the spell of the Hegelian Master in the guise of his
educators, of his employers, of his would-be lovers,
of his fraternal orders and of his own desires to
play god and hero. Jack discovers that to be black
and to live in America is to act out roles of
degradation in a new Birth of A Nation.[53]

The mask of physicality that informs many of
Ellison's dreamy characters is also present in
Joyce's Dublin. During hallucinatory "Circe," Ben
Dollard is transformed into the ape-like sexual
symbol of the Irish, who allegedly are absorbed
and drenched in sexuality:

Ben Jumbo Dollard, rubicund, musclebound,
hairynostriled, hugebearded cabbageared,
shaggychested, schockmaned, fatpapped,
stands forth, his loins and genitals
tightened into a pair of black bathing
bagslops. [p. 521]

Playing a role, assuming false-self systems,
however, is not always negative, defensive or
demeaning in the fiction of Joyce and Ellison.
Paradoxically, certain varieties of role playing can
be a means of liberating subjective inner yearnings.
In Shadow and Act Ellison alludes to the thoughts of
another Irish mentor, William Butler Yeats:

There is a relation between discipline and
the theatrical sense. If we cannot imagine
ourselves as different from what we are and
assume the second self, we cannot impose a
discipline upon ourselves, though we may
accept one from others. Active virtue, as
distinct from the passive acceptance of a
current code, is the wearing of a mask. It
is the condition of an arduous full life.
[p. 53]

Ellison assumes that we can never be totally free
from roles, or from the codes or social systems that
create roles. The search for identity, in fact,
implies that an individual must try out and discard
numerous masks until the most apt persona is found.
Ironically, the origins of this subjective concept of

the formation of the self are basically Protestant.
The Puritans rebelled against the mass conscience, as
it were, of Catholicism, and advocated the formation
of individual conscience created by the person who
could now commune directly with his God. "Masking is
a play on possibility," Ellison argues, "and ours is
a society in which possibilities are many. When
American life is most American it is apt to be most
theatrical." [SA, p. 54] This theatrical spirit in
the American setting results in part from the absence
of a viable past. But this void can become an asset;
former ethnic customs and mannerisms can lose their
tyranny on the present, individuals can create,
indeed self-create themselves.

McConnell describes the Romantic roots of the
theatrical sense of using roles to assert one's
innerness. He argues that role-playing in its more
positive sense is profoundly cinematic, and he cites
Byron's passion for masks as precinematic:

> The Byronic game, played across a potential
> infinity of roles, poses, and situations, is
> in fact the struggle of the poetic intelli-
> gence to find a voice, to invent a structure
> for itself which will make it present in the
> poem. Thus Byron becomes the ancestor of
> all those hero-clowns of modern writing--
> Baudelaire, Wilde, Proust, Joyce, Genet,
> Mailer--who have made their lives a pre-text
> for their work. In all these writers, we
> find the impulse to sacrifice concerns of
> form and decorum and of the traditional
> values of language to the goal of making the
> work manifest the personality of the artist.
> . . .[54]

Certainly Joyce is not Stephen, nor is Jack a fully
accurate portrait of young Ralph Ellison, but, on the
other hand, these characters are, to some degree,
personas for each writer, part of each writer's
Romantic exegesis, part of his need to assert
subjectivity through the constraints of those cinema-
novel hybrids and through the post-Cartesian environment. McConnell goes on to summarize the purpose of
such theatrics in his discussion of Byron:

> And Byron, my nominee for the first star
> actor of the precinema, created an art

which, like the art of Joyce, Chaplin, Cagney, and Pynchon, details the struggle of the self to assert its own existence within a welter of political, cultural, and historical details whose very richness threatens to deprive that self of its vitality.[55]

Roles, then, cannot be discarded completely, and characters in the fiction of Joyce and Ellison often attempt, as Cross Damon puts it, to "dream their own dream." This is part of the meaning of Ellison's Epilogue, for identity, as Joyce punned it, must be "forged," but it is indeed a forgery, an artificial "bricolage," a composite mask woven out of those one emulates, a complex graveyard of role-models that might spur a fresher contact with the inner self. Jack's task is to forge his identity, and he is well on that way in the coalhole. He, like Wright's heroes, must become as Laing argues, a two-dimensional self, "a conjunction of identity-for-others, and identity-for-oneself."[56] If Jack continues to live out more false selves, he can never become "real." Yet if he cultivates a near total subjective identity, if he cuts himself off from others, he, like Stephen Dedalus, will risk becoming unreal. The problem that haunts the reader at the conclusion of Invisible Man has also intrigued and puzzled the 19th century Russian writers, English Romantics, American Transcendentalists, Malraux, Joyce, the Existentialists and many other of Ellison's precursors. For despite Jack's unwarranted sentimentality, how will he function outside the coalhole in the world of ubiquitous stereotypes and incessant racism and metaracism? If we wish to speculate beyond the coalhole, Jack's plight may well be that of most thinking people: the maintenance of a healthy distance between one's self and the crazy yet potentially redemptive American experience, (the sentimentality of the Epilogue to the contrary), the emergence as writer instead of ranter.

In any case, the use of masking can be destructive or liberating. Until America arrives, assuming that it does, multiples of the Jacks, the Fred Daniels and Bigger Thomas's and the Cross Damons will continue to despair in the violent, dreamy, unreal theater of American life; and the national ego will be split and unresolved. On one

level, the integration of the races may be necessary
for the mental health of everyone, or so is the logic
of this fiction.

Ellison's fascination in yet another set of
personas derived from the universal mythology of the
trickster was an interest shared by Joyce, as well.
For the trickster is often able to doggedly assert
himself through wit and trickery. Indeed, the
references made by Joyce in the <u>Wake</u> to Uncle Remus
and Brer Rabbit may have been noted by Ellison for
they offered more proof of the commonalities of the
Irish and black experiences.[57] In "Circe," Bloom
reveals his subversive personality. When he is
stopped by the Watch, he puts on the familiar mask of
the trickster that the oppressed use for survival.
He protests that he is not Leopold Bloom, but rather,
Bloom, the dental surgeon. Next he poses as a member
of the Legion of Honor as his fantasy of deceit
grows; then he is identified with Henry Flower by the
card in his hat. To confuse the Watch further, he
goes on to propose that his is a case of mistaken
identity. Next he pretends to support the British
military exploitation of the Irish in barely disguised satire. He mentions Tweedy's service and goes
on to fabricate his own military record. He finally
compares his use of the trickster mask to the mask
of an American, Jim Bludso. But Bloom assumes the
ultimate mask of the trickster when he tells the
Watch that he is a writer. He concludes his performance by praising the physicality of the military
service, of himself, and of his fellow Irishmen in
his barely guarded satire: "The R.D.F. with our own
Metropolitan police, guardians of our homes, the
pluckiest lads and the finest body of men, as
physique, in the service of our sovereign." [pp.
456-58] In this case Bloom assumes the projected
mask of physicality his oppressors wish him to bear
only to turn the tables on the Watch.

Masking and role playing have a positive value as
means to reach and to protect the "authenticity" of
self. And the cinema metaphor extends this positive
process, as well, for the intuition of the chaotic
unconscious, and its cantankerous dream self becomes
for Jack, as for the Wakean dreamer, an intuition of
an inner kaleidoscope that helps to support the
dialectic between the subjective, Romantic self and
the mechanical models of the human mind and of human
perception.

The Wake has been described as a dream screen
upon which are projected "frames" that contain dream
fragments, superimpositions, which Joyce simulated
through the use of multi-levelled puns. And it
appears that Ellison understood the techniques of
Joyce's eerie simulation of the dream long before
Joyce's critics. In fact, Jack's dream scenarios are
often nearly as superimposed and murky as those in
the Wake, although beyond the use of puns and Joycean
"confusion," Ellison did not attempt to probe the
language of dreams with the intensity of Joyce. But
if Joyce's Wakean language had little impact on
Ellison's style, Joyce's metaphoric linkage of the
projection of unconscious imagery in the dream with
the dreamy cinema medium did capture and fire
Ellison's imagination. Wright also may have recalled
Joyce's unconscious cinema when he spoke of Bigger, a
character posssessed by uncontrollable unconscious
urges, as a dreamy filmic "negative" that Wright
developed, as it were.[58] Ellison, too, continued to
develop such a negative when he metaphorically
compared Jack's intuition of inner mental life with
a mental cinema in passages that recall the
kaleidoscopic Wake.

When Jack lays helpless in the factory hospital,
the doctor quizes him. Jack describes his peculiar
consciousness:

> He began asking questions and I could hear
> myself replying fluently, though inside I
> was reeling with swiftly changing emotional
> images that shrilled and chattered, like a
> sound-track reversed at high speed. [p. 240]

And later Jack compares this introspection into his
inner self as viewing "some crazy movie," when he
leaves the hospital.

> Leaving him and going out into the paint
> fuming air I had the feeling that I had been
> talking beyond myself, had used words and
> expressed attitudes not my own, that I was
> in the grip of some alien personality lodged
> deep within me. Like the servant about whom
> I'd read in psychology class who, during a
> trance, had recited pages of Greek
> philosophy which she had over heard one day
> while she worked. It was as though I were

acting out a scene from some crazy movie. Or perhaps I was catching up with myself and had put into words feelings that I had hitherto suppressed. [IM, p. 243]

In their cinematic glimpses into the ambiguous and kaleidoscopic unconscious, both Joyce and Ellison move beyond the more reductive Freudian assertion of the ultimate intelligibility of the dream work. Of Jack's opening dream in the Prologue and of the many puzzling dreams and hallucinations that follow, Robert E. Abrams reveals that "metaphoric images and situtations suggest multiple meanings simultaneously. Orientation in time becomes problematic. Riddles and puns abound."[59] Abrams compares Ellison's dream scenarios with the oneiric landscapes of Lewis Carroll, but he might compare them to the Joycean "chaosmos" as well. Abrams argues that "Dreams, nightmares, and hallucinations in Invisible Man. . . elude cognitive mastery."[60] For although they invite rational interpretations, they are ultimately indecipherable in contrast to the Freudian optimism that dreams may yield relatively clear and more linear interpretation. The dream landscape of the Wake is such a place and Joyce's labyrinthine journey through the collective unconscious, with all of its identity confusion, its split ego fragments, its unexplained and mysterious guilt, multi-levelled puns, ambiguous riddles and defense mechanisms, appears, along with Alice in Wonderland, to be a probable influence on Ellison's weaving of the unconscious "chaosmos" of Jack, of the "crazy movie."

The oneiric wanderings of Jack reveal dream experiences, then, which rival the superimpositions of the Wakean unconscious. The multi-levelled reefer dream in the Prologue, accompanied by the dissonant music of Louis Armstrong, is representative

And beneath the swiftness of the hot tempo there was a slower tempo and a cave and I entered it and looked around and heard an old woman singing a spiritual as full of Weltschmerz as flamenco, and beneath that lay a still lower level on which I saw a beautiful girl the color of ivory pleading in a voice like my mother's as she stood before a group of slaveowners who bid for her

naked body, and below that I found a lower
level and a more rapid tempo and I heard
someone shout. . . .[IM, p. 9]

The shouting dream revival meeting is riddled with
contradictions:

> "Brothers and sisters, my text this
morning is the 'Blackness of Blackness.'"
And the congregation of voices answered:
"That blackness is most black, brother, most
black. . . ."
> "In the beginning. . ."
> "At the very start," they cried.
> ". . . there was blackness. . ."
> "Preach it. . ."
> ". . . and the sun. . ."
> "The sun, Lawd. . ."
> ". . .was bloody red. . ."
> "Red. . ."
> "Now black is. . ." the preacher
shouted.
> "Bloody. . ."
> "I said black is. . ."
> "Preach it, brother. . ."
> ". . . an' black ain't. . ."
> "Red, Lawd, red: He said it's red!"
> "Amen, brother. . ."
> "Black will git you. . ."
> "yes, it will. . ."
> "yes, it will. . ."
> ". . .an' black won't. . ."
> "Naw, it won't!"
> "It do. . ."
> "it do, Lawd. . ."
> ". . .an' it don't."
> "Halleluiah. . ."
> ". . .It'll put you, glory, glory, Oh
my Lawd, in the WHALE'S BELLY."
> "Preach it, dear brother. . ."
> ". . . an' make you tempt. . ."
> "Good God a-mighty!"
> "Old Aunt Nelly!"
> "Black will make you. . ."
> "Black. . ."
> ". . . or black will un make you."
> "Ain't it the truth, Lawd?" [pp. 9-10]

The unconscious of the dreamer cannot fix boundaries
or identities as can the conscious mind. In the

171

universal unconscious we arrive at incertitude and anarchy that threaten all rational systems. A shrill voice screams at Jack's dream self: "Git out of here, you fool! Is you ready to commit treason?" The wise anarchy of dreams continues when Jack's dream specter becomes "confused" by the "old singer of spirituals":

> "Old woman, what is this freedom you love so well?" I asked around a corner of my mind.
> She looked suprised, then thoughtful, then baffled. "I done forgot, son. It's all mixed up. First I think it's one thing, then I think it's another. It gits my head to spinning. I guess now it ain't nothing but knowing how to say what I got up in my head. But it's a hard job, son. Too much is done happen to me in too short a time. Hit's like I have a fever. Ever' time I starts to walk my head gits to swirling and I falls down. Or it it ain't that, it's the boys; they gits to laughing and wants to kill up the white folks. They's bitter, that's what they is. . ."
> "But what about freedom?"
> "Leave me 'lone, boy; my head aches!"
> I left her feeling dizzy myself.
> [p. 11]

As do these confusing dreams, the dying words of Jack's grandfather become a "constant puzzle" to Jack throughout the novel. Indeed, the dreamy image of Jack's grandfather that emerges from Jack's dreams is one of devious irrationality that would ultimately explode all the perceptual models of the waking world. All attempts to reduce and explain human existence by means of philosophical, social, economic, or theological systems are mocked by Jack's grandfather self. Before his death the old man angerly charges:

> "Live with your head in the lion's mouth. I want you to overcome 'em with yesses, undermine 'em with grins, agree 'em to death and destruction, let 'em swoller you till they vomit or bust wide open." [p. 16]

His advice not only reveals survival tactics for an oppressed group, but it points to the broader theme of the novel: any systemization of life will create its hierarchies, its stereotypes, its false selves, all of which will repress the release of authentic selfhood. This meek man calls for a final guerrilla war on the mind itself, against the human rage for order, so that men might live within the curve of a question mark. The grandfather does not specify the enemy but Jack quickly learns that the rage for order transcends color, that it is found in all men. But how can one protect oneself from becoming unglued in the world of "infinite posssibilities"? This the grandfather will not reveal when he reappears in Jack's dreams.

Trueblood's dream also uncovers a human innerness that is subversive and contradictory. For as Abrams notes, Trueblood longs for sexual release as well as "a lost uterine oblivion beyond sexuality and time," simultaneously. Can the dream, Abrams asks, be ultimately knowable as Freud nervously asserted, or is the self immersed "in polymorphous multiplicity and ambivalence?" [61]

During Jack's climactic dream of castration, the figure of the "iron man," who rises from beneath Jack's hanging genitalia, appears as ambiguous as the censored dream images Trueblood struggles to unravel. This "iron man" may be part of Jack's psyche. Abrams argues:

> His nightmare, in short, would appear to be the nightmare of a fractured, ambivalent ego inhabiting contradictory figures simultaneously. The hallucinating narrator in the foreground, "painful and empty" and reduced to ineffectual laugher, and the "iron man" in the background, heedlessly bent on vengeance, would both seem to be authentic, if polar and contradictory, versions of the same self. [62]

Certainly the goal of the Joycean hero to locate and negotiate the contents of his inner life and arrive at an authentic self that might be released by the artist through revolutionary acts of creation mirror Jack's quest as well as those of the nameless anti-hero of "King of the Bingo Game" and of Todd's in "Flying Home." Nevertheless, Ellison's heroes, armed with their Transcendental optimism and existential faith in the existence of authentic selfhood in all men, will not reach the comic disallusionment that the Wakean dreamer discovers. Norris, perhaps hastily, explains Joyce's final attitude toward the Daedalian quest, the search for authenticity:

> As Joyce's interest shifted from consciousness to the unconscious, he was increasingly forced to recognize the inauthenticity and self-delusion that the artist shares with the philistine. In the world of the dream, every individual is a demon and an angel, a pharisee and a holy man, a charlatan and an artist. The artist enjoys no corner on truth; he merely constructs more elaborate and elegant myths and lies more convincingly than the man on the street.[63]

The Joycean dreamer discovers that he/she is not an isolate entity but a Hegelian "all in all," the bearer of the chaosmos of selves, a graveyard of disparate personalities. For Norris "Joyce comes to maturity" when he replaces the portrait of the artist as "soaring Icarus" with the "subterranean rodent" Shem.[64] The Wakean dreamer discovers the inner nature of man to be chaotic, reptilian, contradictory and ultimately indecipherable.

Ellison locates, perhaps with more optimism than Joyce, an inner self that is as supremely wise as it is mysterious and paradoxical, a self that might be separated out from the dreams that boil in the libidinous kettle, an inner sanctum which most characters never explore in their rage for order, in their struggle against the nets.

The heroes in the worlds of Joyce and Ellison are often, then, doubly threatened by the myth of space that the West has settled upon, for the very fact that they are of oppressed groups means that the dominant cultures ultimately define them as a part of the res extensa, as human chattel, invisible outsiders, who blend in with the sea of matter and become visible only as objects or stereotypes. Kovel's explorations into this process of relegating the oppressed to object status leads him to call upon Alfred North Whitehead to demonstrate that the Cartesian model of reality and our feeling of separation from the world is a dangerous myth badly in need of replacement with a metaphor of unity. Summarizing Whitehead's rejection of the Cartesian metaphor in Science and the Modern World, Kovel reveals:

According to Whitehead, the fantasy imposed on nature by Western scientific man, and confirmed for him by his success in history, is the belief that the material world is composed of lifeless material bodies acted upon by immaterial forces. We see here the nuclear mental operation of Western man in its purest form: nature, which had been experienced in previous eras as an organismic and direct unity, is abstracted and made remote from men. Looking at it from a distance, Western scientific man reduces it to substances, "things"--dead things upon which a force can operate. The nature of the force is unimportant: it may be the Newtonian force of gravity (which was the most brilliant insight permitted by the abstraction) or the conquering force of men. In the primitive, axiomatic, nuclear form of this fantasy, both are equivalent. The result is the death of nature, which becomes "a dull affair, soundless, scentless, colourless; merely the hurrying of material, endlessly, meaninglessly." [65]

For Joyce and for Ellison as well, their heroes can marginally transcend the perceptual traps that would, in turn, mechanize their consciousness. But they do so not in concert, but in their private, emotional moments, best epiphanized by Molly Bloom's memory of the Hill of Howth where she experienced her passion for young Bloom along with feeling of fecund union with the many-flowered hillside, or by Jack's ecstatic loomings in the coalhole amid the brilliant lights, the stereophonic sound, the glistening coal of future potential for men and the earth. The hope of the Wakean dreamer is that a primal unity might be restored between the mind and the outside world, that the split ego might be reunited into a unified self. The coalhole of Jack is likewise a place of unity and synthesis, and on one level it is a model in miniature of a primal attitude toward the external world which is symbolized by the bright light and music Jack so craves, the glistening coal, and the inert electricity that can be used or abused by mankind. Much as jazz syncopation softens and humanizes the harsh military melody and beat in the marching music it is so often fused with, so Jack humanizes his coalhole with music, light, and a consciousness that collapses time into the timeless moment of transcendence.

Joyce's fascination with Giordano Bruno's assertions on the divinity of matter, on the inseparability of soul or essence from matter, and on the basic goodness of the essences of things; Joyce's interest in Blake's esoteric Christianity which refused to devalue the body and repress the "human form divine"; his baptism of Kevin with rice water; his Oriental references in the Wake which imply the ultimate unity of opposites; all of this may point to his own dismissal of Descartes' myth of space. Given the complexity and contrariness of the Wake, we may never be certain if Joyce did indeed dismiss the mechanical models of the mind and of nature. It is likely that for Joyce, as for Ellison, the goal of the unconscious was not always a perverse attempt to confound consciousness; that as Campbell and Robinson assert, for Joyce, deep in the layers of the inner self there was a benign, erotic joissance. This may be part of the message Ellison received from the lower frequencies of Finnegans Wake.

We move in the beast circuls. [FW, p. 438]

A cataleptic mithyphallic! Was this Totem
Fulcrum Est. Ancestor yu hald in Dies Eirae
. . . ? [FW, p. 481]

Secrets, silent, stony sit in the dark
places of both our hearts: secrets weary of
their tyranny: tyrants willing to be
dethroned. [U, p. 28]

Houston paused and stared at the floor.
"You asked me something about civilization.
. . . Civilization," Houston repeated the
word, letting it roll slowing on his tongue.
He looked at Cross, smiled, then asked
teasingly: "You call this civilization? I
don't. This is a jungle. We pretend that
we have law and order. But we don't, really.
We have imposed a visible order, but hidden
under that veneer of order the jungle still
seethes." [TO, 134-135]

CHAPTER IV

Throughout history men have forever sensed, Freud concluded in <u>Moses and Monotheism</u>, "that once upon a time they had a primeval father and killed him."[1] In Joyce's Ireland, primal parricide had been reenacted symbolically: English rule and the fraternal church had unknowingly joined forces to devalue Ireland's fathers and traditions. Then too, the "burrowings" caused by the unrelentless series of invasions and the subsequent intermingling of bloodlines caused the certainty of lineage and "ethnic purity" to atrophy. Old Finn lay in a heap in "confused" Ireland: his mythic authority as progenitor of the Irish "race" more and more remote.

In the Americas of Ellison and Wright, confident fatherhood is also a cold corpse, and the oppression of blacks is a definite cause. And much as in Ireland, miscegenation has created its own geneological stew with a color bar added, for the miscegenation of whites and blacks during the era of slavery, and the forced intermingling of disparate African tribal groups on the plantations rendered family and tribal allegiances far more tentative. The slave trade produced numerous agonizing psychological shocks when uprooted Africans were severed from their tribal chiefs, from their taboos, from their languages, from their kinship systems, and from their names, names which could evoke an identity and a place in the tribe. What was intolerable and agonizing for Africans was unsettling to European and Asian transplants in America, as well, and the black experience of cultural uprooting differs from the ordeal of Europeans and Asians mainly in degree. But in each case the power and prestige of fatherhood lost ground.

The devaluation of fatherhood resulted from other symbolic geldings in America. The Revolution symbolically assaulted the colonial parent, the fatherland, and substituted this authority with the authority of a fraternity. For Ellison, Lincoln offered the hope that fatherhood might be restored in America on the symbolic level, that it might be recreated in a revolutionary land; but in Ellison's imagination the Civil War and the assassination of

Lincoln seem to have succeeded once more in annihilating this restoration, or so he implies in his nightmare of the mutilation of Lincoln in "Tell It Like It Is, Baby." In his attempt to analyze his own dream, Ellison likens the assassinationhe dreams to Greek drama, specifically to Orestes:

> . . . the hero-father murdered (for Lincoln is a kind of father of 20th century America), his life evilly sacrificed and the fruits of his neglected labors withering some ninety years in the fields; the state fallen into corruption, and the citizens into moral anarchy, and with no hero come to set things right. [2]

Interestingly enough, the emptiness Ellison experiences when his dream continues is not unlike the emptiness he suffered after the death of his own father, an event that occurred when Ellison was three years old. Yet Ellison goes on to imply that America simultaneously devalues fatherhood and longs for it.

For Ellison and for many social scientists, capitalism is one more mode of the devaluation process, for American capitalism became the clubhouse of the fraternity in the North. And Christopher Lasch's observation that modern day capitalism appears to be based not on the authoritarian family model, but on a watered down, fraternal one, conforms with Ellison's and Wright's treatment of the world of work. For these writers, much as for Joyce, the unconscious wish to commit parricide, a wish Freud held to be innate in all men, had been re-enacted culturally; the hidden desires of individuals had been vented on a mass scale. Blimin describes the chaos of modern American life in The Outsider:

> We twentieth-century Westerners have outlived the faith of our fathers; our minds have grown so skeptical that we cannot accept the old scheme of moral precepts which once guided man's life. In our modern industrial society we try to steer our hearts by improvised, pragmatic rules which are, in the end, no rules at all. If there are people who tell you that they live by traditional values and precepts--as the English sometimes pretend--then they are

either lying to you or to themselves; maybe they are lying both ways. . . . There is no modern industrial nation on earth today that makes decisions based upon anything remotely resembling the injunctions of the Old or New Testament. . . . [p. 358]

Ellison further revealed that America has failed to follow the Founding Father's advice that it become a nation of equality. For Ellison, America's failure to adhere to the melting-pot ideal is a cause for its lack of direction, of tradition, and of order. America is still a confused fraternity:

So perhaps we shy from confronting our cultural wholeness because it offers no easily recognizable points of rest, no facile certainties as to who, what or where (culturally or historically) we are. Instead, the whole is always in cacophonic motion. Constantly changing its mode, it appears as a vortex of discordant ways of living and tastes, values and traditions; a whirlpool of odds and ends in which the past courses in uneasy juxtaposition with those bright, futuristic principles and promises to which we, as a nation, are politically committed. In our vaguely perceived here and now, even the sounds and symbols spun off by the clashing of group against group appear not only alarmingly off-key, but threatening to our inherited eyes, ears, and appetites. Thus in our intergroup familiarity there is a brooding strangeness and in our underlying sense of alienation a poignant--although distrusted--sense of fraternity. Deep down, the American condition is a state of unease.[3]

Indeed, Ellison's Senator Sunraider, or "son-raider," as America itself, would block cultural amalgamation. He would continue the fraternal brother battles between the races that prevent his recognition of Daddy Hickman as moral interpreter of American values on the personal level, and his recognition of democratic idealism on the political level. And generally in the works of Joyce, Ellison and Wright, the sons run wild in the streets; genuine fatherhood atrophies.

Ellison and Wright, much as Joyce and T. S.
Eliot, were writing under the cross-cultural spell of
late 19th and 20th century depth psychology and com-
parative anthropology. Assuming much of the
"Romanticism" of Hegel, Freud and Sir James Frazer,
Ellison and Wright explored the possibility that men
and society might be freed of the compulsions of the
unconscious through introspection and rational articulation of its murderous and libidinous impulses.
The modern day rituals of sacrifice, of the scapegoat, which symbolically re-enact Freud's description
of the primal murder in Totem and Taboo, might be
neutralized by means of a rational, psychoanalytical
consciousness. The grip of the archaic archetypes on
modern life might themselves be slaughtered through
art.

     That Joyce, Ellison and Wright assumed Freud's
alleged, innate parricidal urges and sacrificial
remanifestations to be universally shared in the
unconscious of all races and individuals appears to
be an accurate account of their survey of
"unconscious politics" and points to their reliance
on a Frazerian and Freudian use of the mythopoeic eye
in describing events and characters in their fiction,
on a double perspective that locates unconscious
motivation in seemingly conscious acts. At West
Point, Ellison explained his view of a fictional
character:

     My task would be to give him the surface and
     then try to take him into the internalities,
     take him below the level of racial struc-
     turing and down into those areas where we
     are simply men and women, human beings
     living on this blue orb, and not always
     living so well.[4]

In "A Very Stern Discipline" Ellison spoke of the
universal unconscious where archetypes reveal "their
basic humanity" in a "timeless and raceless"
dimension. [5]

     In Shadow and Act he focused a mythopoeic eye on
Charlie Parker and Louis Armstrong. In a review of
Robert Reisner's Bird: The Legend of Charlie Parker,
Ellison described the slow death of Parker as the
dismemberment of a fertility god straight from the
pages of Frazer's The Golden Bough. Parker becomes

181

a sacrificial figure whose struggles against
personal chaos, on stage and off, served as
entertainment for a ravenous, sensation-
starved, culturally disoriented public which
had but the slightest notion of its real
significance. While he slowly died (like a
man dismembering himself with a dull razor
on a spotlighted stage) from the ceaseless
conflict from which issued both his art and
his destruction, his public reacted as
though he were doing much the same thing as
those saxophonists who hoot and honk and
roll on the floor. [p. 227]

The Parker melody, "Oh, they picked poor robin
clean," that echoes in Invisible Man becomes for
Ellison a music from the unconscous depicting a
primitive scapegoat ritual complete with the
sacrifice of a totem bird:

For each of us recognized that his fate was
somehow our own. Our defeats and failures--
even our final defeat by death--were loaded
upon his back and given ironic significance
and thus made more bearable. Perhaps
Charlie was poor robin come to New York and
here to be sacrificed to the need for entertainment and for the creation of a new jazz
style and awaits even now in death a
meaning-making plucking by perceptive
critics. The effectiveness of any
sacrifice depends upon our identification
with the agony of the hero-victim. . . .
[SA, pp. 231-32]

If Parker fell into synch with the primitive
archetype, Armstrong was able to distance himself
from the role of clown-performer-scapegoat by
assuming that the clown mask was to be worn only in
the act of "make believe." [SA, p. 227] But Ellison
was all too aware that make believe was hard to
sustain in a country where blacks were too often
perceived by whites as scapegoat figures to be used
in several cathartic ways. Ellison, like Freud,
realized sadly that "In order to have a human society
you are going to have some form of victimization."
Ellison's pessimistic observation was tempered by
the hope that the national goat need not be racially
determined in years to come.

Indeed, much of Ellison's jazz and literary criticism draws upon the assumptions of depth psychology. He attempts to illuminate the unconscious landscape of the American, that shadowy place which generates the primitive mechanisms resulting in racism, exclusion and national bloodletting.

No doubt, Wright and Ellison discussed the politics of the unconscious thoroughly in the early days of their association. In "How Bigger Was Born," Wright reveals his own desire to mine the universal archetypes of the unconscious, "the implicit, almost unconscious, or preconscious, assumptions and ideals upon which whole nations and races act and live." [NS, p. xviii] Native Son offers a chilling look at the impulsive, half-controllable compulsions of Bigger, compulsions which reveal the reign of the unconscious not only over his acts, but over many of the acts of white America. For if Bigger's crimes are horrible, so too are society's. Max condemns the court in its attempt to enact its own conscious scapegoat ritual, the execution of Bigger, and offers a plea that the court would attempt to recommend that the forces which create the Bigger Thomas's of America be isolated and irradicated. Max challenges the judge:

I say, your Honor, that the mere act of understanding Bigger Thomas will be a thawing out of icebound impulses, a dragging of the sprawling forms of dread out of the night of fear into the light of reason, an unveiling of the unconscious ritual of death in which we, like sleep-walkers, have participated so dreamlike and thoughtlessly. [p.354]

In The Outsider Blimin proposes that out of the terror of primitive man's life was created a lust for "Untruth." Armed with other fictions, early man "stuffed his head full of myths" rather than face the alternative of dying from fear. [p. 356] Communist Blimin reasons that the myths and rituals of primal men linger in men today despite the preponderance of rational thought:

The ravaging scourge that tore away the veil of myth worlds was science and industry; science slowly painting another world, the

real one; and industry uprooting man from
his ancestral, ritualized existence and
casting him into rational schemes of living
in vast, impersonal cities. A split took
place in man's consciousness; he began
living in the real world by the totems and
taboos that had guided him in the world of
myths. But that could not last for long.
Today we are in the midst of that crisis. .
. . The real world stands at last before
our eyes and we don't want to look at it,
don't know how to live in it; it terrifies
us. All of the vast dramas which man once
thought took place in the skies now
transpire in our hearts and we quake and are
moved compulsively to do what we know
not. . . . [p. 357-58]

Cross Damon's attempt to subtract religious myth
and ritual from his mind can go only so far according
to Houston, who argues,

"You saw through all the ideologies,
pretences, frauds, but you did not see
through yourself. How magnificently you
tossed away this God who plagues and helps
man so much! But you did not and could not
toss out of your heart that part of you from
which the God notion had come." [p. 424-25]

For Houston the bottom line of the psyche is
"desire," "the mad thing," "a restless, floating
demon." [p. 425] Wright describes this demon at
rest in Cross, early in The Outsider:

His movements were mechanical. The dingy
walls seemed to loom over against him,
asking wordlessly questions that he could
not answer. Nothing made meaning; his life
seemed to have turned into a static dream
whose frozen images would remain unchanged
throughout eternity. [p. 102]

Indeed, Cross Damon's life produces a profound irony.
In his phenomenological attempt to strip himself of
illusions and societal restraints, this would-be,
existential anti-hero has freed up the murderous
unconscious demon and unwittingly enslaved himself to

184

the heroic role with all its archetypes. Houston explains to Cross that Cross' attempt to make his own situational ethics has resulted in his becoming a "little god." Houston leaves Cross to his mental hell: "Didn't you know that gods are lonely?" [p. 430] Cross' assumed act of liberation, his devaluation of God and the moral codes sanctioned by religion, amounts symbolically to parricide, and the rational attempts at controlling the compulsions of the unconscious become more remote as Wright's vision becomes increasingly tragic.

The "sacrifice" of Chris in The Long Dream carries with it all the qualities of a primitive scapegoat ritual. When Dr. Bruce examines Chris' mangled, castrated body, he tells the brooding group:

"You have to be terribly attracted toward a person, almost in love with 'im, to mangle 'im in this manner. They hate us, Tyree, but they love us too; in a perverted sort of way, they love us--" [6]

Dr. Bruce is learning his anthropology the hard way, for in the scapegoat ritual the successful purgation of guilt can only be accomplished if those sanctioning the act of sacrifice can identify with the victim. It must be they too who are being symbolically punished by death. Chris' death temporarily relieves the whites of their own unconscious, rebellious and parricidal urges; he is castrated in place of them; he serves both as the rebellious son and as the castrating father. Dr. Bruce begins to understand America as a country where repressions have been weakened, where the scapegoat ritual can be acted out not in dreams or in minor violence but in actual murder.

In White Man, Listen! Wright summarizes his fictional probe into the unconscious and offers clues toward a psychology of racism in the West:

It is a racism that has almost become another kind of religion, a religion of the materially dispossessed, of the culturally disinherited. Rooted in my own disinheritedness, I know instinctively that this clinging to, and defense of, racism by Western whites are born of their psychologi-

cal nakedness, of their having through
historical accident, partially thrown off
the mystic cauls of Asia and Africa that
once too blinded and dazed them. A deeply
conscious victim of white racism could even
be strangely moved to compassion for that
white man who, having lost his mystic vision
of a stern Father God, a dazzling Virgin,
and a Dying Son Who promises to succor him
after death, settles upon racism! What a
poor substitute! What a shabby, vile, and
cheap home the white heart finds when it
seeks shelter in racism! One would think
that sheer pride would deter Western whites
from such emotional debasement! [p. 81]

Fatherless men who through no real choice of
their own discover themselves in a world where God
the father has become invisible, must, like the
sons in Freud's symbolic Primal Horde, become a law
unto themselves and spill their repressions onto
scapegoats who will bear the guilt of the primal
murder: onto the Tod Cliftons, onto the Chris'. In
Black Power Wright cringes at the human sacrifice
practiced by the Ashanti. He echoes Freud when he
reflects on the barrel of human heads discovered by
the British after the death of an Ashanti chief:

If you fear your ancestor, it's because,
psychologically, you feel guilty of something. But of what? That guilt, no matter
how confused or unconscious, stems from
one's having wanted to kill that dead
ancestor when he was alive. In the life of
the Akan people the thought that is too
horrible to think finds its way into reality
by identifying itself with the dead
ancestors. Killing for that dead ancestor
is a way of begging forgiveness of that
ancestor; their own murderous conscious
assumes the guise of their ancestor's
haunting them. . . . [pp. 292-93]

Such is "the wild dark poetry of the human heart"
that haunts the fictional worlds of Ellison and
Wright, and the world of Joyce, as well, a poetry
that forms yet another link in the Joyce-Ellison con-

nection. [BP, p. 293] For each of these writers view all killing as ritual killing when it is observed through the Frazerian-Freudian mythopoeic eye. Life becomes understandable when that eye is employed, for as Jack discovers in Invisible Man, human experience resembles a "sacrificial merry-go-round." [p. 494] To fully appreciate this link in the connection it will be necessary to review Freud's influential theory of sacrifice developed both in Totem and Taboo (1913) and in Moses and Monotheism (1939), while we assess the Freudian impact on these writers.

In his attempt to prove that the incest taboo, totemism, and the fraternal nature of "political" and social organization resulted from the conscious and unconscious recollection of the primal slaying and the eating of the leader of the Primal Horde, Freud expanded on Darwin's theory of this Primal Horde, and used that theory along with anthropological obser-vations of Frazer and other anthropologists as a cornerstone for Totem and Taboo. For Freud, a cataclysmic event, the killing of the horde leader, a leader who held the women of the tribe as his exclu-sive possessions, began the repetition-compulsion of religion and politics:

> One day the expelled brothers joined forces, slew and ate the father, and thus put an end to the father horde. Together they dared and accomplished what would have remained impossible for them singly. Perhaps some advance in culture, like the use of a new weapon, had given them the feeling of superiority. Of course these cannibalistic savages ate their victim. This violent primal father had surely been the envied and feared model for each of the brothers. Now they accomplished their identification with him by devouring him and each acquired a part of his strength. The totem feast, which is perhaps mankind's first celebra-tion, would be the repetition and commemoration of this memorable, criminal act with which so many things began, social organization, moral restrictions and religion.[7]

The band of brothers had gained their sexual freedom; they could copulate with the liberated women without fear of castration. But this orgy was short-lived; soon the sons were battling among themselves for the choice females. Then, too, they began to feel a "longing for the father," for the authority and guidance that their primal father had provided. They felt the lack of a model to emulate, to both fear and to respect. To fill this psychological vacuum, many generations after the primal event the clan would replace the dimly remembered primal father with the totem animal. And this animal symbolized the spirit of the dead patriarch in the unconscious of the clan members. The veneration of the totem animal welded the whole clan into a consanguineous "family" bond that was stronger than its later vestige, the modern family with all its variants. No member of the totem group, they decreed in a social contract, could copulate with any other member of that totem. Only members of different and prescribed totem clans were allowed to mate. The incest taboo, exogamy, symbolically resembled the original possession of the women by the primal father.[8] Relative order returned when a type of "group marriage" emerged which blocked random copulation, cooled down the brother battles, and extended the family. Freud explained

> that a man not only calls his begetter "father," but also every other man who, according to the tribal regulations, might have married his mother and thus, become his father; he calls "mother" not only the woman who bore him, but also every other woman who might have become mother without violation of the tribal laws; he now calls "brothers" and "sisters" not only the children of his real parents, but also the children of all the persons named who stand in the parental group relation with him, and so on.[9]

Freud further noted that traces of this family structure appear today in concepts such as "Sisters in Christ."[10] The incest taboo, then, was one form of self-imposed repression, and it existed concurrently with the more liberal tolerance of homosexual laisons within the brother band. Homosexuality was yet another way of sublimating the chaotic sexual appetite. Other social modifications developed in the fraternal, totemic order as well. In Moses and Monotheism Freud went on: "a fair amount of the absolute power liberated by the removal of the father passed over to the women; there came a period of matriarchy."[11]

The elevation of the totem allowed the fraternal band to both atone for and repress any memory of the murder of the primal father. The clan was forbidden to kill or eat the totem except during prescribed periods when the totem would be ritualistically killed and eaten in a ceremony of shared guilt. Freud explained the need for the totem feast: It allowed the brothers to symbolically release their innate parricidal wishes, while at the same time, divide the power of the father as totem through their partaking in the meal. As a result, "No one could or was allowed to attain the father's perfection or power, which was the thing they had all sought."[12] An unsettling "equality" resulted; the fraternal band fulfilled its longing for the father and its contrary parricidal desires symbolically and in acknowledged ways during the totem feast, the primal holiday.

The social order evolved, according to Freud. Soon patriarchal families developed, and eventually "godlike kings" were able to "transfer the patriarchal system to the state."[13] Thus the longing for the father allowed his repression to be established through this strange evolution. And these kings were able to placate the libidinous urges of their subjects by ordaining human sacrifice. For the evolving social order, the concept of an omnipotent God finally emerged from both totem animal and kingly authority. Freud went on: "Sacrifice, as it is now constituted, is entirely beyond their responsibility. God himself has demanded or ordained it."[14] As the authority of the God projection became seated in the power of kings, the kings themselves would be sacrificed to the higher authority during observed seasonal changes. When the idea of kingly sacrifice was eventually abandoned, a doll or criminal would be sacrificed instead. Freud concluded:

Thus the memory of that first great act of sacrifice had proved to be indestructible despite all attempts to forget it, and just at the moment when man strove to get as far away as possible from its motives, the undistorted repetition of it had to appear in the form of a god sacrifice.[15]

189

When Christianity was finally patched together, the parricidal impulse was sublimated again. For Freud, man's sense of "original sin is undoubtedly an offence against God the Father" who is ultimately, of course, a representation of the immutable memory of the primal father.[16] Through Christ's crucifixion, the faithful were able to vicariously punish themselves for their dimly intuited parricidal desire and to seek a reconciliation with God. But this is not all. Freud continued:

> In the same deed which offers the greatest possible explanation to the father, the son also attains the goal of his wishes against the father. He becomes a god himself beside or rather in place of his father. The religion of the son succeeds the religion of the father. As a sign of this substitution the old totem feast is revived again in the form of the communion in which the band of brothers now eats the flesh and blood of the son and no longer that of the father, the sons thereby identifying themselves with him and becoming holy themselves. Thus through the ages we see the identity of the totem feast with the animal sacrifice, the theanthropic human sacrifice, and the Christian eucharist, and in all these solemn occasions we recognize the after effects of a crime which so oppressed men but of which they must have been so proud. At bottom, however, the Christian communion is a new setting aside the father, a repetition of the crime that must be expiated. We see how well justified is Frazer's dictum that "the Christian communion has absorbed within itself a sacrament which is doubtless far older than Christianity."[17]

Christianity was unable to successfully channel the libidinous urges of men into sublimation and displacement. The need to expiate the free floating guilt over the unacknowledged desire to kill the father endured in their hearts. A long bloody string of scapegoats and martyrs, to say nothing of holy wars, would reveal the mixed blessing of Christianity. The unconscious would be fed.

Freud concluded that the desire for parricide and incest are innate, indestructible components of the collective unconscious. "Modern" man then is a reincarnation, albeit dulled, of his "primitive" ancestors; he is quite capable of reenacting the barbarism of the fraternal band through the wars and immolations that mark the 20th century.[18] Thus, for Freud, all murder is ritual murder either of the parent image or of the embodiment of the rebellious son.

For Joyce, especially in the Wake, this Freudian scenario of the origins of history revealed itself as an unconscious reel of film, run off and rewound ad infinitum in everyman's mind; and printed in negative with libidinous archetypes. Freud's assertion that primitive man is "still our contemporary" was well received by Joyce when he depicted history as a filmic continuous present which telescoped the modern with the savage, the totem feast with both the Holy Communion and with the scapegoat rituals of "modern" times. For Freud, the evolved religions such as Christianity and Judaism were able to accomplish a marginal repression of libidinous desire by projecting an invisible, sexless father-god, and that god hovers over Joyce's Dublin, over Ellison's Harlem, or over Wright's Chicago and Wright's South. In Moses and Monotheism, Freud described the results of such sublimation:

A sensory perception was given second place to what may be called an abstract idea--a triumph of intellectuality over sensuality or, strictly speaking, an instinctual renunciation, with all its necessary psychological consequences, allowed the projection of a God whom one cannot see.[19]

The Hangman God was born. "We move in the beast circuls" quipped Joyce in Finnegans Wake. [p. 481]

Campbell and Robinson noted the influence of Totem and Taboo in "The Children's Study Period" in Book II, chapter two of the Wake: "Joyce here is burlesquing Freud's Totem and Tabu, but at the same time coordinating the psychologist's view with the mythological vision of Vico."[20] Several critics, most notably Margot Norris, have attempted to trace the influence of Freud's metaphor of the Primal Horde in the Wake. According to Norris, Joyce's interest in the problems of selfhood and his later concern with the Viconian social theory required a vehicle for the simultaneous expression of psychoanalytic and social processses. This need was aptly filled by the Oedipus myth, which was familiar to Joyce from a number of perspectives, including the Freudian one. In the Oedipus myth, private acts have public consequences, personal crimes become civic crimes, parricide is also regicide, and the quarrels between brothers-in-law threaten to result in civil war. Freudian psychology elaborates this myth in the theory that infantile instincts persist in the character of the adult, that familial relations express themselves collectively in the conduct of nations, and that colonial revolutions can therefore be treated as analogues of infantile parricidal wishes.[21]

For Joyce, as for Freud, the emergence of "civilization" is tied to the repression of parricide and incest. Joyce's task was to explore the results of that repression in the unconscious of his Dubliners.

Ellison and Wright also adapted the Freudian myth of the Primal Horde as well as numerous Frazerian scenarios to provide mythic frames for many of their short stories and novels in a manner reminiscent of Joyce and Eliot. In fact, Ellison directly alludes to Totem and Taboo, for a copy of the book is eyed by Jack on the desk of Emerson's son. It is likely that Joyce's double perspective greatly impressed Eliot when Eliot constructed his telescopic The Waste Land. That Ellison, especially, would follow Eliot's reaction to Joyce's pioneering effort is a crucial link in the Joyce-Ellison connection. We have already noted that on one level Invisible Man is a deliberate parody, if not a literary essay in criticism, as well, of Joyce's A Portrait. James B. Vickery has offered a detailed study of the probable influence of Frazer and other anthropologists on Joyce's themes and imagery. In A Portrait, especially, Stephen couples "the sights, sounds, smells, and feelings generated by early twentieth century Dublin" with "the scenes and sensations of ancient and primitive life, registered in The Golden Bough" and in "the expanding horizons of myth." [22] Such myths for Freud, as for Joyce, were viewed as the collective representations of individual neurosis.

This coupling, which began as early as Dubliners, reaches its crescendo in the Wake where the collective unconscious described by Vico, Freud, Frazer and others is laid bare in the dream of old Finn, the mythical primate of Ireland, its dying and reviving god. If Freud, heavily saturated with Frazer's anthropology, presented history as a kind of murder mystery, if he attempted to mine the repressed desires for parricide and incest, then Joyce, Ellison and Wright would offer their own versions of the mystery in partial homage to Totem and Taboo. The failure of Christianity to end blood sacrifice, the ubiquitous reemergence of the sentiments of the myth of Ham, the general need for scapegoating and war in 20th century life and in politics revealed to them that parricidal impulses fueled history, politics and everyday human interaction. Joyce's mythopoeic eye was greatly admired by Ellison, much as it was by Eliot before him, and Ellison, along with Wright, developed his own variations on the persistence of the unconscious in American culture and race relations.

As we have argued earlier, many forces have combined to devalue fatherhood in these various fictional worlds: cultural uprooting brought about by forced or by voluntary migration; actual political oppression and discrimination practiced by church and state, or colonizing nation; political revolution; and the fraternal structure of capitalism. It is as if the Primal Father had been slain again, this time not literally, but, subliminally, with the help of these abstract forces. Fiedler's view of the American who had overcome the British ogre through Revolution as a fatherless man, an eternal son of the mother, serves as an analogue to the American whom Ellison, Wright and other American writers describe. The predominance of incest as a complex theme in both Irish and American literature must have certainly struck Wright and Ellison, as well, as did Joyce's fascination with the commonality of the Irishman's fate with the fate of the archetypal American, Rip Van Winkle.

In Invisible Man, the Primal Father seems to exist, however, only as a projective fantasy: the

joke image of Norton as a monstrous, miscegenous,
phallic predator; the shrivelled, wiry, rabbitman
Brockway who renders Jack a mock castration with
false teeth; and the composite image of all the
lynchers of consciousness Jack has suffered fused
into one castrating father arising from his dream of
dismemberment after his escape from the riot. Only a
fantasy. The father, in his primal animalism, is
long dead in Ellison's America. But unfortunately
so is, for the most part, viable fatherhood. For
despite Jack's desire to kill Bledsoe, Wrestrum,
"Marse" Jack, and Hambro, we come to realize that
these men are already psychologically castrated; that
they are a band of conniving brothers, parodies of
true paternity. As Joyce puts it in the Wake, the
father has become "the bung king, sung king, or hung
king." [p. 25] In a parody of the Lord's Prayer,
Joyce reflects the symbolics of the primal murder,
"In the name of the former and of the latter and of
their holocaust. Allman." [FW, p. 419] In the
fiction of these writers, the father remains only as
a shadow image to be unwittingly projected by their
heroes onto characters.

The random copulation of the newly emancipated
brothers seems to resurface symbolically, however, in
the history of miscegenation and rape inherent in the
acts of oppression committed in Ireland and in
America. Ras protests that one result of oppression
is "a race of bahstards" produced and ambivalently
tolerated by white progenitors. [IM, p. 364] The
opening dream in the Prologue reveals the rage of
the black boys who have been fathered but not claimed
by the white Master. Both these boys and Jack
discover that in America one must become one's own
father. For oppression, on a world wide scale, has
attempted to turn an exploited colony into both a
mine or cheap labor and a complex psychological and
physical brothel. Joseph Conrad contemplated the
"nowhere" of exploited Africa much as Joyce, Ellison
and Wright surveyed the malaise of Ireland and
America where the dominant cultures could, if often
only in fantasy, express their repressed desires for
incest (miscegenation) and parricide (the murder and
brutalization of the oppressed).

Norris has brilliantly analyzed the effects of
patriarchal devaluation in Joyce's fiction although
she does not always link the father's fall to

194

oppression. For Norris, HCE symbolizes all the
Irishmen that have internalized the British stereotypes of the Irish and all that have betrayed true
paternity. HCE has committed a mysterious and
ancient crime linked with parricide, incest, and the
confusion of races and lineages. His identity and
race cannot be determined. Even his real name is
unknown or non-existent. He reveals a "low
visibility"; he is called "a spoof of visibility," "a
vague of visibilities," "Noman" and "Nemo in Patria."
[FW, pp. 49, 175, 229, 608] He is guilty of a symbolic parricide because both as an Irish Uncle Tom
and as "Hugest Commorcial Emporialist" he had aided
the British Empire and willingly offered up the Irish
to the domination of their invaders. [FW, p. 374]
"Our Forhmer who erred in having" is haunted by
incest desire and dread. [FW, p. 500] His type
recalls Erebus, the god of the underworld, mentioned
by Vico in The New Science. Erebus, the son of
Chaos, oversees the lower frequencies of human
desire, of Vico's "infamous promiscuity," when the
son enjoins "the confusion of human seeds."[23] Vico
recalls that through Erebus' underworld

> runs the river Lethe, the stream of
> oblivion, for those men who left no name of
> themselves to their posterity, whereas the
> glory of heaven eternalizes the names of
> illustrious heroes.[24]

Joyce's Liffey may become that river Lethe, and
Jack's fears of drowning in the river he views after
he parts from Sibyl also evoke this classical image.
The guilt charged dreams of incest and miscegenation
in the Wake, and the resultant Honuphrius case, where
Joyce described the history of love throughout the
ages as a torrid knot of incestuous desire brought
about in part by cultural uprooting and oppression,
may be possible sources for Ellison's antihero's
dreamy descents into the tangled lineages of multi-
ethnic America in the Prologue, into the miscegenous
undercurrents at the Golden Day, into Trueblood's
dream, into the Chthonian, and into the bedrooms of
the white women.

For Norris, then, the Wakean family is in crisis,
a crisis that may well have influenced Ellison's
x-raying of the American psyche. Norris explains:

Through incest and parricide, family roles
and family relationships are violated in
such a way that figures can no longer be
defined. Consequently identities are
unstable and interchangeable, and the self
is constantly alienated from itself and
fails to know itself. This self-alienation
is manifested in a language which is
devious, which conceals and reveals secrets,
and therefore, like poetry, uses words
and images that can mean several, often
contradictory, things at once.[25]

Indeed, the "confusion" that echoes both in Joyce's
works and Invisible Man may well be Viconian, as each
writer updates this Neapolitan's view of purgatory.

It was stated that Joyce coupled Viconian
mythological vision with Freud's psychological
perspectives on human history. This synthesis of
ideas directly influenced Ellison, and Ellison's
adaptation of Viconian thunder imagery more than
resembles Joyce's creative use of such imagery in the
Wake. For Vico's primal man was not so different
from Freud's. Indeed, Vico's wandering bands of men
thought the roaring thunder to be the voice of an
angry God calling the lost sons of Ham and Japheth to
enter into monogamous marriage that would end the
chaos of random copulation. Vico explains:

The descendants of Ham and Japheth and the
non-Hebraic descendants of Shem, having wan-
dered through the great forest of the earth
for a century or two, had lost all human
speech and institutions and had been reduced
to bestiality, copulating at sight and
inclination. These dumb beasts naturally
took the thundering sky to be a great
animated body, whose flashes and claps were
commands, telling them what they had to do.
The thunder suprised some of them in the act
of copulation and frightened copulating
pairs into nearby caves. This was the
beginning of matrimony and of settled
life.[26]

Eliot used thunder imagery at the end of The
Waste Land much as Vico prescribed. For there the

196

angry thunderous God commands obedience and discipline from his misguided 20th century children.

Joyce, however, decided to turn the imagery around. Norris explains that in the Wake the ten thunder claps or hundred letter words are associated with "male conflict, presumably the father's fall, 'the hundering blundering dunder, funder of plunder-sundered manhood.'"[27] Indeed, for Norris, the thundrous sounds in the Wake may imitate the sounds of the father falling down the stairs, his guilty stutter, his defecation, or the gun shots directed toward him. Rather than merely commanding monogamy, thunder in the Wake will often serve as a stuttering confession of the father's incestuous desires.[28]

Vico also proposed that language originated from fears evoked by thunder during his Divine Age. Since thunder was assumed to be the voice of God, a language which imitated that thunder was valid, sanctioned; and the names of those who worshipped that God were sacred and certain names. Norris argues that for Vico "The father corresponds to the semantic function of language; he is, as it were, the legal equivalent to the law of speech which fixes each in its place."[29] Norris goes on

> The Christian tradition defines the source of authority as the Word. The authority of the symbolic father lies therefore in his name, because he names himself, designates his own function, and creates his own identity.[30]

The Father-God can say "I am who I am," and hence, names derived from a language system of the thunder-clap can be given to human offspring to insure the children's certain identity, their link to the God, their place in the network of kinship laws allegedly sanctioned by God.

In the "chaosmos" of the Wake, where countless invasions have mixed the clans of Europe into a geneological Irish stew, the Primal Father is fallen; names, identities are uncertain.[31] The thunder is now the guilty stutter of the Wakean Father, who speaks an incestuous language and who reveals a dif-fuse identity, a father image who is a product of the confusion of kinship that invasions and uprooting create. This state of incertitude helps to explain the anxiety Stephen Dedalus experiences when he broods over names and their reality in A Portrait. It manifests itself again in Jack's hesitation and nervousness when he is asked to give his name in Invisible Man.

Each time the thunderwords echo from the dream landscape of the Wake, the father's fall is implied. Bernard Benstock notes their appearance and their implications:

> The first thunderclap is the basic fall motif: "bababadalgharaghtakamminarronnkonn-bronntonnerronntuonnthunntroyarrhounawnskaw-ntoohoohoordenenthurnuk!" (3.15-17); the second is the slamming of Jarl van Hoother's castle door (23.5-7); the third announces the ballad written by Hosty (44.20-21); the fourth is an obscene rumble during the trial, suggesting the fall in the park (90.21-33); the fifth is the babble of the gossipy letter (113.9-11); the sixth is the slamming of the Earwicker door after the children have come in from their play (257.27-2); the eighth is the noise of the radio static preceding the Crimean War broadcast, as well as the orgasm during the seduction of Anna Livia (332.5-7); the ninth is Shaun's cough as he clears his throat in preparation for the recounting of the Ondt-Gracehoper fable (414.19-20); and the last follows soon after (424.20-22), Shaun's angry rumble of abuse against Shem serving as the basic thunderclap of destruction before the Cabalistic regeneration begins. The complete destruction of the established order is thus indicated as the end of sephiroth, the blending of One and Zero into the perfect union of Ten prefiguring the birth of a new world.[32]

The cycle of history, Viconian or otherwise, is exhausted in the Wake: God and fatherhood have become invisible, lingering ghosts. Yet as we shall see, Joyce regards the fall of the Father-God as a fortunate one indeed; the confusion of races and language systems as a gain rather than a loss for our common humanity; the breakdown of clannishness into a more international outlook as a movement upwards along the spiral of human consciousness.

Ellison appears to have adapted Viconian thunder much as Joyce had done, but Ellison gave his adaptation a modern, existential twist.[33] Instead of containing the divine command for monogamy alone, thunder roars and lightning flashes in the secular world of Ellison's America when Jack and other characters wax inauthentic, untrue to their folk heritage, or unresponsive to the guilt that arises in them heralding their existential bad faith. Although the Joycean hundred letter thunderword only occurs once in Invisible Man when Wheatstraw imparts his folk wisdom to an ambivalent Jack, thunder itself is a dominant motif that sounds actually or metaphorically at crucial points throughout the novel. In fact, the imagery of thunder or lightning occurs nine times in the novel, and the blaring music and glaring 1369 lights in Jack's coalhole may well serve symbolically as the tenth Viconian roar and flash as Jack steals the "divine" force.

Since the advice of Peter Wheatstraw reveals the hundred lettered thunderword, this incident will be examined first. When Jack first arrives in Harlem, he encounters the singing junkman who hauls a cart full of discarded blueprints:

> "She's got feet like a monkey
> Legs like a frog--Lawd, Lawd!
> But when she starts to loving me
> I holler Whoooo, God-dog!" [IM, p. 170]

The one-hundred letters recall the sephiroth as well as the Egyptian mythology of Osiris, Isis, and Anubis, a mythology which spread to Greece and to the strange Dogon tribe that today lives on the River Niger. Anubis, the god with the head of a dog and the body of a man, was associated by all three with the twin star of Sirius, the invisible Sirius B, which took one hundred months to orbit Sirius. Peter's blues links God to fertility rather than to abstraction, and Peter's last name as well as his cart, a cart which recalls the wagon of the sun mentioned by Frazer, all point to his being a kind of pimitive anomaly who has somehow found himself in the urban jungle of Harlem.[34] As in ancient fertility religion, Wheatstraw's folk logic has not split the chthonic, "devillish" nature of man from the rest of human nature; for he's the "Devil's only son-in-law," who, much as his black folk counterpart for whom he appears to be named, would explore the totality of human nature much as Jack finally must do in the coalhole.

These curious stacks of blueprints displayed on this junkman's cart might be a symbol of Ellison's art, as well, for Peter is a complex character who recalls, by way of analogy, the ever improvising "biocoleur" described by Claude Lévi-Strauss.[35] The bricoleur saves and juxtaposes heterogeneous materials in order to create new combinations. He can be a repairman or an artist. Joyce, Ellison and Wright also resemble the bricoleur when they create verbal collages of past and present literary styles and allusions, juxtapositions of ancient and modern sensibilities, in their fiction. The artist as bricoleur realizes that there is no new thing under the sun, only novel combinations of old myth fragments. The works of Joyce, Eliot, Ellison, and Wright, as well as those of numerous other 20th century writers, often resemble fictional kaleido-scopes of telescoped time. Peter, much as the "bricoleur," is able to pour over his borrowed blueprints and his junk collection, to dream of new combinations, while he improvises new blues verses, as well. Peter reveals both a pride in his black heritage and a healthy desire to combine his experience into new wholes, much as the bluesy brico-lage of his verses combines African and Western musical elements. He advises Jack:

"All it takes to get along in this here man's town is a little shit, grit and mother-wit. And man, I was bawn with all three. In fact, I'maseventhsonofaseventhso-nbawnwithacauloverbotheyesandraisedonblackc-atboneshighjohntheconquererandgreasygreens-" he spieled with twinkling eyes, his lips working rapidly. "You dig me, daddy?"
"You're going too fast," I said, beginning to laugh.
"Okay, I'm slowing down. I'll verse you but I won't curse you--My name is Peter Wheatstraw, I'm the Devil's only son-in-law, so roll 'em! You a southern boy, ain't

you?" he said, his head to one side like a
bear's.
"Yes," I said.
"Well, git with it! My name's Blue and
I'm coming at you with a pitchfork. Fe Fi
Fo Fum. Who wants to shoot the Devil one,
Lord God Stingeroy!"
He had me grinning despite myself. I
liked his words though I didn't know the
answer. I'd known the stuff from childhood,
but had forgotten it: had learned it back
of school. . . . [IM, pp. 172-73]

Wheatstraw is an embodiment of buoyant self-
determination and the rebelliousness of the slave
High John the Conquerer, and like his own blues,
Wheatstraw is a human bricolage as he echoes the
past and eyes the future. His slang phrase for Jack,
"daddyo," implies that in a fatherless world Jack
must create himself out of the cultural kaleidoscope
that is America. Naive Jack senses Wheatstraw's
power, but he is torn between "pride" and "disgust"
when he listens to Wheatstraw's bluesy chords in the
distance. [p. 174] Jack will learn later that he,
like Wheatstraw, must be his own devillish initiator;
that he must create himself out of the fragments of
experience; that he must view the surfaces and depths
both of experience and of his own mind to find
wholeness and marginal freedom within the limits;
that he must allow his folk past to help form his
identity. The thunder that roars in Wheatstraw's
voice reveals that Ellison, much as Joyce, celebrates
the father's fall, the loss of certitude, for the
thunderword encourages Jack to explore Jack's fallen
world without blinders, to probe the depths of his
mind to reach an authenticity of self. Wheatstraw's
jam-packed wheelbarrow may also derive in part from
the wheelbarrow motifs in the Wake which include
Kate's wheelbarrow at the Museum, "Junkermenn
Funagin," and the word play "Toborrow and toburrow
and tobarrow," all of which point to the theme that
the human unconscious represented by the dreamer of
the Wake is a vast, eternal, archetypal bricolage, an
"all in all." [pp. 503, 455] [36]

Thunder haunts Jack's emerging conscience
throughout Invisible Man. Modified Viconian thunderclaps first resound when fallen Jack recovers from
the battle royal to address the townspeople. When he

gives his speech, he confuses "social responsibility" with "social equality" and when he corrects his "mistake," he is rewarded with a "thunderous applause" from the fraternal gathering for his endorsement of segregation. [p. 31] In fact, applause becomes a negative sound in the novel. It often occurs when Jack or other characters become trapped in a role, a false self. When the brown girl is captured by her humanity during the a cappella hymn, she is greeted with "no applause," but with the appreciation of "profound silence." [p. 115] Applause reverberates, however, in inauthentic ways throughout the novel.

Thunder is used ironically, after Trueblood recounts his apparent incestuous dream and "dream sin" to Norton and Jack. He recalls that after Kate wounded him, he expected to hear thunder or get struck by a "bolt of lightnin," but instead he saw "the sun comin' up," and he heard the birds "chirpin." [p. 64-65] For Ellison, Trueblood's act may be taboo, but it is no sin. Like the chapel singer, Trueblood has followed the will of his unconscious and its more benign desire. His dream sin would not be understood as such by "endogamous" royal families throughout many parts of the world.[37] For Trueblood's sexual act with Matty Lou recalls the endogamy Freud noted among Australian tribes, an endogamy that sanctioned sexual intercourse among immediate blood relatives. And Norton's "envy" of tabooed Trueblood recalls Freud's discussion of endogamy:

An individual, who has violated a taboo, becomes himself taboo because he has the dangerous property of tempting others to follow his example. He arouses envy; why should he be allowed to do what is prohibited to others?[38]

Norton, like Trueblood and all men, cannot escape the buried desire for incest, and, on the subliminal level, Norton reveals an incestuous desire for his own dead daughter when he gazes at her photograph. Trueblood, like the chapel singer, has not violated his inner self. No thunder threatens a warning to him, only the inauthentic howls of Kate. Ellison too has modified Viconian thunder.

202

Thunder echoes again before the speech of Homer
Barbee. When Bledsoe, the white trustees, Barbee,
and the guests are "herded" toward their elevated
chairs on the platform, the thunder of the organ
begins, but the subversive organist moves his feet
"as though dancing to rhythm totally unrelated to the
thunder of his organ," a thunder obviously selected
to appease the trustees upon whom Bledsoe has just
"placed his hand . . . as though exercising a powerful magic." [p. 113] Later in this "meaningless
ritual," Barbee recalls how Dr. Bledsoe had once
continued a speech for the Founder after the Founder
had "tottered" from the excessive emotion of the
event:

"And the Founder pauses, then steps forward
with his eyes spilling his great emotion.
With his arm upraised, he begins to answer
and totters. Then all is commotion. We
rush forward and lead him away.
    The audience leaps to its feet in
consternation. All is terror and turmoil, a
moan and a sighing. Until, like a clap of
thunder, I hear Dr. Bledsoe's voice ring out
whiplike with authority, a song of hope.
And as we stretch the Founder upon a bench
to rest, I hear Dr. Bledsoe stomping out the
time with mighty strokes upon the hollow
platform, commanding not in words but in the
great gut-tones of his magnificant basso--
oh, but wasn't he a singer? Isn't he a
singer still today?--and they stand, they
calm, and with him they sing out against the
tottering of their giant. Sing out their
long black songs of blood and bones:
    Meaning HOPE!
    Of hardship and pain:
    Meaning FAITH!
    Of humbleness and absurdity:
    Meaning ENDURANCE!
    Of ceaseless struggle in darkness,
meaning:
    TRIUMPH. . . ."[pp. 123-24]

Bledsoe's thunderous voice and Barbee's fall on the
platform are reminiscent of the shouts and falls of
the fallen fathers in the Wake.[39]   No father,
Bledsoe, as prophet of black humility, would appease
the white trustees by preaching the old stereotypes,
by limiting rather than liberating the students.

Both modified Viconian lightning imagery and
thunder are employed to herald quantum leaps in the
hero's growth. The explosion in the industrial hell
of Liberty Paints is one example. Here Jack has been
involved in another symbolic act of bad faith, the
mixing white paint with black dope to make the white
paint whiter still. The explosion, "a blind flash,"
recalls the uterine explosion and Trueblood's fetal
immerson in Trueblood's dream. It plunges Jack into
a more authentic self, for folkloric echoes surface
during the hospital scene, echoes which hasten Jack's
movement toward genuine conscience.

When Jack presents his speech on dispossession to
the Brotherhood meeting, he assumes the dangerous
heroic role, and, ironically, praises the fraternal
structure of America:

> "I feel that I can see sharp and clear
> and far down the dim corridor of history and
> in it I can hear the footsteps of a militant
> fraternity! No, wait, let me confess. . . I
> feel the urge to affirm my feelings. . . I
> feel that here, after a long and desperate
> and uncommonly blind journey, I have come
> home. . . Home! With your eyes upon me I
> feel that I've found my true family! My
> true people! My true country! I am a new
> citizen of the country of your vision, a
> native of your fraternal land. I feel that
> here tonight, in this old arena, the new is
> being born and the vital old revived. In
> each of you, in me, in us all.
> "SISTERS! BROTHERS!
> "WE ARE THE TRUE PATRIOTS! THE
> CITIZENS OF TOMORROW'S WORLD!
> "WE'LL BE DISPOSSESSED NO MORE!"
> The applause struck like a clap of
> thunder. I stood transfixed, unable to see,
> my body quivering with the roar. [pp.
> 337-38]

Jack temporarily assumes, then, the role of an
emergent fallen father when he extols his fatherless land, during this "confused" betrayal of
authenticity.

Lightning flashes again "across the eastern sky"
on the day of another abortive experience, the day

that Jack experiences a "revolting ritual," his date
with Sibyl. She constantly stereotypes him into
roles such as stud, "Brother Taboo," Joe Louis, Paul
Robeson, and "buck." He wonders if her ambivalent
affection for him may not hide "an unconscious
expression of revulsion." Jack, much as a scapegoat,
is being used by Sibyl in an unconscious ritual which
allows her to vent her sexual desires on thingified
Jack. ". . . I feel so free with you" she tells him,
and he recognizes his invisibility once again. [pp.
505ff] Viconian imagery frames this scene, then, to
herald bad faith and to reveal the undercurrents of
the black and white sexual free-for-all that Sibyl
craves.

The Harlem riot reveals more modified Viconian
imagery. And "a thunderous sound" causes Jack to
enter the psychological landscape of the exploding
libidinous desire the riot inspires. As we shall
see, the Harlem riot is largely a Freudian "holiday,"
or a Frazerian Saturnalia, rather than an effective,
political act. Jack finds himself estranged from his
inner self; his personality melts into the mass
hysteria of the crowd, for "a thunder of footfalls"
roars again when Jack participates in the burning of
the tenement. This act itself may be pragmatic, but
the surrender of selfhood that threatens Jack, if not
the wiser Dupre, becomes yet another act of bad
faith. Jack discovers that his "personality" is
"blasted." [pp. 335-37]

Later in the riot, the voice of Ras reechoes the
sound of thunder when he commands the crowd to hand
over Jack. Jack comes to a realization of his
invisibility once again, as well as to an
acknowledgement of the "confusion" of "American
identity." [p. 546] For he must reject Ras'
nationalism and repudiate Ras' admonitions of racial
purity and self-imposed sexual and social
segregation.

The coalhole itself, with its "music of
invisibility" and its brilliant, rational lights, may
well symbolize the final thunder and lightning of
the novel. Like Joyce's tenth thunderword that contains the 101 letters for <u>ricorso</u> (which recall the
ten circles of the sephiroth of the Kabbala),
Ellison's mystical, triadic 1369 may also imply a
hopeful future for a more psychologically articulate
Jack.[40]

Thunder and lightning, then, occur when Jack and other characters have failed to experience true conscience and autonomy. Much as in the Wake, the image pattern indicates the fall from true manhood and authenticity. Thunder is no longer the voice of God calling his children, but in a godless world, it becomes the sign of approval from the myth-imbued mob. But now we need to examine in more detail the threats inherent from such flashes and sputters in the fictional worlds of these psychoanalytically inclined works.

In Totem and Taboo Freud speculated that during the long interlude after the slaying of the horde leader both a fraternity and a matriarchy ascended to power. Joyce and Ellison partially draw upon Freud's speculations when they examine the emergence of such power displacement in Irish and American life. The preponderance of brother rivals throughout Joyce's works: Stephen and his rival Mulligan (an adversary with his horse's face and oakgrained hair who recalls the Frazerian challenger to the king of the wood at the grove at Nemi);[41] the battling twin brothers in "Nausicaa"; the mob and priests opposed to Parnell (an Irish hero who recalls the Frazerian chieftain and fertility deity complete with his emblematic holly for the chieftain tree and ivy for the dying and reviving nature god);[42] Bloom versus the citizen; Old Hamlet and his rival brother Claudius; Hamlet and Laertes; Shem and Shaun; Joyce and Stanislaus; and, indeed, all the multiple variants of brother rivals in the Wake who wander through the labyrinthine folds of matrifocal Dublin, appear to have influenced Ellison in his own delineation of fraternal, fatherless America. For in Ellison's America, would-be father figures, with the exception of Jack's grandfather, Vet, Peter Wheatstraw, Trueblood, and the old black man who sings at Tod's funeral, are really mindless members of a vast fraternal brother band. A type of endless cold war of brother against brother is evident in the Dick Tracy cartoon world of the novel. When Jack reflects on the Brotherhood, he harps on the constant spying that goes on: "Is everyone reading Dick Tracy these days?" He wonders: "What was this obsession with enemies, anyway?" when he discovers Tobbit's conspiracy against him. [pp. 395-96] Wrestrum's advice that the brothers must constantly watch themselves further unnerves Jack.

As in Freud's fraternal band, the brothers are
battling among themselves not for women but for symbolic turf. They are determined to block the rise of
a new patriarch from their number who might return
them to the conditions of the half-remembered image
of the Horde. And the "committee" that determines
the Brotherhood's policy and punishes assertive
members is reminiscent of the social contract insti-
tuted by the brother band in Totem and Taboo.
Norman O. Brown characterizes the concept of
"brotherhood" in terms that recall Joyce's and
Ellison's critiques: "Brotherhood is always a
quarrel over paternal inheritance. . . the dear love
of comrades is made out of mutual hate."[43] A naive
Jack, who could proudly call America a "fraternal
land," will later realize the pathos involved in such
a pronouncement. Indeed, the "brotherhood" in
Ellison's America recalls that "spirit of quarrelsome
comradeship" Stephen observes among his peers in
A Portrait. [p. 332] And the truth of Brown's
observation is only too evident in Joyce's fiction
and in Irish history, for the bloody reprisals of the
Irish Civil War, for example, plunged I. R. A.
comrades into such an internal housecleaning that in
little more than six months the Free State executed
three times the number of comrades than the British
had killed in the entire Anglo-Irish conflict of two
and one half years.[44] And to return to fiction, if
the dreamer is in a kind of psychic limbo near the
close of the Wake, a Conradian "nowhere" of the
unconscious, so Ellison's America resides in Ras'
"nowhere," in the interregnum of Totem and Taboo.

If Freud's band of brothers found it necessary to
resort to homosexual relations among themselves
during the interregnum in order to bind their libidinous desires for the women, so, too, do the charges
of "buggery" and homosexual relations of all kinds
surface in Joyce's fiction. We need only recall the
perverse, homoerotic, relationship betwen Corley and
Lenehan, or Stephen's suspicions of rampant buggery
among the priests, or the appearance of "Lady Boyle"
in A Portrait, as well as the frequent references to
anal impregnation or impalement in the Wake to
discover the perverse "homosodalism" that exists in
the fantasy life and perhaps in the sexual activity
of many of Joyce's fraternal Dubliners.

During Jack's encounter with Emerson's son, a
nervous son inclined to read Totem and Taboo, this

white nameless one confesses seductively that he is a homosexual, a "Huckleberry." Naive Jack misses the point and the pass as well. While the son attempts to lure Jack into a brotherly mood, the son laments: "With us its still Jim and Huck Finn." [IM, p. 184] Ellison may well have had Joyce, Freud and Leslie Fiedler in mind when he constructed this guarded suggestion of the persistence of homosexual or homoerotic urges in the fraternal disorder of America. [45]

During "The Ballad of Persse O'Reilly" in the Wake, three soldiers accuse HCE and his variants of buggery in Phoenix Park:

"He was joulting by Wellington's monument.
Our rotorious hippopopopotamuns
When some bugger let down the backtrap of the omnibus
And he caught his death of fusiliers.
. . ." [p. 47]

Then, too, in the Wakean comedy HCE is accused of exhibiting a "homosexual catheis of empathy between narcissism of the expert and steatopygic invertness" in a parody of psychological jargon. [p. 522] Such references are common in the scatological Wake where even Shem's coalhole can become an anus, and these references often imply the influence of Totem and Taboo, along with a psychoanalytical critique of culture.

Still more facets of Freud's sexology of primitive man haunt the family in the fictional worlds of Joyce and Ellison. Freud held that a form of "group marriage" evolved after the primal deed, as we saw earlier. That all possible mates for the real parents were regarded as "mother" and "father" to children in the exogamy of totemism seems to echo not only in the Wake, where characters assume roles like dream chameleons, but in Invisible Man as well. Not only are the familiarities "brother" and "sister" ubiquitous, but, also, slang pronouns such as "mama," "daddyo," "baby," which we have mentioned earlier in connection with the undercurrent of incest that permeates Invisible Man. Jack's need to feel as if his audience at the dispossesion of the Provos were a new family or kin and that the Provo's are "like my

mama and papa" reveals this vestigial emotional need.
For Freud and for Ellison, the consanguineous ways
still exist in modern life.

In reality, the Brotherhood attempts to fuse two
fraternal orders, the black membership and the white
membership, an effort that adds yet another sexual
dimension to the novel. For when the Brotherhood
splinters apart along racial lines, the two brother
clans emerge. Ras sees through Brother Jack's phony
promise of brotherhood for the black membership. For
Ras, the white brothers offer up some of the unwanted
women to the black members in order to convince the
black wing that it has freedom. And indeed, Jack's
affairs with white women during his affiliation with
the Brotherhood resemble a parody of the exogamous
exchange of women from different totem clans.

Both Joyce and Ellsion describe their respective
milieus as caught in the grip of a fratricidal cold
war right off the pages of <u>Totem and Taboo</u>. For
Ellison, the war gets hot during the murder of Tod
and during the Harlem riot. And, indeed, the division that rocks the Brotherhood recalls Brown's
shrewd analysis of the archaic base of politics, the
struggle of two moieties for the dismembered pieces
of the Primal Father:

> Political parties are primitive secret
> societies: Tammany's Wigwam; caucus; mafia;
> cabal. The deals are still always secret,
> in a smoke-filled room. Political parties
> are conspiracies to usurp the power of the
> father. . . antagonistic fraternities, or
> moieties. . .[46]

The depictions of the death of Tod and the
ensuing riot are framed in highly intricate and
penetrating double perspectives that combine the
narrative events with the ancient scenarios of blood
sacrifice, of mourning, and of Saturnalia that inform
<u>Totem and Taboo</u> and <u>The Golden Bough</u>. Although
Ellison has clearly fashioned his mythopoeic eye from
the double perspectives employed by Eliot and Joyce,
we will limit discussion to the probable literary
influence of Joyce.

Much as Joyce presents characters who recall
archetypal figures from ancient myth and religion:

Stephen as priest-poet, scapegoat and dying god; Molly as fertility goddess; Mrs. Daedalus as Ishtar, Semele, and the ravenous Hangman God; Bloom as scapegoat, dying god, sun hero; the whores of nighttown as sacred prostitutes; Mulligan and Carr as threatening replacements and denigrators of Stephen's heroic postures; Shem and HCE as final expressions of the scapegoats and dying gods, so too does Ellison create characters fitted with these archaic masks, characters that risk immolation on the altar of the unconscious politics that fuel history.[47] In his study of the probable influence of The Golden Bough on Joyce's conception of characters and themes, Vickery observes that the major anthropological pattern of Ulysses implies the generation of archetypal figures, characters who are simultaneously individual persons and anthropological archetypes.

And, indeed, Joycean characters often come to a realization that they are haunted by ancient fertility, scapegoat, and dying god rituals. Stimulated by his anthropolgical interests, Bloom will explore and resign himself to the ancient unconscious forces that haunt the modern mind; he will accept with caution and cunning his role as scapegoat and return "compassion for contempt and acceptance for rejection."[48] Stephen will also probe the unconscious depths of human motivation and reach the epiphany that all men bear a collective unconscious which can reduce them to puppets of archaic impulse when he discovers "the mystery of an invisible person." [U, p. 202] Like Frazer and Freud, Bloom and Stephen, especially, plunge into the primeval heart of darkness and attempt, however successfully, to purge its grip upon their daily lives through rational articulation of their psychological night journeys. Stephen refuses to surrender his artistic freedom of thought to his bitch-mother's ghost in "Circe," and Bloom attempts to understand and tolerate his Dublin victimizers with a kind of passive resistance. Joyce and Ellison both reflect the Frazerian view that secular society forgets the original religious significance of its rituals, its totems and taboos, which it nonetheless enacts in often truncated rituals with a frightening blindness. The impact of anthropology has been quite thoroughly documented in the works of Joyce, but a detailed examination of the impact of works such as The Golden Bough and Totem and Taboo on Invisible Man also needs further attention.

In Totem and Taboo Freud recalls much of his
Frazer when he reconstructs the sequence of the totem
feast. It is this archetypal meal and its ramifica-
tions that help to inform both Tod's ritual sacrifice
and the events of the Harlem riot. The first event
of the totemic ritual involves the killing of the
totem animal. Freud explains:

> Thus we have the clan, which on a solemn
> occasion kills its totem in a cruel manner
> and eats it raw, blood, flesh, and bones.
> At the same time the members of the clan
> disguised in imitation of the totem, mimic
> it in sound and movement as if they wanted
> to emphasize their common identity. There
> is also the conscious realization that an
> action is being carried out which is forbid-
> den to each individual and which can only be
> justified through the participation of all
> so that no one is allowed to exclude himself
> from the killing and the feast. [49]

A period of ritual mourning follows:

> After the act is accomplished the murdered
> animal is bewailed and lamented. The death
> lamentation is compulsive, being enforced by
> the fear of a threatening retribution, and
> its main purpose is . . . to exculpate
> oneself from responsibility for the
> slaying.

The last stage reveals itself as a period of general
license, a holiday:

> A holiday is permitted, or rather a
> prescribed excess, a solemn violation of a
> prohibition. People do not commit the
> excesses, which at all times have charac-
> terized holidays, as a result of an order to
> be in a holiday mood, but because in the
> very nature of a holiday there is excess;
> the holiday mood is brought about by the
> release of what is otherwise forbidden. [50]

Freud assumed that the killing of the totem reenacted
on the unconscious level the original slaying of the
Primal Father: hence, the seemingly contradictory
acts of mourning and mirth. The act of eating the

animal allowed the clan to maintain its strength, its solidarity, its certain identity derived from its ingestion of the totem, and, at the same time, the act provided for the orderly release of repressed parricidal desires.

Frazer discusses the last stage of the three-fold ritual, the holiday, at great length. In agricultural societies the holiday persisted and often occurred during a marked change in the season, such as mid-summer. For when summer began to wane, the dreaded death of nature required fertility cults to plan for the selection and the death of a king, a scapegoat, or of a victim who would serve as a fusion, a scapegoat-king. For in ancient times the withering, scorched vegetation symbolized the correspondent weakening of the king. The unfortunate king would often be killed ritualistically, and throughout Europe the act of sacred murder often occurred around the Eve of St. John on June 23rd. Eliot's "The Fire Sermon" in The Waste Land recalls that the lighting of the "need fires" on the "holiday" both purged sins and insured the return of Spring. Stephen Dedalus' role as a mummer in a school play that is presented on Whitsuntide reveals a fossilized vestige of the holiday in A Portrait.[52]

The three-fold ritual of the totem feast may well have evolved into such vestiges as St. John's Day and the pagan Saturnalia, both reconstructed by Frazer:

> a conspicuous feature of the Carnival is a burlesque figure personifying the festive season, which after a short career of glory and dissipation is publically shot, burnt or otherwise destroyed, to the feigned grief or genuine delight of the populace. If the view here suggested of the Carnival is correct, this grotesque personage is no other than a direct successor of the old King of the Saturnalia, the master of the revels, the real man who personated Saturn, and, when the revels were over, suffered a real death in his assumed character.[53]

Joyce appears to link Bloom to this "grotesque personage" in "Circe." Frazer discusses the Saturnalia:

> This famous festival. . . was properly sup-
> posed to commemorate the merry reign of
> Saturn, the god of sowing and of husbandry,
> who lived on earth long ago as a righteous
> and beneficent king of Italy, drew the rude
> and scattered dwellers on the mountains
> together, taught them to till the gound,
> gave them laws, and ruled in peace. His
> reign was the fabled Golden Age: the earth
> brought forth abundantly: no baleful love
> of lucre worked like poison in the blood of
> the industrious and contented peasantry.[54]

The Saturnalia recalled a mythical golden age of
equality much as do its remnants such as Mardi Gras.
To evoke the era of equality in the Saturnalia, the
slaves wore the outfits of their masters and the
masters dressed as slaves. Frazer notes, however,
that the Golden Age of Saturn was not without "the
dark shadow" of human sacrifice.[55] Reacting to
Frazer's reconstructions, Freud reveals in <u>Totem and
Taboo</u> that as the original totem holiday underwent
its evolution, the human sacrifice of the king was
replaced by symbolic substitutions for the king, such
as a stranger or a criminal. Eventually, dolls were
used as a king substitute when the human taste for
blood was further sublimated.[56]

As Ellison no doubt observed, the "Circe" section
of <u>Ulysses</u> is a comic attempt to articulate the
violent drives of the unconscious, for the section
interfaces the Frazerian Saturnalia and the totem
hunt with Bloom's masochistic fantasies of his heroic
role as mock king and his death and rebirth as
Dublin's scapegoat and dying and reviving nature
deity. For in "Circe" all of the scapegoating that
has been directed toward Bloom on June 16, 1904
reaches its clamorous epiphany. He is hunted and
flagellated by the crowd; he confesses to sexual
crimes and thus serves as a fertile "stinking goat of
Mendes"; he is sentenced to hang; he is likened, as
is Stephen, to the Wren King in Joyce's St. Stephen's
Day parody; he promises, as mock-king, a golden age
of free love and "weekly carnival with masked
license"; he is castrated by the nymph with the
Frazerian Druid's knife as the dying and reviving
nature god of Frazerian ritual; and he, like Stephen,
eventually enacts a marginal escape from the Ishtars,
the bitch goddesses, the composite bovine god of

nighttown. [pp. 480ff] Stephen, too, assumes the mask of the dying and reviving god when he symbolically dies during this dance of death, only to be later reborn from the fetal position after his rough and tumble with Carr and after his deliverance by Bloom. All of this comic, hallucinatory probing of the haunted unconscious occurs during the "midsummer madness" of "Circe." [57]

Finnegans Wake deepens the plunge into the haunted mind of modern man. Ellison may well have observed that Finn becomes a dying and reviving god who "wakes" when, as Finnegan of the Irish-American ballad, he is splashed with whiskey; that Hosty serves as the spirit of both the dying god and the declining year; that Persse O'Reilly, Parnell, HCE, Finnegan, Shem, and their counterparts are linked to ancient scapegoats and nature gods; that Frazerian birds, symbolic of the soul of the slain fertility god or king, take flight after HCE's ritual hanging; that totem animals and Horde fathers haunt the Wakean dreamer. [58] The "longing for the father" expressed in the creation of totems is just as real a factor in the Wakean dreamer's unconscious as it was in primitive man's ritualized clans. And many of the totems in the Wake may well have found their way into Invisible Man. Tod Clifton's name may be derived from several sources: the German word for "death," "tot," and totems such as Tod Lowrie, the Scottish fox, Swiney Tod, the Welsh fox, and the "Tad" for "Dad," all of which appear in the Wake. These are likely sources for Tod, who serves ritualistically as a father-figure, totem animal, and scapegoat on the unconscious level when the cop and the amused crowd react to his death. Then too, the bear image in Invisible Man recalls the Wakean "Brookbear" totem and the European "Bogie," as well, while the source for Charlie Parker's cock robin appears to be European. And this scapegoat bird flutters through the Wake during the Russian General sequence. And if Stephen assumes the mask of his imagined bull totem in A Portrait, that "Bous-Stephaneforos," Jack will similarly name himself "Jack the Bear." Foxes, bears, bulldogs, rabbits all fuse with characters in Invisible Man as Ellison reviews the folklore and archaic animal worship, in a manner reminiscent of Joyce, that still cling to modern men. [59]

Much as Stephen, Bloom, and the dreamer of the Wake peer dimly into the unconscious images of the human race, Jack, too, must articulate and hopefully control the dangerous compulsions of his unconscious. The events surrounding the death of Tod finally begin to jolt Jack into a wariness of the compulsive forces that stem from the unconscious. The events leading to Tod's death fall into a pattern for the anthropologically oriented reader of Invisible Man. For the decay of nature that triggers dying god and scapegoat rituals becomes the sultry summer heat wave in Harlem which produces a mental heat in the city; and Tod's physical description hints at the deeper psychological reverberations of his murder. He is about Jack's age; and he reveals, in a more compulsive way, Jack's short temper and violent outbursts of rage. He wears a crossed bandage on his "Afro-Anglo-Saxon face" which hides a wound won in a fight with the Black nationalists; and he sports hair described as "Persian lamb's wool." [pp. 352ff] Then too, Tod seems, like Otto Rank's hero, to be without family: He mentions no relatives. Tod's kingly appearance, his association with a lamb, fit the Frazerian qualities of the sacrificial scapegoat-king. And the dolls, with their grinning grotesque faces, recall the description of various dolls in The Golden Bough and in Totem and Taboo, ritual dolls that were substituted for the clown in scapegoat sacrifices. Indeed, Tod is a composite of a variety of victims, and he recalls a character in Ellison's earlier short story, "Flying Home."

Joseph Trimmer has discussed Todd's attempt in "Flying Home" to flee the experience of DuBois' "double consciousness" by no longer seeking recognition from the death oriented army.[60] Since the whites have militarized even the skies, Todd's goal of becoming a pilot reveals his need to be accepted and defined by a dehumanized power structure. His final decision to abandon his career results in his acceptance of the old black man Jefferson as a kind of foster father and bearer of a skeptical, black American tradition that is clearly more sane to Todd than the death-orientation of the white world. And Jefferson is not only a foster-father but also Todd's initiator into genuine manhood, a manhood Todd comes to discover after his "fortunate fall" as an Alabama Icarus.[61] Trimmer explains the imagery which, for our purposes, suggests Stephen Dedalus' ordeal in A Portrait:

Todd, like Icarus, has tried to fly too
close to the sun, and his fall has taught
him his conceit. But like Adam's, Todd's
fall can be seen as fortunate for it eventually occasions his salvation. The
Daedalus figure, Jefferson, has taught his
"son" the error of his ways.[62]

Trimmer revals that Todd's acceptance of his
"community identity" saves him from psychic suicide;
that his identification with the defiant tradition
of men like Jefferson allows his phoenix-like
rebirth:

Once he accepts this community identity,
Todd, like the buzzard-jimcrow, is transformed into the bird of flaming gold. Like
the Prodigal Son, Todd was dead and is now
alive again and ready to begin his flight
home.[63]

Tod Clifton finds no such redemption when he attempts
to locate meaning and secure an identity in the confusion of Americn life. A community identity alone
will no longer suffice. Tod Clifton cracks up not
only because white America will not accept his black
heritage, but also because it will not accept his
humanity as part of its own.[64]

Tod's life is drawn toward alienation. He
thwarts the Brotherhood's attempt to control him. He
will not be one of the band of brothers; he will
strive, like Jack, for self-definition, but the
contradictions of the black experience become too
much for him. For Tod, human relations are twisted,
contorted. Despite his emulation of Marcus Garvey,
he cannot tolerate Ras' racial bombastics. Yet he is
seduced by Ras' logic and Ras' loving praise of him
as a remnant of black royalty. Tod knows that whites
threaten his humanity from another direction. The
white brothers, for example, will use him in a power
game, but they will not accept his uniqueness or
even his value as a person. The contradictions cannot be reconciled. After knocking Ras down, Tod
admits: "It'll run you crazy if you let it." [p.
367] Then Tod confides in Jack: "I suppose sometimes a man has to plunge outside history. . . .
Plunge outside, turn his back . . . otherwise he
might kill somebody, go nuts." [p. 368] Tod recalls

Malraux's Gisor in Man's Fate, but he fails to escape
unconscious politics, and Tod becomes another victim
of Saturn. Tod demands recognition and reciprocity
by America; he wants his existence validated by
meaningful human relationships. Jack will go another
route; he will become his own father, he will seek
inclusion into the pantheon of estranged, self-
reliant tricksters who will offer reciprocity and
recognition. But Jack must bear more unnerving
experiences before he may preside over his own birth
of conscience.

Before Jack encounters Tod's exhibition of Sambo
dolls, Ellison is careful to discuss the weather in
Harlem. It is early July, and very, very hot. The
trees are scorched. Everyone seems to be on edge,
nervous. Jack too is edgy. He is furious at Brother
Jack and wishes to kill him for selling out the black
membership. Jack's anxiety increases; he searches
for Tod. He enters Barrelhouse's Jolly Dollar (a
place where as in The Sun Also Rises, Jack, like Jake
Barnes, discovers that money can be the real welding
force of "brotherhood"), "a dark hole of a bar and
grill" in search of Brother Maceo and for a clue to
Tod's whereabouts. Jack is immediately accosted by
two men at the bar for calling them "brothers." Mac
Adams mocks Jack, "Shit, he ain't no kin of mine."
[IM, p. 413] Barrelhouse stands up for Jack and
tells Mac Adams that he is not offended by Jack's
familiarity. Jack apologizes. Unconsciously, clan
loyalties, the essence of racial hostility, are
emerging. Mac Adams retorts to Barrelhouse: "You
just tell your brother he ought to be careful 'bout
who he claims as kinfolks." [p. 416] The bar, the
city vibrate with nervous energy. As Frazer
revealed, a change in weather can trigger violence
in the human unconscious when the need for a scapegoat becomes shared by a group. Wright said much the
same about links between seasonal changes and
lynchings in the South. But Jack decides not to
enter into a brawl with Mac Adams, a name which is
itself ironic. For if this bar, with its fraternal
secret society, is reminiscent of Barney Kiernan's
pub in Ulysses, then this "Son of Adam" is really a
fatherless, fraternal monster cut along the lines of
Michael Cusak. Barrelhouse continues to talk with
Jack. He admits that jobs are tight, and he implies
that this economic situation is a cause of the fric-
tion in the bar. Black labor is seen as a threat,

then, along with the intolerable heat. The
Erotherhood's design to abandon blacks is shared by
the workforce. Jack leaves the bar and once again
joins the hot, sweating masses of pedestrians. Then
he sees a peculiar and ominous sight: "In a hot
sidestreet I came upon a couple striking matches
along the curb, kneeling as though looking for a lost
coin, the matches flaring dimly in their faces."
[IM, p. 417] This apparently insignificant detail
fits the pattern of events that is about to unfold,
for this kneeling scene recalls, in miniature,
visions of the St. John's Day fires, complete with
the appeasement of the waning sun, symbolized here by
the coin. In the afternoon sun, Harlem appears
haunted by the past, "a city of the dead."

Then Jack sees a Sambo doll:

I'd seen nothing like it before. A
grinning doll of orange-and-black tissue
paper with thin flat cardboard disks forming
its head and feet and which some mysterious
mechanism was causing to move up and down in
a loose-jointed, shoulder-shaking, infuriat-
ingly sensuous motion, a dance that was
completely detached from the black, mask-
like face. It's no jumping-jack, but what,
I thought, seeing the doll throwing itself
about with the fierce defiance of someone
performing a degrading act in public,
dancing as though it received perverse
pleasure from its motions. [p.421]

An unidentified man spiels a jingle when the
scapegoat dolls gyrate. And the audience chuckles at
the grotesque vision:

"He'll make you laugh, he'll make you
sigh, si-igh.
He'll make you want to dance, and
dance-
Here you are, ladies and gentlemen,
Sambo,
The dancing doll.
Buy one for your baby. Take him to
your girl friend and she'll love you, loove
you!
He'll keep you entertained. He'll make
you weep sweet tears from laughing.

                    Shake him, shake him, you cannot break
      him
                    For he's Sambo, the dancing Sambo, the
      prancing,
                    Sambo, the entrancing, Sambo Boogie
      Woogie paper doll." [p. 421]

Jack himself feels the lure of the scapegoat when he
struggles "between the desire to join in the laughter
and to leap upon it with both feet." Like Trueblood,
Jack is "paralysed" by this unacknowledged projection
from the unconscious. Tod spiels on:

                    "Look at that rumba, that suzy-q, he's
      Sambo-Boogie,
                    Sambo-Woogie, you don't have to feed
      him, he sleeps collapsed, he'll kill your
      depression
                    And you dispossession, he lives upon
      the sunshine of your lordly smile. . . ."
      [p. 423]

Jack discovers, finally, that it is Clifton who is
running this show, and the ritual procedes: "Who
else wants little Sambo before we take it on the
lambo?" Tod rails. [p. 423] Jack feels "betrayed";
the sight of the doll causes a "rage" to well up in
him. He picks up a doll when Tod moves the show
around the corner. He tries to check himself: "I
might forget myself and try to attack him." [p. 423]
He walks away to cool down, and in the hot sun of
Bryant Park, through the cars that speed by, images
of the show become dreamy "seeming to unfold in my
mind like a slow-motion movie run off with the sound
track dead." [p. 425] Jack notes the nervous
pigeons; they swirl in the street. A policeman and
Tod struggle. The policeman is described in fascist
imagery: ". . . I could see the cop push Clifton
again, stepping solidly forward in his black shirt,
his arm shooting out stiffly. . . ." [p. 425] Tod
knocks the officer down; pigeons fly into the air,
after the officer shoots. Strangely paralysed, Jack
is unable to interfere. Clifton falls to his knees
"like a man saying his prayers." [p. 426] The
officer looks down on Clifton's crumpled body "as
though surprised." His act has been a ritual murder,
part of an unacknowledged, impulsive ritual, and Jack
senses his own lack of interference as complicity.
Jack's slow-motion movie perception freezes the scene

into a mythic timelessness in a scene that recalls this filmic cliché in Robert Penn's ending to Bonnie and Clyde, for example. Jack also has the strange feeling that he has suffered along with Clifton, for amid the noise of the flapping Frazerian birds, Jack walks "blindly" down the street. Jack notices a boy with "Slavic eyes" who is caught up in an "ecstasy" as the boy also indulges in the ritual. [p. 426] Jack faces the policeman and Trueblood's dream re-echoes silently: "I opened my mouth but nothing would come." It has all been a kind of waking dream, a frightening projection of archaic ritual from the unconscious. The officer asks Jack: "What's your name?" [p. 427] We recall that same question asked of Jack in the hospital room during Jack's earlier plunge into the unconscious, where personal identity was lost and archaic masks or childhood memories assumed control. Jack, like Stephen, is sounding "the mystery of an invisible person." And in the process he is discovering that he, too, is complicit in this unconsciously motivated ritual which partially transcends race; that he, too, felt the same impulses as the officer when he first saw that strange man with the dancing doll.

A policeman gives Tod's epitaph: "He's a cooked pigeon, Mac." [p. 427] A boy unwittingly validates Tod's worth as a sacrifice and Tod's ability to evoke identification among the bystanders to insure their own purgation: "Your friend sure knows how to use his dukes. Biff, bang! One, two, and the cop's on his ass." [p. 428]

Jack's subsequent wanderings; his sense of communion with the three young hipsters who live on the fringes of history; his unsuccessful attempts to repress the slow-motion replay of Tod's death cause him to feel a new sense of isolation when he begins to understand the ritual and to realize his need to dislodge himself from the boomerangs of unconscious and daylight history.[65] His mind again awakes: "I'd been asleep, dreaming" in the jungle of Harlem. [p. 433]

Several critics have observed that Tod serves as a kind of "doppelganger" for Jack. We have noted the similarities between Tod and Jack earlier, and we might further note that the sacrifice of the double is a common theme in literature. In fact, the

Wake teems with "doblingangers." On one level, Tod's likeness to Jack facillitates Tod's initial success as scapegoat for him. In The Long Dream Wright employs the double in much the same manner as Ellison does in Invisible Man. For both Fishbelly and Chris share a near compulsion to experience sex with a white woman. When Fishbelly hears of Chris' ritual dismemberment, he feels a momentary sense of independence. Chris' death as a scapegoat figure has unwittingly worked its catharsis on Fishbelly, for he dies a little, too, and experiences vicarious punishment for his own guilt that resulted from buried desires for white women.⁶⁶ Tod's death may well flaw Invisible Man, as Eleanor Wilner has suggested, for it prevents a fuller treatment of the double-bind inherent in the black experience.⁶⁷ But, in any case, Jack dies a little too when the realization of Tod's death hits home. He, unlike Tod, will retreat from violence and settle upon an approach to existence that admits an Emersonian as well as existential mea culpa for the bad faith of living out the white stereotypes of blackness. Tod's death allows Ellison to table the exploration of the double-bind and to strike out for a less tragic view of possibilities in the Epilogue. And certainly Jack is far more complex than Fishbelly, for even though Jack was initially complicit in the mockery and revulsion against the mysterious man with the dolls, his growing detachment and isolation from history and his painful introspection into his own mind allow him to begin to articulate the bondage that all men experience under the reign of unconscious rituals. But Jack must first experience the funeral and the riot before he is able, like Bloom, to reach a fuller humanity.

The impact of Frazer and Freud on Ellison's critique of the "unconscious politics" of history continues. Jack's ill-defined guilt, which appears to stem from his own acknowledgement of his impulsive participation in the scapegoat ritual, causes him to plan for a funeral: "I seized upon the idea as though it would save my life." [p. 439] Indeed, Jack has trouble sleeping before the funeral; he also eats very little. At the funeral, perfumed as it is by the "sick smell of some female dogs in season," Tod's coffin is carried "like a heavily loaded ship in a channel." [p. 440] The archetype of the soul-ship combines with the sexual aroma to again reinforce the libidinous, totemic nature of the ritual. The "old plaintive, masculine voice" causes Jack to leap to his childhood and, recalling Norton's envy, he feels "a twinge of envy" toward this mysterious old man, who like tabooed Trueblood, appears to have survived his transgressions against the limits placed upon men. Jack looks closely at the face of the singer: "It was a worn, old, yellow face and his eyes were closed and I could see a knife welt around his upturned neck as his throat threw out the song." The song evokes Jack's mysterious inner self: "I was listening to something within myself," but he still does not have the wisdom to explore those feelings that are deeper than "protest, or religion." [p. 442]

Jack admits that he has "no idea of ritual" as he prepares for the funeral speech. He is correct, for he violates the Frazerian taboo of the dead, which obviated for primitive man that the name of the deceased not be spoken for fear that the dead might hear and come in their loneliness to claim the living. In his discussion of mourning, Freud argued in Totem and Taboo that the ritual was designed to appease the dead so they would not avenge themselves on the mourner. For Freud and Frazer, primitive man experienced the dead as demons, jealous lonely demons who sensed that the living wished them dead. The coffin which floats as a ship during Tod's funeral fits into this primitive fear, for these living-dead in Harlem put some distance between themselves and the deceased with their own unacknowledged ritual. Of this phenomena of distancing the dead from the living in primitive society, Freud remarks:

The living did not feel themselves safe from the persecutions of the dead until a body of water had been put between them. That is why it was preferred to bury the dead on islands or to bring them to the other side of a river: the expressions "here" and "beyond" originated in this way. [68]

Jack's funeral speech further reveals Ellison's awareness of archaic motives buried in all men. His annoyance at the crowd, who would turn the funeral into a "holiday celebration," may reflect an annoyance at himself as well, at his earlier momen-

222

tary enjoyment of the dancing dolls. Jack dispenses with funeral euphemisms and bravely repeats the name of Clifton over and over again. His growing maturity reveals itself when he demythologizes Tod: Tod is not a hero, he has not safely departed into the land of the dead. Instead, he is rotting in the box that stands before the audience, much as the Harlemites are rotting in their tenements. Jack will not cast Tod as a dying and reviving hero: "And don't be fooled for these bones shall not rise again." [p. 447] In fact, Jack rules out any religious interpretation of Tod's death: "Tod Clifton was underground." [p. 448] Through his anti-oration, Jack, on the mythic level, tries to free the crowd and himself from the masks of the archaic ancestors, from the alleged naiveté of fertility ritual and of religious salvation. His near-impuslive speech does just that: "And as I took one last look I saw not a crowd, but the set faces of individual men and women." [p. 448] Temporarily, at least, Jack's street existentialism has triumphed; this group cannot realize a holiday, they cannot unite in "clan" solidarity, they cannot unwittingly complete the rituals of the totem feast, for Jack has touched them.

What the audience accomplishes during the funeral gathering is not enough to block the Saturnalia that has been set into motion. The Saturnalia is certainly not new to this novel. We recall the upside down world of the Golden Day where Norton becomes the goat, or the aftermath of Jack's speech on dispossession amidst the clutter of the Provo household where the crowd acts as one "huge man" as it taunts the police and moves the Provos' possessions back into the tenement. It all seemed "like a holiday." [p. 275] But the holiday was contained. The Harlem riot, cannot be contained and Saturn is about to triumph much as his spirit does throughout Joyce's fiction and in the influential Man's Fate. Jack will learn more anthropology in the streets.

We need now to take a closer look at the events of the Saturnalia. For this event harkens back to an imaginary golden age where equality and justice prevailed, if at the expense of blood sacrifice. The election and execution of a one-eyed "mock king" probably served to release repressed parricidal urges

as well as the free floating guilt so indigenous to
agrarian cultures which hoped to appease nature and
insure fertility by offering sacrifice.⁶⁹ Interestingly enough, the sequence of events in the Harlem
riot offers a point for point comparison with the
Pagan Saturnalia.

The riot, ironically on the Fourth of July,
becomes a spontaneous release of the anxiety that has
plagued sweltering Harlem. This date is one-eyed
Brother Jack's birthday as well, and he might serve
symbolically as a 20th century Saturn. Tod's death
does not in fact cause the riot, and none of the
rioters really know exactly why they are out in the
streets. Scofield attempts to explain the cause.
First he tells Jack that "a cop shot a woman or
something." Jack concludes that it is "a night for
Clifton." But then Scofield offers another
explanation:

> "Aw man, don't tell me," Scofield said.
> "Didn't I see it with my own eyes? About
> eight o'clock down on Lenox and 123rd this
> paddy slapped a kid for grabbing a Baby Ruth
> and the kid's mama took it up and then the
> paddy slapped her and that's when all hell
> broke loose."

Dupre counters: "Don't nobody know how it started."
[p. 528-29] While Jack wanders through the surreal
dream landscape of this modern day Saturnalia, he
sees black women wearing looted "blond wigs" and
rioters sporting stolen guns from a pillaged navy
store. [p. 531] The oppressed are clothed in the
trappings of their oppressors. Saturn is triumphing.
As he dodges a policeman's bullet, Jack's mind suddenly moves into a "brilliant suspension of time."
He plunges into mythic timelessness, into the
unconscious landscape of a "blue dream." In this
dream the repressed desires of the unconscious have
emerged:

> There was something I had to do and I know
> that my forgetfulness wasn't real, as one
> knows that the forgotten details of certain
> dreams are not truly forgotten but evaded.
> I knew, and in my mind I was trying to reach
> through a gray wall that now seemed to hang
> behind my eyes as opaquely as the blue cur-

tain that screened the street beyond the
safe. The dizziness left and I managed to
stand, holding onto my briefcase, pressing a
handkerchief to my head. Up the street
there sounded the crashing of huge sheets of
glass and through the blue mysteriousness of
the dark the walks shimmered like shattered
mirrors." [p. 525]

With his nicked head Jack has become a Trueblood; he
has looked into the heart of darkness of the human
psyche. He has survived.

After Jack drinks the ritual whiskey stolen by
Dupre's men, he joins Dupre's band of looters. But
he resists loosing himself in the Saturnalia and
questions the purpose of the riot: "I stood there in
the dark feeling a rising excitement as their voices
played around me. What was the meaning of it all?
What should I think of it, do about it?" [p. 531]
As Dupre's men prepare to burn the tenement, Jack's
strange inability to interfere recalls his paralysis
at the Clifton shooting: "It didn't occur to me to
question. . ." But Jack finally realizes that
Dupre's act is sound, for "No one laughed," when
kerosene is dumped in the rooms. Dupre's act is not
part of the ritual, not a retaliation nor a reaction.
It is a mature act, designed to destroy the filthy,
rat infested tenement. Jack reflects:

And now I was seized with a fierce sense of
exaltation. They've done it, I thought.
They organized it and carried it through
alone; the decision their own and their own
action. Capable of their own action. . ."

Yet this moment of autonomy is lost. Jack begins to
enter into the mass hysteria of the "holy holiday,"
to enjoy it, with his "personality blasted."
[p. 536-37]

Jack's revulsion toward the hanging white dummy
on the lamp post reveals to him his own complicity
with the others in this stange ritual that is masking
his individuality. For the scapegoat ritual is now
being enacted by the black community, as well;
Clifton's symbolic dolls are not so unlike the hanged
dolls. the dummys littering the street from the
looted store, or, for that matter, from the

"distinguished" dignataries on the platform at the
college chapel service , who to Jack, looking at them
as through "a reversed telescope," seem "small.
doll-like" while they act out a "meaningless ritual."
[p. 115] But Jack is more intricately caught up in
the rituals of the riot, for he must encounter Ras.
who to Ellison comes to symbolize a "mock king."
Jack glimpses the surreal Ras and Ras' band:

> They moved in a tight-knit order. carrying
> sticks and clubs, shotguns and rifles, led
> by Ras the Exhorter become Ras the Destroyer
> upon a great black horse. A new Ras of a
> haughty, vulgar dignity, dressed in the
> costume of an Abyssinian chieftain; a fur
> cap upon his head. his arm bearing a shield.
> a cape made of the skin of some wild animal
> around his shoulders. A figure more out of
> a dream than out of this Harlem night. yet
> real. alive. alarming. [p. 544]

If on the subliminal level Ras will become the ritual
sacrifice to bleed off the tensions of Harlem. from
Jack's point of view Ras must be stopped to prevent
the riot from becoming a bloodbath:

> They moved up around the horse excited and
> not quite decided, and faced him, knowing I
> was no worse than he. nor any better. and
> that all the months of illusion and the
> night of chaos required but a few simple
> words , a mild. even a meek, muted action to
> clear the air. To awaken them and me.
> [p. 545]

Jack hopes to awaken himself and the crowd from the
grip of their compulsions. from this tragic holiday.
but after Ras threatens to hand Jack over as an Uncle
Tom and to display Jack's body next to the dummies,
Jack protests to the crowd. "Can't you see it? They
want you guilty of your own sacrifice!" [p. 545] He
faces Ras and realizes that unless he acts. he will
become the next scapegoat in Harlem:

> I stood there facing them. and it seemed
> unreal. I faced them knowing that the mad-
> man in a foreign costume was real and yet
> unreal. knowing that he wanted my life. that
> he held me responsible for all the nights

226

and days and all the suffering and for all
that which I was incapable of controlling,
and I no hero, but short and dark with only
a certain eloquence and a bottomless capacity for being a fool to mark me from the
rest; saw them, recognized them at last as
those whom I had failed and of whom I was
now, just now, a leader, though leading
them, running ahead of them, only in the
stripping away of illusionment. [p. 546]

To avoid his own sacrifice, Jack, helplessly inside
history, delegates the mask to Ras. As an emergent
anti-hero, he must, paradoxically, complete the
symbolic action of the Saturnalia in order to save
himself. He fires the spear and unhorses Ras; he
acts not to participate in a ritual, but to save
himself.

After Jack escapes from the angry crowd, he hides
and overhears some men joke about Ras' theatrics and
laugh at Ras' desire to kill rather than to loot.
Relieved, Jack, like Trueblood, feels "rescued from
drowning." [p. 550] He has emerged from the
unconscious landscape of the Saturnalia. Jack wonders why the discussion he overhears of Ras' battle
with the police that night is described by the men
only as a comic event. In fact, for Ellison, Ras is
one more doll to these men, another scapegoat clown
with his exaggerated appearance.

The entry into the coalhole is "a kind of death
without hanging." [p. 554] In the coalhole, which
on one level symbolizes the unconscious, Jack is able
to symbolically illuminate the human heart of
darkness first with a match and then with his blazing
electric lights in a kind of tribute to Frazerian,
Freudian, and Hegelian rationality, to the light of
anthropological and philosophical introspection.
Jack attempts to burn the Sambo doll he had picked
off the street. The doll burns "stubbornly," but
Jack is now able to symbolically neutralize his
uncritical subservience to the unconscious. He is
self-consciously "all in all." He is now able to
evaluate and transcend his unconscious politics, to
awake from the nightmare of history, or at least
dodge the boomerangs he himself refuses to throw.
Like Bloom or Trueblood, Jack is now taboo. He has
stepped off the "sacrificial merry-go-round."

Phillip Reiff's evaluation of Freud's "Romanticism" is applicable at least in part to Jack's catharsis:

> Freud's end, processionally and valuationally, was to outwit tradition for the sake of a personality type unknown to history thus far, the psychological man--man emancipated by rational analysis from commitments to the prototypal past. Because tradition and the repressions have failed him, psychological man must now admit that he can be all things to himself, as well as to all other men. His identity is for him to choose; none can choose him, as in the days of the living gods and imposing fathers. [71]

Jack's abandonment of the heroic role also allows him to defer a willing acquiescence to the scapegoat ritual. For in the end, the hero is the scapegoat. As Brown argues, heroes are invented to enact the tabooed deeds which the community is unable to perform. [72] The hero, however, soon becomes the scapegoat; he allows his community's redemption. The community's need for a hero, for Ellison, is an act of bad faith, of substitution. The visible signs of the devious unconscious, myths and rituals, which are really forms of institutionalized mental illness, try to imprision men, unless, like Stephen, Bloom and Jack, men dare to awake.

Ultimately then, the uprooting American experience may prove to be more positive than negative for Ellison. In Shadow and Act he recalls how his childhood in Oklahoma spurred his aspirations of becoming a Renaissance Man:

> But to ourselves we were "boys," members of a wild, free outlaw tribe which transcended the category of race. Rather we were Americans born into the forty-sixth state, and thus, into the context of Negro-American post-Civil War history, "frontiersmen." And isn't one of the implicit functions of the American frontier to encourage the individual to a kind of dreamy wakefulness, a state in which he makes--in all ignorance of the accepted limitations of the possible-- rash efforts, quixotic gestures, hopeful

testings of the complexity of the known and given? [p. xv]

The "dreamy wakefulness" of America, with its confused lineage, its dedication to the future, its dim memory of European, African, or Asian pasts, may be an ultimate strength rather than a weakness, a redemption rather than a curse. For Ellison, as for Joyce, the acceptance of the "chaosmos" is a fortunate fall; the loss of a certain identity, a requisite for genuine freedom; the lack of a new covenant, a formula for a wiser conscience, an invitation to be one's father or to model oneself after free spirits such as old Jefferson, the grandfather, Douglass, Trueblood and the rest. If the Irish and American experiences opened the heart of darkness so that its impulses were released almost unchecked, they also left a crack wide enough to let in a ray of light.

Had Pyrrhus not fallen by a bedlam's
hand in Argos or Julius Caeser not been
knifed to death? They are not to be thought
away. Time has branded them and fettered
they are lodged in the room of the infinite
possibilities they have ousted. But can
those have been possible seeing that they
never were? Or was that only possible which
came to pass? Weave, weaver of the wind.

<u>U</u>, p. 25

"And remember, the world is full of
possibility if only you'll discover it."

<u>IM</u>, p. 154

Now, as never before, his strange name
seemed to him a prophecy. So timeless
seemed the grey warm air, so fluid and
impersonal his own mood, that all ages were
as one to him. A moment before the ghost of
the ancient kingdom of the Danes had looked
forth through the vesture of the haze-
wrapped city. Now, at the name of the
fabulous artificer, he seemed to hear the
noise of dim waves and to see a winged form
flying above the waves and slowly climbing
the air.

<u>P</u>, p. 430

CHAPTER V

If Stephen wishes an awakening from the nightmare of history, from the recurrent bloody myths of the past, from the grip of unconscious archetypes, he also reveals an opposite desire: He nostalgically longs for initiatory myths and heroic archetypes from mythology that might hasten or insure his birth of conscience. Rites of passage that would perform this task have atrophied in Dublin. The father is fallen, unsure of his functions as initiator, and even usurped of those responsibilities by the church. Stephen's nostalgia for the Daedalus myth, his rejection of the rites of the church, his frantic search for conscience, and his half-hearted desire to raise up both Ireland's "fallen language and tradition" and "his father's fallen state" by restoring a sacred meaning to the "profane world" all point to his exertions to restore primitive rites and an heroic, Greek ambiance to "dear, dirty Dublin." Stephen's longing for heroic models from mythology, and his seemingly contradictory revulsion at the possession of the present by icy tradition are preoccupations that need not be seen as contradictory. For much like Nietszche's efforts to restore a Greek vigor to the West, Stephen would select those myths and heroes which make life here and now sacred, rather than relegate the sacred to Plato or to the dio boia. Indeed, Stephen ultimately would transcend time by annihilating it as did primitive man in ancient ritual. Stephen would inject the myths and heroes of sacred time into the present. He would forge a much needed rite. This quest defines his nostalgia, his need for ancient rites of passage, a nostalgia that causes him eventually to provide his own rite of passage, to become his own initiator, the father of himself. And this nostalgia was carefully observed by Ellison, as we shall see.

As Stephen becomes more and more alienated from the lethargy of Dublin, from Dublin's impacted authority, he longs, then, for a meaningful transition out of the perpetual adolescence shared by the hypermasculine Dubliners. But he encounters only perverted rituals of the sacred rites, withered ritual stumps. Mircea Eliade's discussion of the perversion and decline of ancient rites helps to

clarify both Stephen's frustration and the similar
ordeals experienced by characters in the fiction of
Ellison and Wright:

> . . . it was as <u>homo</u> <u>religiosus</u> that man
> first became conscious of his own mode of
> being. Whether he wants to or not, the
> nonreligious man of modern times continues
> the behavior patterns, the beliefs, and the
> language of <u>homo</u> <u>religiosus</u>--though at the
> same time he desacralizes them, empties them
> of their original meanings.[1]

Eliade reveals that ostensibly non-religious
activities in the modern world,

> public ceremonies, spectacles, sports
> competitions, youth organizations, propa-
> ganda by pictures and slogans, literature
> for mass popular consumption--all still
> preserve the structure of myths, of symbols,
> of rites, although they have been emptied of
> their religous content.[2]

In a world of atrophied ritual, the primal needs
still exert themselves, the "religious" unconscious
retains the themes and symbols that are not given
proper expression in the milieus these fictional
heroes inhabit. According to Eliade, modern man,
across the boards, is no longer truly religious in
the primitive sense:

> since there is no longer any religious
> experience fully or consciously assumed,
> initiation no longer performs an ontological
> function; it no longer includes a radical
> change in the initiand's mode of being, or
> his salvation.[3]

Human lives, then, continually reveal "a series of
ordeals," of "deaths," and of "resurrections."[4] But
the inner needs for intense symbolism and ceremony
are ungratified: culture largely fails to understand
and to incorporate into its rituals the powerful
demands of the unconscious of its children for
effective rites of passage.

Indeed, Stephen's driving need to "forge" his own
conscience and that of his Irish "race" is a

necessary consequence of the collapse of effective ritual in oppressed Ireland and in the "freer" world, as well. Stephen's impetus, however, is quite the opposite of the transformation that occurs in primitive rites of passage, rites which, as Eliade explains, "make" the man, while incorporating him into the mysteries, the world view, the history and the fellowship of the tribe or secret society: "For archaic thought, . . . man is made--he does not make himself. It is the old initiates, the spiritual masters, who make him." [5] But the old initiates are themselves acting in accordance with mythic scripts. Eliade goes on:

> But these masters apply what was revealed to them at the beginning of Time by the Supernatural Beings; indeed, in many cases they incarnate them. This is as much as to say that in order to become a man, it is necessary to resemble a mythical model. [6]

Rites of passage accomplish the two objectives that would most benefit Stephen. They create the new personality of the initiand by providing him an identity with the tribe, with its mythical, heroic progenitor and with it's timeless mythology, while they allow the initiand to undergo a radical separation from his mother and the profane, maternal, temporal world. Eliade explains the rationale in leaving the maternal world of childhood behind:

> The maternal universe was that of the profane world. The universe that the novices now enter is that of the sacred world. Between the two, there is a break, a rupture of continuity. Passing from the profane to the sacred world in some sort implies the experience of death; he who makes the passage dies to one life in order to gain access to another. [7]

In Stephen's frenetic attempt to sever his emotional dependence on his mother and to seek out a mythic hero-initiator, he only undergoes a series of perverted rites of passage which will not further his accomplishment of either objective. Eliade describes both Ulysses, and Eliot's The Waste Land as works where "initiatory themes are discernable." [8] Perverted

and truncated themes, we might add, for in both
simulations of the modern consciousness, meaningful
initiation is thwarted, and such failure informs
Joyce's earlier fiction as well.

Dubliners teems with young adult characters who
are unable to pass from childhood to genuine
adulthood. For their role models often appear as
hypermasculine failures or as static, grown-up
infants, who live out lives of perpetual adolescence.
In Stephen Hero Joyce more actively explores the
failure of rites of passage in Ireland. For Stephen
harbors an aversion to games which have indeed become
gamey, sport-encrusted Dublin's equivalent to ritual.
When Heally asks Stephen to join in playing handball,
Stephen echoes Hamlet, "I'm a poor player." [p. 57]
The rites of sport appear as ineffective as Stephen's
abortive initiations into sexuality. He describes
his desire to fornicate with Emma as tantamount to a
"distorted ritual," a black mass perhaps, for young
Stephen feels that Catholicism has so perverted any
natural, open expression of sexuality that he can
only join in a counter-perversion. [p. 193] The
linkage of ritual and sexuality becomes more developed in A Portrait when Stephen telescopes time
during his fervent sexual meanderings. Vickery
explains that Stephen uses ritual imagery to describe
nighttown. The streets form a maze; the gas street
lights are "burning as if before an altar." [P,
p. 352] According to Vickery,

> Stephen sacralizes the world of prostitution
> in a way that provides a rationale for the
> romanticizing of the prostitute and his loss
> of virginity later in the same scene:
> "Before the doors and in the lighted hall
> groups were gathered arrayed as for some
> rite. He was in another world: he had
> awakened from a slumber of centuries."[9]

Vickery explains Stephen's leap in time to the ritual
of the ancient world:

> To find himself in another world centuries
> old entails for Stephen the instinctual
> recognition that the loss of virginity is
> neither trivial nor moral but momentous and
> religious. In effect, for him the Dublin
> whore is not simply a contemporary street

walker but a woman functionally similar to
the sacred prostitute of The Golden Bough,
who serves the god of fertility by cohab-
iting with strangers, each of whom may be a
manifestation of the god.[10]

Since sacred prostitution was an ancient initiation
rite for women, we see that its degenerate form can
serve no corresponding purpose when fertility is
desacralized in Dublin.

One after another the rites fail in A Portrait.
Stephen's desired entry into the priesthood would
provide two important elements of the ancient rite of
passage: he would be separated from the maternal and
sexual realm through celibacy, and he would be
initiated into the sacred mysteries of the Trinity.
Sensing the simony of the church, Stephen finally
recoils from the church's hollow and empty ritual
after his desperate struggle with faith and finally
searches for the sacred, here and now. Feeling that
his own art is the true divinity that might take its
place with the god-like creations of previous
artists, Stephen seeks his place within an apostolic
succession of artists; he fantasizes his own initiation and rebirth as Daedalus. Yet the myth he
embraces is an abortive one as well, and in Ulysses
he realizes that he is not Daedalus but a "lapwing"
Icarus who has plunged into the maternal sea of
Dublin's paralysis. In "Circe" Stephen boasts: "No,
I flew. My foes beneath me. And ever shall be.
World without end. (He cries.) Pater! Free!" But
the cartoon image of his father undercuts Stephen's
flight:

"That's all right. (He swoops uncertainly
through the air, wheeling, uttering cries of
heartening, on strong ponderous buzzard
wings.) Ho, boy! Are you going to win?
Hoop! Pschatt! Stable with those half-
castles. Wouldn't let them within the bawl
of an ass. Head up! Keep our flag flying!
An eagle guiles volant in a field argent
displayed. Ulster king at arms! hai hoop!
(He makes the beagle's call giving tongue.)
Bilbul! Burbibibrurblbl! Hai boy!"[p. 572]

In his parody of the rite, Mr. Dedalus is both a
mock masked initiator and a joke initiatory animal

who serves an ineffectual god. He characteristically
gives reverence to gamey Dublin's perverted rites:
games, horse racing, the hunt and chauvinistic flag
waving. Stephen reluctantly admits, however, that
his rejection of Simon and his own attempt to become
a reborn Daedalus have failed, for Stephen is a
fallen lapwing, the son of a buzzard-father, a father
whose fallen world Stephen will increasingly come to
accept as more real than his own megalomania for some
vague sacral transformation of life through art.

Eliade mentions that rites of passage can be
oriented around sky god mythology or the more
chthonic earth god rituals.[11] Having failed to learn
the wisdom of a Daedalus, Stephen must endure another
rite in "Circe." With Bloom presiding, Stephen makes
the descent to the initiatory underworld where primal
chaos will return in the physical and mental worlds,
chaos that might begin the transformation of his personality. For according to Eliade, if a rite of
passage is to succeed, it must simulate the first
chaos of the creation to facilitate a new birth into
adulthood: "Every ritual repetition of the cosmogony
is preceded by a symbolic retrogression to Chaos. In
order to be created anew, the old world must first be
'annihilated.'"[12] Psychic chaos is a constant with
adolescent Stephen, but it is never successfully
channelled. His Jesuit chaos is projected outward
into his end of the world fantasy, a dirge that
recalls Gabriel's similar apocalyptics in "The Dead."
Stephen relates his "monstrous dreams":

> Rain was falling on the chapel, on the
> garden, on the college. It would rain
> forever, noiselessly. The water would rise
> inch by inch, covering the grass and shrubs,
> covering the trees and houses, covering the
> monuments and the mountain tops. All life
> would be choked off, noiselessly: birds,
> men, elephants, pigs, children: noiselessly
> floating corpses amid the litter of the
> wreckage of the world. Forty days and forty
> nights the rain would fall till the waters
> covered the face of the earth. [P, pp.
> 370-371]

In the successful ritual, chaos must also be
accompanied by or symbolized by ritual death. Eliade
again:

237

In the scenario of the initiatory rites, "death" corresponds to the temporary return to Chaos; hence it is the paradigmatic expression of the end of a mode of being-- the mode of ignorance and of the child's irresponsibility. Initiatory death provides the clean slate on which will be written the successive revelations whose end is the formation of a new man. [13]

William Fitzpatrick cites Eliade when describing the initiatory birth imagery in "Oxen of the Sun" and in Stephen's ritual descent into nighttown; for, as Eliade explains, rites that involve a womb-return allow the initiand's rebirth into "a new mode of existence (involving sexual maturity, participation in the sacred and in culture; in short, becoming 'open' to the Spirit)." [14] In "Oxen of the Sun" Bloom and Stephen both enter the symbolic womb-hospital where, as Joyce revealed, the nurse is the ovum, Bloom, the spermatozoan, and Stephen, the embryo.[15] Fitzpatrick notes that both Stephen, who is faced with his irrepressible obsession with his mother, and Bloom, preoccupied as he is with the progress of Molly's adultery, are emotionally drained, and, on the mythic level, "both individuals have returned to the well of life," the liquid womb of the hospital.[16] Here Stephen and Bloom can regroup their wits and reaffirm their wonder and awe at the rhythms of birth, the temporary defeat of death. As Stephen points out to his drinking companions, the artist can also conquer the cycles of generation: "Mark me now. In woman's womb word is made flesh but in the spirit of the maker all flesh that passes becomes the word that shall not pass away. This is the postcreation." [U, p. 391] "Oxen of the Sun" prefigures "Circe," for if Stephen is to fulfull his artistic ambition, he must undergo a rite; he must be reborn; he must transcend the haunting chill of his dead mother and of the church and replace these morbidities with an exuberant creativity. Fitzpatrick notes that Stephen recapitulates both the history of language in "Oxen of the Sun" and its gradual, historical steriliza- tion. Stephen must use this degeneration of language. Fitzpatrick explains:

The symbolic shattering of that tradition concludes the episode, forming a kind of Viconian chaos, the terminal state of Vico's tripartite cyclical series, signifying the necessity of a _ricorso_, after which language would become primal gesture.[17]

The Viconian thunderclap follows. Mina Purefoy gives birth. Will Stephen give birth to the word? Before he can, the mythic frames of this novel suggest that he must undergo an initiation rite under the guidance of fatherly Bloom. The rite will be attempted in the chthonian brothel. Of the "Circe" section Fitzpatrick observes:

> "Circe" provides the occasion on which Stephen and Bloom face their pasts, and such confrontation leads to the obliteration and disintegration of that past. There is a breaking apart, a reversion to chaos so that a new cycle may commence.[18]

As in primitive initiation rites, primal chaos is simulated when Stephen and Bloom confront the debilitating power of the labyrinthine female world of Bella Cohen's brothel. Zoe's question to Stephen, "What day were you born?" evokes a questionable reply from him, "Thursday. Today." [p. 562] But Stephen can only feebly strike the chandelier after he and Bloom encounter the various perversions of the maternal world: Bello; the old sow image; Granny Gummy; the hallucinatory image of May Dedalus' rotting corpse; the Nymph; and the rest. When Stephen lays stunned in the street during the Joycean battle royal, only a parody of death and rebirth occurs: Stephen struggles to rise to his feet from the fetal position. Stephen has not been transformed from ranter to writer, and the "Circe" section ends on a downbeat note. The image of dead Rudy, not reborn Stephen, fills Bloom's final hallucinations. Bloom's ability to undergo the torments of Bella/Bello and to turn the tables on her/him during his sadomasochistic fantasies, finds no counterpart in Stephen's similar attempt to separate from the maternal forces.[19] And, indeed, Bloom's recapturing of the potato, a _momento mori_ of his mother, hardly implies that Bloom has put the maternal world behind him. For Bloom is "manchild in the womb." He has failed to conduct the rite with any but marginal success, and he seems barely qualified to officiate over Stephen's rite. If Bloom will collapse into the amniotic warmth of Molly's bed, Stephen will figuratively wander in the amniotic nostalgia for ancient Ireland, Tara.

Rites, then, are clearly perverted and ineffectual in Joyce's Dublin. The maternal world has triumphed and Stephen's sky rite, his trip to Paris, has brought him no genuine rebirth in Ulysses; nor has his chthonic descent into the nighttown of his unconscious. He is still well within the grip of his internalized maternal demons and of incompetent father images.

That Ellison was intrigued by rites of passage and their perversion in modern life is evident not only in Invisible Man but in several of his short stories, where a Joycean influence often appears unmistakably present.

In "Mr. Toussaint" (1944), the theme of perverted rites first emerges. Sky god, initiation imagery occurs as the down-home barnyard images, robins and chickens, become surrogates for Buster and Riley. During their self-enacted rite, the boys may hopefully separate themselves, by the success of their animal surrogates, from the matriarchal Aunt Kate. These two fatherless boys are burning for a rite. But Aunt Kate can only repress their urges by setting the limits on possibility when she chides them for hoping to become presidents of the United States. Ellison's mythic frame implies that she has usurped the role of the male; hence, sky god symbolism is deflated. Not a rebirth into adulthood, but a Christian death-wish is her interest, for she sings:

> ". . . that
> Ah had wings of-vah dove
> Ah'd fly to mah Jesus and
> Be at res' . . . ."

But Riley gets his revenge on her negativism when he counters with his own verses:

> "If I had wings of a dove, Aunt Kate,
> I'd eat up all the candy, Lawd,
> An tear down the White House gate."

He goes on:

> "Amazin grace, how sweet the sound. A bull-
> frog slapped his gramma down."[20]

That these boys long for a fatherly initiator who
might aid them in their separation from the maternal
Aunt Kate is revealed in the ensuing discussion about
their favorite heroes and in their admiration of "the
Louis Armstrong of the chickens," the rooster Ole
Bill, who flaps his wings and lords over the hens.
[p. 7] Riley would be a rooster. He would escape
his mother's philosophy of crying "before you kin
feel good" and from the shame her philosophy evokes
in him. [p. 6] Yet Buster must remind Riley that
roosters cannot fly.

Then they hatch the idea of putting parachutes on
some baby chickens and dropping them from the roof of
the barn. The chickens become surrogate images of
the boys, and, at the same time, the boys figuratively assume the father's role of initiator. When
Buster drops the chicks, the chutes fail to open.
Aunt Kate discovers their abortive ritual. When she
scolds the boys, Riley closes his eyes in fear before
he lashes out at her: "I hate yuh . . . I wish you
had died back in slavery times. . ." [p. 10] The
story concludes as Perseus-Riley sustains another
wound to his pride:

> ". . . if I jus hadn't looked at her," he
> thought. His eyes swam. And so great was
> his anguish he did not hear the swift rush
> of feathers nor see the brilliant flash of
> outspread wings as Ole Bill charged. The
> blow staggered him and, looking down, he saw
> with tear-filled eyes the bright red stream
> against the brown where the spur had torn
> his leg.
> "We almost had 'em flying," said
> Riley. "We almost. . ." [p. 11]

As Klein notes, Riley is symbolically castrated at
this initiation, once by the rooster, who is incapable of real flight, and, we might add, subliminally, by Aunt Kate, who causes Riley to close his
eyes.[21]

Initiatory airplane imagery, a modern analogue to
the sky god myths of the ancient rites of passage,
frames the short story "Flying Home" (1944), when
this time another abortive ritual ultimately leads to
a more successful one.

As a fictional counterpart in Tuskegee's air
school, Todd wishes to enter into the army, which
was, at the time of this story, a closed fraternity
indeed. As Joseph F. Trimmer has observed, Todd suffers from Dubois' "double consciousness," for Todd
feels he must "measure himself against the mirror of
other men's appreciation."[22] In his abortive flight,
which reveals much of the imagery of initiation,
Todd, like Icarus, flies too high; he tries to
discover who is on the other end of the string of a
flying kite and falls to earth in his plane like a
"pitchin' hoss." A buzzard panics him, and he goes
down in what becomes, as Trimmer notes, a kind of
fortunate fall complete with mythic wound, a broken
ankle.[23] He regains consciousness only to be greeted
by a character he at first regards as a disgusting
old black man, Jefferson. But Jefferson comes
finally to serve as an initiator for Todd. The old
man relates a symbolic fable to him:

> "Once I seen a hoss all stretched out like
> he was sick, you know. So I hollers, 'Gid
> up from there, suh!' Just to make sho! An'
> doggone, son, if I don't see two ole
> jimcrows come flying right up outa that
> hoss's insides! Yessuh! The sun was
> shinin' on 'em and they couldn't a been no
> greasier if they'd been eating barbeque."
> [p. 259]

Jefferson then links Todd to that buzzard: "Saw him
just like I see you." [p. 259]

For our purposes the imagery in Jefferson's fable
recalls initiation imagery from primitive rituals.
Eliade describes an initiation rite among the Bantu:

> . . . the boy, before being circumcised, is
> the object of a ceremony called "being born
> anew." The father sacrifices a ram, and
> three days later wraps the boy in the
> animal's stomach membrane and skin. But
> before being wrapped up, the boy has to get
> into bed beside his mother and cry like an
> infant. He remains in the ram skin for
> three days.[24]

The subliminal meaning of the imagery in "Flying
Home" is clarified by such rituals: Todd is the buz-

zard that flies out of the dead horse-airplane in a rebirth that allows him to accept Jefferson and the black world. The uterine return from the symbolic horse, or, from its referent, the airplane, is presided over by his symbolic father-initiator, Jefferson, who teaches him that collusion with the whites in turning the peaceful sky into one of death is to be shunned.[25] Only by avoiding such collusion would Todd retain his humanity and define his own values. And the broken ankle completes the subliminal initiation imagery of ritual circumcision. When he imparts allegorical wisdom to Todd, Jefferson relates a fantasy of his own flight in heaven where he was banned from flying because of his excessive skill. In the fantasy, St. Peter gives Jefferson a parachute and Jefferson falls to Alabama. As Trimmer notes, Jefferson's fable implies "that aspirations of flight are not bad but are simply limited by the existing power structure."[26] Jefferson, then, like primitive initiators, offers "confused" Todd a view of reality, an identity with the group and a group-mythology. The Dabney Graves' of America have perverted the land and the skies; Todd needs to take pride in his more benign black heritage and not allow the white power structure to define him.[27] For Trimmer, then, Todd's fall is a fortunate one; Todd accepts a "communal identity" with Jefferson when he is reborn from buzzard into a golden phoenix in an epiphanic ending reminiscent of Joyce's tendency to end chapters of _Ulysses_ with transcendent images such as the Rosvean vessel, the dream image of Rudy, the image of cheese, the bar of rising soap, or Molly's seedcake.

Ellison explores this double consciousness in _Invisible Man_, as well, for Tod Clifton (Todd's literary reincarnation) struggles with ethnic and national concepts of identity with far less resolution. Jack will modify both approaches to identity and enter the coalhole of the universal mind where ethnic identity is in no way discarded but placed instead into the context of possible universal understanding. Todd discovers that if he must choose identity concepts, the communal, ethnic one may be more viable given the perversions of the national one committed by the dominant white culture. But for Jack, self-definition will fuse and, paradoxically, transcend both of these approaches to identity.

The symbolic use of a machine, in this case the airplane, as a uterine image anticipates the abortive rite in the hospital room in Invisible Man. Todd feels "naked" outside his airplane. He argues that the plane is "Not a machine," but "a suit of clothes that you wear." ["FH," p. 256] Those clothes must be shed if Todd is to experience some "being for itself"; if he is to strive for a genuine conscience. Fatherless Todd, much as Stephen, will gain some wisdom from his spiritual father Jefferson, and indeed, as in Ulysses, where Bloom is mistaken for Stephen's father, Jefferson is mistaken for Todd's. Dedalus is in Tuskegee now, complete with the Joycean imagery of the fortunate fall and the lapwing Icarus. And like Stephen, who finally comes to accept his father's earthy, fallen world, Todd is able to accept and feel pride in his communal identification with old Jefferson.

Ellison has had much to say about the obsessive imagery of initiation in his novel. He has revealed his interest in various hero myths and their relation to ancient initiation rites. His study of Lord Raglan's The Hero and of Otto Rank's The Myth of the Birth of the Hero opened the door to an obviously broad anthropological study that is reflected throughout his novel. Speaking of the occurrence of rites in Invisible Man, Ellison focused on the battle royal episode during an address at West Point:

. . . the narrator of the story goes through a number of rites of passage, rites of initiation. And as I tried to tell my story, I began looking at the meaning of certain rituals. No one had ever told me that the "battle royal" was a rite but I came to see that it was. It was a rite which could be used to project certain racial divisions into the society and reinforce the idea of white racial superiority. On the other hand, as a literary person trying to make up stories out of recognizable experience, and as one who was reading a lot about myth and the function of myth and ritual in literature--it was necessary that I see the battle royal situation as something more than a group of white men having sadistic fun with a group of Negro boys. Indeed, I would have to see it for

what it was beyond the question of the
racial identities of actors involved: a
ritual through which important social values
were projected and reinforced.[28]

Ellison goes on to acknowledge the perversion and the
failure of rites in America, and he points to the
greater efficiency of rites in primitive cultures:

. . . in our democratic society, which is
relatively unstructured as societies go (an
unstructured society precisely because we
had to play it by ear as we got it going),
such patterns are not widely recognized for
what they are, or at least they are not
codified and, thus, they are not institutionalized. Primitive societies are much
more efficient and consistent. They are
more concerned with guiding the young
through each stage of their social development while we leave much of this to chance,
perhaps as part of the responsibility of
freedom.[29]

Ellison cautions the overzealous reader and critic,
however, not to view characters and their ordeals on
the mythic level alone. For despite his assertion
that "novels are ritualistic and ceremonial at their
core," characters and events must be understood on
the level of the "specific form of social reality"
from which they are drawn. [SA, p. 57] With this
caution in mind, we need to locate the primitive base
implicit in many of the abortive and self-
administered rites in the fiction of Ellison and
Wright, and posit evidence for any Joycean influence,
as well.

According to Ellison the central theme of his
novel is "the initiation of a greenhorn." But the
novel also conveys the nervous, "confused" state of
blacks in America who are often not allowed to fully
share in the fruits of this land, who are often not
allowed to feel accepted by the dominant culture and
share in a national identity. For blackness can put
you "in the whale's belly"; the experience of being
black in Jack's opening dream can often lead to a
uterine entrapment, an inability to enact the ritual
of rebirth. We have already noted that the cyclic
structure of Invisible Man reveals on one level a

parody of the repetitive, often static, narrative style of A Portrait.[30] Stephen's failure to success- fully experience a rite of passage or initiation, his constant need for his mother or for mother surro- gates, continue to the end of the novel. In his exuberence to transcend the nets of Ireland with his Paris journey, he invokes his mythical father Daedalus, but his confessional cry, "Old father, old artificer, stand me now and ever in good stead" is a desperate plea. For he is still haunted by initiatory animals in his dreams:

> A mother let her child fall into the Nile.
> Still harping on the mother. A crocodile
> siezed the child. Mother asked it back.
> Crocodile said all right if he told him what
> he was going to do with the child, eat it or
> not eat it. [pp. 522-23]

And Stephen's image of his father recalls "More mud, more crocodiles." Stephen languishes in extended adolescence, and this paralysis haunts him throughout Ulysses. The initiatory crocodile is not an agent of rebirth but of mastication, instead.[31]

Klein has said of Invisible Man.". . . it is all an initiation rite." He goes on to argue that "the novel has no real progress except that at each stage it clarifies and reinforces the hero's dilemma."[32] Klein believes that the Epilogue of the novel asserts an undue optimism that is not justified by the novel itself:

> One asks this hero how he is to come out and
> be socially responsible? Upon what ground
> in reality can he affirm any positive prin-
> ciple? Just what is he going to do?
> Everything in the novel has clarified this
> point: that the bizarre accident that has
> led him to take up residence in an abandoned
> coal cellar is no accident at all, that the
> underworld is his inevitable home, that
> given the social facts of America, both
> invisibility and what he now calls his
> "hibernation" are his permanent condition.[33]

Echoing Eliot's "Burnt Norton," Jack's end does become his beginning, but what do "end" and "beginning" imply? Unaccommodated man? That the core of self one develops when a child needs to be rediscovered in maturity after false selves have been exposed? What of Jack's admission, "I was whole." Jack is nearly whole, but his culture is not. Klein's view needs to be tempered. Jack's socially responsible role is to write in the tradition of the alienated American novelist-critic; to define the oldness at the heart of America to others, so that they might work a cure upon themselves even in isolation, if necessary. Since white culture will not accept Jack and initiate him into the mainstream of American activity, Jack has successfully, unlike Stephen, enacted a patchwork rite of his own. He has learned of the mysteries of his own mind, of his own impulses to be Hegelian "lord," of his own archetypal urges, and he has learned the purpose of life, as he sees it: to subvert the mechanizers of consciousness with the pen. We now need to scrutinize the slow birth of Jack's conscience, along with some Joycean parallels.

Jack ends up quite stillborn in the battle royal. For although this ritual reveals on its surface the symbolic attempt to define the sexual and economic limits of the black males and to perversely and vicariously project white sexual urges onto them, it also contains archaic imagery and undercurrents. Indeed, the blindfolds the young men wear at the battle royal recall similar blindfolds used by archaic man to simulate the darkness of the womb for the initiands in order to facilitate their rebirth into adulthood. As unwitting victims of this rite of exclusion, the "blind" young men at the battle royal, however, are not revealed any tribal mysteries; rather, they are barred from such revelations and told, symbolically, that they can never be men in the eyes of whites, never be meaningfully integrated. The only mystery revealed to them is the flesh of the naked white woman, but it is a mystery they dare not act upon, except in their fantasy life. Frederick L. Radford explains the twists and turns:

> These white men, being who they are in that town at that time, are enjoying the violation of their own most religiously upheld taboo, in a controlled ritual situation without risk. To them, the exposure of a white woman, any white woman, naked to the eyes of black boys is the equivalent of

rape, and if anything approaching such
action were to be initiated by the boys
themselves their fate would be that of Emmet
Till. When this is added to the Krafft-
Ebing sadism of the boxing ring and the
electrified mat, where the black boys are
ritually punished for observing the white
woman, the moral collapse of the white self-
image is complete.[34]

Ironically, the coins on the rug are used theater
tokens emphasizing, symbolically, that not materialistic gain but only the fantasy of gain is open to
these boys, just as the fantasy of white flesh and
not the reality of it is their sexual option. The
infliction of bloody wounds in the ring completes the
archaic imagery. But these wounds, unlike their
primitive counterpart, circumcision, lead nowhere.[35]
The black boys leave with no new state of maturity
but with the possible recognition of their alleged
inferiority and of their alienation from each other.
In an interview, Ellison spoke of Jack's desire to be
a hero and a leader, an ambition which Jack first
reveals in his speech at the conclusion of the battle
royal:

He went through the agony of the "battle
royal" because he wanted to go on following
an ideal, wanted to become a leader; and
this experience is an initiation into the
difficulties of an heroic role, especially
given his background and place in society.[36]

It will take some time for Jack to abandon that goal,
but first he must, like Stephen, suffer new rituals.

The Golden Day sequence has remarkable parallels
to the "Circe" section of Ulysses. For a descent
into the repressed layers of the self, into halluci-
nation and paranoic role playing, emerge when drunken
Supercargo, the "superego," disappears upstairs. The
crowd becomes more and more excitable; it has
"absolutely no inhibitions." [IM, p. 75] The animal
imagery reveals the triumph of the unconscious, of
chaos. Even high-brow Norton exhibits "amazingly
animal-like teeth." [p. 75] Sexual desire is let
loose as well. One vet calls Norton his grandfather,
and the ubiquitous and often repressed desire for
miscegenation is charged. The banter continues
between the drunken men. One says of Norton:

"Look at those features. Exactly like
yours--from the identical mold. Are you
sure he didn't spit you up from the same
earth, fully clothed?"
"No, no, that was my father," said the
man earnestly.
And he began to curse his father
violently as we moved for the door.
[p. 77]

Bloom's self-origination parody in "Circe" echoes
here as well as the desperate need for men in a
fatherless land to create themselves, to provide
their own rites. The mock description of Norton as
"the Messiah" also recalls Bloom's unconscious
politics in "Circe." The chaos continues as the
antics of Supercargo, and the hurling of whiskey
bottles supply the sterile chaos of a perverted rite.
Yet this is not the necessary disorder required for
a successful rite. Chaos leads nowhere in the
fatherless Golden Day. One of the drunks yells at
Supercargo. "Here I'm forty-five and he's been
acting like he's my old man." [p. 82] The crowd
turns on Supercargo, symbolically now a primal father
and a scapegoat. Jack wishes to join this ritual
within a ritual:

Men were jumping upon Supercargo with both
feet now and felt such an excitement that I
wanted to join them. Even the girls were
yelling, "Give it to him good!" "He never
pays me!" "Kill him!" [p. 82]

Much like Bloom, again, Supercargo becomes the butt
of a mock scapegoat ritual. Supercargo is finally
subdued as Joyce's nighttown reverberates in Alabama:

With Supercargo lying helpless upon the bar,
the men whirled about like maniacs. The
excitement seemed to have tilted some of the
more delicately balanced ones too far. Some
made hostile speeches at the top of their
voices against the hospital, the state and
the universe. The one who called himself a
composer was banging away the one wild piece
he seemed to know on the out-of-tune piano,
striking the keyboard with fists and elbows
and filling in other effects in a bass voice
that moaned like a bear in agony. One of

the most educated ones touched my arm. He
was a former chemist who was never seen
without his shining Phi Beta Kappa key.
[p. 84]

If we are reminded of the chaos of "Circe" at
Ellison's Golden Day, we might also recall Bloom's
end of the world fantasy which may have influenced
Ellison here; for as one of the vets reveals:

"The world moves in a circle like a roulette
wheel. In the beginning black is on top, in
the middle epochs, white holds the odds, but
soon Ethiopia shall stretch forth her noble
wings! Then place your money on the black!"
His voice throbbed with emotion. "Until
then, the sun holds no heat, there's ice in
the heart of the earth. Two years from now
and I'll be able to give my mulatto mother a
bath, the half-white bitch!" he added,
beginning to leap up and down in an
explosion of glassy eyed fury. [p. 80]

This confused, enraged, apocalyptic fury reveals more
anger than mixed-up Bloom's integrative hallucinations, however, as Ellison attempts to create a verbal schematic of the infernal regions of the black
experience.

One scapegoat follows another in this Alabama
nighttown when Norton, described as "an aged doll,"
becomes the next "sacrifice" to emerge after
Supercargo is subdued. [p. 84] And Bloom's transformation into an infant during his sado-masochistic
fantasy is recalled too when Norton is described by
one of the prostitutes as "Just a little white baby."
[p. 86] Then the prostitutes threaten Norton, much
as the Dublin whores intimidate Bloom:

"You just like white men, Edna. That's
all," the skinny one said.
Edna shook her head and smiled as
though amused at herself. "I sho do. I
just love 'em. Now this one, old as he is,
he could put his shoes under my bed any
night."
"Shucks, me I'd kill an old man like
that."

> "Kill him nothing," Edna said. "Girl,
> don't you know that all these rich ole white
> men got monkey glands and billy goat balls?
> These ole bastards don't never git enough.
> They want to have the whole world."
>   The doctor looked at me and smiled.
> "See, now you're learning all about
> endocrinology," he said. "I was wrong when
> I told you that he was only a man; it seems
> now that he's either part goat or part ape.
> Maybe he's both!" [p. 86-87]

This not so mad glimpse at Norton's repressed
sexuality, at his comic affinity to an old goat, and
to an aged, sexual scapegoat in this mock reversal,
then, carries Joycean undertones.

     The women are sent away and Norton is safer under
the care of the Vet, but Norton must endure the Vet's
life story and a much deserved insult before the
nighttown experience ends: "To some, you are the
great white father, to others the lyncher of souls,
but for all, you are confusion come into the Golden
Day." [p. 91-92] It is this modified Joycean
"confusion," this American "confusion," resulting
from the oppression and the resultant mutilation of
the psyches both of the Hegelian "lord" and of the
"bondsman," that reveals the most profound similarity
between the "Circe" section and the Golden Day
episode.

     When Ellison parodied "Circe," however, he did
not mean to equate Norton with Bloom, for Norton
could never conceive of Bloom's magnanimity, but
rather, Ellison seems to have inserted much of the
Joycean schema into his x-ray vision of the American
unconscious in recognition of the fact that the black
experience bears analogies to the Irish ordeal, and
further, that the effects of oppression will produce
some rather universal phenomena: role playing,
paranoic delusions, scapegoating, and a general sense
of "confusion" and psychological chaos that leaves
both cultures in a "nowhere" state of mind. And, as
in "Circe," where initiatory chaos is parodied and
found perverted, so in the Golden Day episode, the
chthonic descent into the psyche yields only marginal
transformation. Vet does, however, impart some
wisdom concerning the Hegelian duo, Norton and Jack,
which will stew in Jack's mind for years before it is
finally understood:

"He believes in you as he believes in the beat of his heart. He believes in that great false wisdom taught slaves and pragmatists alike, that white is right. I can tell you his destiny. He'll do your bidding, and for that his blindness is his chief asset. He's your man, friend. Your man and your destiny. Now the two of you descend the stairs into chaos and get the hell out of here. I'm sick of both of you pitiful obscenities! Get out before I do you both the favor of bashing in your heads!" [p. 94]

Joycean influences and archaic imagery continue to inform the double perspective of Ellison's novel. Barbee's speech to the regimented students and trustees recalls the long Jesuit diatribe that so terrifies Stephen in A Portrait. And, as in Joyce's novel, another abortive rite is to occur. The students enter the squat, vine covered chapel which appears to be "more earth-sprung than man sprung." The sound of the bells, their "doomlike" ring, is oppressive to Jack. He walks by "the rows of puritanical benches straight and torturous, finding that to which I am assigned and bending my body to its agony." [p. 108] The "defeated" students are to hear a modified rite of white America, "a black rite of Horatio Alger," which is

performed to God's own acting script, with millionaires come down to portray themselves; not merely acting out the myth of their goodness, and wealth and success and power and benevolence and authority in cardboard masks, but themselves, these virtues concretely! Not the wafer and the wine, but the flesh and the blood, vibrant and alive, and vibrant even when stooped, ancient and withered. [p. 109]

This secularization of bread and wine into the business of religion contains elements of ancient ritual in an atrophied state. For this rite is to describe "the limitations of our lives and the boldness of our aspirations. . . ." [p. 110] Barbee and Bledsoe serve as the initiators who will not, of course, reveal the creation of the world as enacted

by the ancient god-hero, but, instead, the creation
of the American Dream, of the new, materialistic god,
wrought by the secular god-heroes: the millionaires,
the trustees--who themselves become the student's
"thunder and lightning." Ironically, it is to Susie
Gresham that Jack must turn in this desacralized
chapel for an initiatory lesson, for like Lorraine
Hansberry's strong mother, who preserves her dead
husband's tough dream in A Raisin in the Sun, Susie
bears the correct interpretation of possibilities
which was taught to her by the Founder. Jack
dedicates his singing to her:

> Ha! Susie Gresham, Mother Gresham, guardian
> of the hot young women on the puritan
> benches who couldn't see your Jordan's water
> for their private steam; you relic of
> slavery whom the campus loved but did not
> understand, aged, of slavery, yet bearer of
> something warm and vital and all-enduring,
> of which in that island of shame we were not
> ashamed--it was to you on the final row I
> directed my rush of sound, and it was to you
> of whom I thought with shame and regret as I
> waited for the ceremony to begin. [p. 112]

Certainly Bledsoe is no proper initiator, for
Jack describes him as "a portly head waiter," an
English butler, who, nonetheless, conceals a perverted manna as the white man's lackey while he
interprets and enforces white definitions of black
roles and aspirations to his charges in this euphe-
mistic and "meaningless ritual." [pp. 112, 115]

Barbee proceeds to interpret the grandiose deeds
of the Founder when he casts the man's life into the
heroic mold during the histrionics that follow:

> "And into this land came a humble prophet,
> lowly like the humble carpenter of Nazareth,
> a slave and a son of slaves, knowing only
> his mother. A slave born, but marked from
> the beginning by a high intelligence and a
> princely personality; born in the lowest
> part of this barren, war scarred land, yet
> somehow shedding light upon it where'er he
> passed through. I'm sure you have heard of
> his precarious infancy, his precious life
> almost destroyed by an insane cousin who

splashed the babe with lye and shrivelled
his seed and how, a mere babe, he lay nine
days in a deathlike coma and then suddenly
and miraculously recovered. You might say
that it was as though he had risen from the
dead or been reborn." [p. 116-17]

Barbee's need to embalm real life with myth is
laughable to Jack, and Ellison may well agree with
Rank that the hero myth is basically a "paranoic
structure" reflective of individual neurotic
behavior.[37] For in that myth, the hero's fatherless
state may indicate the hero's neurotic wish-
fulfillment to eliminate the father and possess the
mother by becoming the father of himself. This
appears to be implicit in Barbee's account of the
Founder. And the "insane cousin" in Barbee's sermon
recalls Rank's observation that the child may project
this hatred of the father onto a surrogate, a surrogate feared as a murderous persecutor by the child.

Outlines of the hero myth derived from Rank and
Raglan are parodied by Ellison as Barbee's mythological hype continues. The Founder is self-exiled; he
leads his people across a "blood-red sea" of
lingering Civil War hatreds; his initiation is presided over by an "emissary direct from above"; and
although he is shot in the head, he undergoes a mira-
culous rebirth. [pp. 118-19] Indeed, a skillful
slave, not unlike the Vet, a slave who knows his
medicine and serves as the town's scapegoat, becomes
the Founder's initiator, and Barbee's imagery
suggests both symbolic circumcision and rebirth
during his account of the Founder's escape:

"For he shaved our skull, and cleansed our
wound and bound it neat with bandages stolen
from the home of an unsuspecting leader of
the mob, ha! And you recall how you plunged
with the Founder, the Leader, deep into the
black art of escape, guided at first,
indeed, initiated by the seemingly demented
one who had learned his craft in slavery."
[p. 120]

Barbee's mythomania continues when he describes the
death of the Founder in solar imagery as "the great
sun going down." Comic deflations of Barbee and
Bledsoe reveal Jack's contempt for such mytholo-

gizing. For Ellison sharply undercuts their exuberence. And the revelation that Barbee is blind implies that he suffers from spiritual blindness, that he has never been reborn. This rite is false from the start. And a mature Jack, reminiscing from his coalhole, sees that rite as one which enforces limitations on possibilities, much as Stephen, who senses that the Jesuit sermon would wilt human freedom and autonomy through bloodless myth, rejects his Jesuit indoctrination. This rite of Horatio Alger becomes as hollow for Jack as the sermon finally becomes for ambivalent Stephen, and the tendency to cast the chaos of life into the assurances of myth will largely be rejected by both young protagonists.

Vet's advice to Jack will offer an alternative to the desacralized rite. Although Vet admits that there is no "cure" for his own soul sickness, he does prescribe some medicine for Jack during the train ride. First, he recommends that Jack not see the world through mythological eyes, but understand it as an ever-changing game instead.

"Play the game but don't believe in it--that much you owe yourself. Even if it lands you in a straightjacket or a padded cell. Play the game but play it your own way--part of the time at least. Play the game but raise the ante, my boy. Learn how it operates, learn how you operate--I wish I had more time to tell you only a fragment. We're an ass-backward people, though. You might even beat the game though. Its really a crude affair. Really pre-Renaissance--and that game has been analysed, put down in books. But down here they've forgotten to take care of the books and that's your opportunity. You're hidden right out in the open--that is, you would be if you only realized it. They wouldn't see you because they don't expect you to know anything, since they believe they've taken care of that. . . ." [pp. 151-52]

America has muddled its own mythology, but it has unwittingly left some openings, dropped its guard in a few places. Vet's advice would allow Jack, and the oppressed in general, to stretch the limits and sub-

255

vert the dominant culture's attempts to keep blacks
down. Vet's initiation of Jack continues:

> "Now is the time for offering fatherly
> advice," he said, "but I'll spare you that--
> since I guess I'm nobody's father except my
> own. Perhaps that's the advice to give you:
> be your own father, young man. And
> remember, the world is full of possibility
> if only you'll discover it. Last of all,
> leave the Norton's alone, and if you don't
> know what I mean, think about it.
> Farewell." [p. 154]

Vet's advice seems to echo Stephen Dedalus' self-
originating fantasies as well as Stephen's conviction
that history might reveal infinite possibilties, that
it is largely a web of chance combinations of events,
an "open" system. Stephen reflects in "Nestor":

> Had Pyrrhus not fallen by a bedlam's hand in
> Argos or Julius Caeser not been knifed to
> death? They are not to be thought away.
> Time has branded them and fettered they are
> lodged in the room of the infinite possibil-
> ities they have ousted. But can those have
> been possible seeing that they never were?
> Or was that only possible which came to
> pass? Weave, weaver of the wind. [U, p.
> 25]

Vet's advice, like Stephen's reflections, reveals
that history is a game of chance and its movement,
therefore, is partially arbitrary and beyond human
control. His advice serves as Jack's most successful
approach to an initiation. And when Jack leaves the
train, archaic animal imagery of initiation is
apparent, for he feels "like something regurgitated
from the belly of some frantic whale." [IM, p. 156]
But Jack is still naive, and this initiation,
although more successful than Barbee's perverted
rite, is not fully understood by Jack. Experience
will offer his final rite, and he will conduct his
initiation, as Vet says he must, as the father of
himself, with more success perhaps than Stephen.

Peter Wheatstraw appears, on the mythic level, as
another possible initiator for Jack. Peter's "Fe Fi
Fo Fum" echoes both folklore and Joyce's Ulysses.

Wheatstraw's rhetoric of giants immediately follows his utterance of the Joycean-Viconian thunder word. Eliade notes that in ancient rites thunder was often simulated by the initiators in order to acknowledge the presence of the divine god or of the heroes. Wheatstraw's "Fe Fi Fo Fum," then, links him to the giants from folklore who appear in initiation rites. In Ulysses, Stephen muses over such folklore when he sits by the sea: "I'm the bloody well gigant rolls all them bloody well boulders, bones for my steppingstones. Feefawfum. I zmellz de bloodz odz an Iridzman." [pp. 44-45] Of Stephen's remembered images from the distant past, Vickery notes:

> In the nursery tale of the bloodthirsty giant and the hero there lurks analogues both to the Homeric Polyphemus and to the Frazerian giant who figured in initiation ceremonies of young men.[38]

And, as Trudier Harris has revealed, Wheatstraw tries to initiate Jack into the use of the trickster mask and to align Jack with West African folklore. But Jack refuses to wear the rabbit mask or to play the dozens.[39] Wheatstraw grows in complexity for he is a blend of many folkoric elements, with the African element a component. In any case, although Jack fails to grasp much of Wheatstraw's meaning, Jack's memory does record this encounter and its impact is understood in his subsequent thoughts.

The cyclic structure of Invisible Man continues when uninitiated Jack meets another victim of the confused and impotent rites of fatherless America, Emerson's son. The son's belief that no one in America has any identity serves to epiphanize the problem of rites of passage in the novel and to emphasize that this problem is a multi-racial one. And certainly Jack is not much better off than the son at this point in the novel, for Jack's lingering dependence of the mother-surrogate Mary Rambo reveals that he has yet to separate from the maternal world.

And Jack undergoes yet another truncated rite when he descends into the chaos of the gooey, womb-like paint factory. Paranoid Brockway serves as Jack's inept initiator into a world of work where knowledge of the job is withheld rather than given.

Jack recalls that during the explosion he "seemed to sink to the center of a lake of heavy water and pause, transfixed and numb with the sense that I had lost irrevocably an important victory." [p. 225] His womb-like immersion leads to no rebirth but only serves as a prelude to the horrors of the next symbolic womb Jack languishes in, the hospital machine.

In the hospital episode archaic initiation imagery again underlies much of the action, and Jack moves still closer to the primal chaos that this per- verted rebirth obviates. Tongue-tied Jack recalls Eliade's description of the prohibition against speech that occurs in many primitive rites of passage, a prohibition "open to. . . twofold interpretation--as death, and as return to earliest infancy. The neophyte is either dead, or scarcely born--more precisely, he is being born."[40] Jack describes his regression to earliest infancy in similar terms:

> I tried to remember how I'd gotten here, but nothing came. My mind was blank, as though I'd just begun to live. When the next face appeared I saw the eyes behind the thick glasses blinking as though noticing me for the first time. [p. 228]

Jack finds himself in the belly of a mechanical initiatory monster: "I was not lying on an operating table but in a kind of glass and nickel box, the lid of which was propped open." [p. 228] The doctor's desire to extinguish Jack's earlier self fails utterly, however, and the real spirits of the dead enter Jack's mind to subversively initiate Jack, when he recalls memories and folkloric motifs from his childhood identity:

> Oh, doctor, I thought drowsily, did you ever wade in a brook before breakfast? Ever chew on sugar cane? You know, doc, the same fall day I first saw the hounds chasing black men in stripes and chains my grandmother sat with me and sang with twinkling eyes:
>> "Godamighty made a monkey
>> Godamighty made a whale
>> And Godamighty made a 'gator
>> With hickeys all over his tail. . ."
> [p. 229]

Eliade's observation on the return of dead ancestors
in the initiation ceremony seems to apply here, and
the now familiar animal imagery appears again when
Jack recalls an old wisdom.   But the doctor would,
on the mythic level, view the hospital machine as a
divine agent in Jack's electric birth.   He warns his
colleagues, ". . . from now on do your praying to my
little machine, I'll deliver the cure."   [p. 230]
When electricity flows through Jack's body, the rug
at the battle royal is recalled, for one of the
hospital attendants cries, "Look, he's dancing.
. . ." The voice Jack hears suggesting "Why not
castration, doctor?" recalls, again, the circumcision
or stomach wound the novices often received in primitive puberty rites. [pp. 231-32][41] Then, too, Jack's
temporary blindness recalls the blindfolded boxers at
the battle royal and the motif of blindness in the
ancient rites. Chaos returns to him once more:

> I seemed to have lost all sense of
> proportion. Where did my body end and the
> crystal and white world begin? Thoughts
> evaded me, hiding in the vast stretch of
> clinical whiteness to which I seemed con-
> nected only by a scale of receding grays.
> No sounds beyond the sluggish inner roar of
> the blood.   I couldn't open my eyes.   I
> seemed only to exist in some other
> dimension, utterly alone. . . .   [p. 233]

Jack's inability to answer the doctor's question,
"WHAT IS YOUR NAME?" recalls, too, the motif in
ancient rites where the old name of the novice must
be forgotten.   [p. 334]   And the theme of the
separation from the mother is perversely restated
here when Jack, echoing Stephen, recalls:

> Mother, who was my mother? Mother, the one
> who screams when you suffer--but who? This
> was stupid, you always knew your mother's
> name. Who was it that screamed? Mother?
> But the scream came from the machine. A
> machine my mother? . . . Clearly I was out
> of my head. [p. 235]

Of the hospital machine and Jack's mechanical
rebirth, William J. Schafer has noted:

> The apparatus which resurrects the invisible
> man is a mechanical womb, complete with

umbilical cord attached to his stomach which
is finally cut by the doctors: he is
delivered of the machine, and the doctors
pronounce his new name--yet he remains
nameless.[42]

But luckily for Jack the dead come to rescue him when
he recalls his old rabbit masks from childhood,
"Buckeye, the Rabbit" and "Brer Rabbit."[43] The
electricity has literally shocked Jack back to
himself; he is becoming authentic; he is consciously
aligning himself with rabbit men, with the tricksters
of his folk heritage, with his grandfather, and with
Wheatstraw. Much as Trueblood is not destroyed by
his initiatory plunge into the womb and the underworld of the unconscious; much as he realizes that
"A man ain't nothing but a man;" so Jack discovers
part of the mystery of life: "When I discover who I
am, I'll be free." [p. 237] Ironically, Jack is
being joined to his folk heritage and to that inner
self, despite the doctor's intentions. The spirits
of the dead have returned in the form of once
forgotten memories to work their curative and
initiatory magic.

The experience Jack endures at the Chthonian
serves as yet another perverted rite. Jack is
welcomed to the Brotherhood in a confused series of
events which remind him of his initiation into his
college fraternity, and, on the mythic level, recall
initiation rites into primitive secret societies.
His initiators, however, become both Brother Jack and
Emma, for unlike primitive secret societies, this
moeity is sexually "integrated." Distorted echoes
from primitive rites continue. Brother Jack asks
Jack to forget any former identity, to "put aside"
the past, to refrain from writing to his family, to
move away from Mary's boarding house. But it is Emma
who reaches "into the bosom of her taffeta hostess
gown" to offer Jack the notification of his new identity in the form of an envelope containing his new
name. [p. 302] Eliade's description of the rebirth
and the common custom of giving new names to the
novices that accompanies initiation, is pertinent
here if we are to understand the mythic level of
Jack's night in the Chthonian.[44] But the rite is, of
course, a failure. In fact it is not perceived as a
rite by the Brotherhood, and Emma's role in the
unacknowledged event recalls the confusion of male

and female authority rampant in Joyce's nighttown.
Jack is not reborn in the Chthonian except on the
superficial level; no profound inner transformation
occurs; his slow, dark birth is still pending. The
tearing of his eyes after the drunk's Freudian
slip during the confused rendition of "St. Louis
Blues," "St. Louis mammieeeee-with her diamond
riiiings. . .," links the initiatory wound with
subliminal castration. [p. 305] But the rite is a
dead end; Jack shares no fundamental feeling of
brotherhood with a group that would exclude him and
eventually use him to unglue Harlem.

Jack's subsequent rejection of the Brotherhood
and his temporary flirtation with the masks of
Rinehart offer other variations on the theme of
rites of passage:

> It was as though by dressing and walking in
> a certain way I had enlisted in a fraternity
> in which I was recognized at a glance--not
> by features, but by clothes, by uniform, by
> gait. [p. 474]

But the Rinehart philosophy Jack momentarily espouses
in this strange rite reveals another parody of initiatory chaos. In the symbolic dark glasses, Jack
would be forever blindfolded, forever unborn:

> His [Rinehart's] world was possible and he
> knew it. He was years ahead of me and I was
> a fool. I must have been crazy and blind.
> The world in which we lived was without
> boundaries. A vast, seething, hot world of
> fluidity, and Rine the rascal was at home.
> Perhaps only Rine the rascal was at home in
> it. It was unbelievable, but perhaps only
> the unbelievable could be believed. Perhaps
> the truth was always a lie. [p. 487]

Jack goes on to contemplate possibility gone mad, a
possibility that obscures human identity, when he
emerges from this perverted rite:

> You could actually make yourself anew. The
> notion was frightening; for now the world
> seemed to flow before my eyes. All bound-
> aries down, freedom was not only the
> recognition of necessity, it was the

261

recognition of possibility. And sitting
there trembling I caught a brief glimpse of
the possibilities and turned away. It was
too vast and confusing to contemplate. [p.
488]

Jack learns his existentialism on the streets; he
discovers the terrible burden of freedom in the
chaotic yet static ghetto.

The events of the Harlem riot reveal further
analogies with the motifs of the rite of passage.
This cyclic novel reveals one of its most grueling
cycles when Jack once again is plunged into initiatory chaos. And one of Jack's initiators is
Dupre, a street version both of existential man and
of rugged American individualism. For Dupre does not
wish to be a leader; instead, he wants each man in
his group to feel individually responsible for his
own actions despite the fact that these acts might be
committed in concert with the acts of the others.
Yet Jack describes Dupre's men as blind moles who
work deep in the earth, and he begins to recoil from
his own absorption of selfhood into the mass hysteria
of the riot. Although Jack finds Dupre's self-
determination admirable, Jack must reject the
violence of the riot as being yet another dangerous
flirtation with chaos that leads nowhere. For Jack
is slowly realizing that in America, the rite of
passage may well need be an existential one, self-
administered.[45]

And Jack's experience in the underground coalhole
reveals such a self-administered rite of passage
complete with archaic imagery. For previously, in
Jack's dream of castration, which preceded his fall
into the coalhole, Jack asserted his new found
selfhood against history and history's mechanizers of
consciousness. In the dream he loses all sense of
time. He enters an initiatory chaos that will continue in the underground coalhole until he is ready
to come out. For Jack's hole is symbolic of the initiatory womb of rebirth and not of death in the womb.
For it is in the underground that Jack nurtures and
develops that sense of wholeness he experienced at
the close of his dream of castration. And it is
here, too, that Jack is finally able to separate from
the regressive maternal world, from the lure of Mary
Rambo. Jack finally emerges from the underground

with his novel, as a writer instead of a ranter. The
"initiation of a greenhorn," as Ellison put it, has
finally been accomplished. And unlike less intact
Stephen, Jack has "forged" his conscience, for Jack's
social responsibility as a writer induces him to help
his public strip dangerous illusions. Jack is now an
anti-hero, whereas Stephen still basks in the heroic
role at the end of A Portrait. Yet, like Stephen,
Jack links himself to an apostolic succession, to
those anti-heroes past and present who have in turn
stripped illusions, to Armstrong, to his grandfather,
to the black youths on the subway, to Wheatstraw, to
Trueblood and the characters of folklore, to Vet, to
Douglass, and to all the rest who have discovered the
positive power of true invisibility. The culture and
rites of America are in disarray. But from the
fragments of remaining folk wisdom and motherwit, he
creates a conscience from an anti-rite, as it were,
from an initiation into the role of inveterate
subversive.[46]

Yet although Jack finally rejects the heroic
role, the hero myth does inform his final assertion
of conscience. For much like Stephen Dedalus, Jack
must, unwittingly and paradoxically, course stages of
the hero myth in order to escape heroics. As Ellison
has revealed, his own readings of Raglan's The Hero
and of Rank's The Myth of the Birth of the Hero
influenced this novel. Then too. Joyce may well
have been influenced by Rank's treatise on the hero
as Shechner has noted. for Rank published it in
1909.[47] Indeed, Schechner argues that Stephen's
theory of fatherhood and sonship in Ulysses appear to
be very close to Rank's description of these estates
in the various hero myths Rank examines.[48]
Basically, the myths can be broken down into child's
fantasy that he was born of noble parents, but he has
since been abandoned, stolen, or misplaced in
infancy; that he was raised by a second set of
parents in less lavish circumstances, and that he
eventually returned to his high born parents. Freud,
Rank's teacher, spoke of two periods in the family
romance--a pre-oedipal period during which the child
doubts the authenticity of his father and mother, and
a later sexual stage, where the mother is seen as
biologically certain but the father is denied as
incertus. Shechner reveals:

> The similarity of certain of Stephen's
> remarks to Freud's description of the sexual

phase is striking. Freud attributed the
change in the family romance to the child's
discovery of parental sexuality: "When
presently the child comes to know of various
kinds of sexual relations between fathers
and mothers and realizes that 'pater semper
incertus est,' while the mother is
'certissima,' the family romance undergoes a
peculiar curtailment; it contents itself
with exalting the child's father, but no
longer casts any doubts on his maternal
origin, which is regarded as something
unalterable."[49]

Hence, the hero may opt, as do Stephen and Jack, for
a spiritual father. But Ellison varies the apostolic
theme. Jack exalts his grandfather while he ignores,
for the most part, any mention of his biological
parents. Jack's new lowly parents become, as Clipper
argues, his Alma Mater, controlled by Bledsoe, the
"coal black daddy," as well as the Brotherhood and
Mary Rambo.[50] Stephen's rage against his father in
Stephen Hero is reminiscent of Jack's rage against
Bledsoe and other lowly father surrogates: Brockway,
Brother Jack, and Ras. Stephen argues that

Armor matris, subjective and objective
genitive, may be the only true thing in
life. Paternity may be a legal fiction.
Who is the father of any son that any son
should love him or he any son. [U, p. 207]

In Ulysses, Daedalus is replaced by Shakespeare as
the spiritual father as Shechner notes, and this
cuckolded mentor serves Stephen better "because as
father, the unmanned Shakespeare has already been
wounded in accordance with the parricidal wishes of
the son who aspires to succeed him."[51] Stephen's
adherence to the Sabellian heresy also reveals

that Stephen fancies himself not merely a
spiritual son, but the true apostolic suc-
cessor, who is in all ways consubstantial
with the him who came before. As the son,
he is the father or, in Sabellian terms, a
mode of the same being. Thus it is possible
for Stephen to fancy himself both Hamlet
pere and Hamlet fils, ghost and prince, all
in all.[52]

Thus, the hero myth allows Stephen to neutralize his real parents and "Instead of the hero as secret prince, Stephen gives us the hero as selfmade man."[53] Shechner continues, "if the father and the son are identical in essence, no mother is needed, for the son, as Stephen puts it, is 'an androgynous angel, being a wife unto himself.'"[54] Of Stephen's narcissistic triumph, Shechner concludes:

> The autonomous creator-God is free from the authority of the father, the treachery of the brothers, and the seductions of the mother, for he has triumphed over childhood and sexuality. As bisexual creator of his own family, he is not only free from anxiety and guilt, but, as creator of his own parents, is free of the infantile help-lessness and filial dependence. He is infallible.[55]

For as artist, Stephen can create and manipulate his biography in order to control and define his parents and his enemies by casting them into fictional characters. He is an artist-god. And paranoia and narcissism are clearly the stuff of these heroics, heroics both Stephen and Jack will finally attempt to transcend. Stephen's self-naming as "Autontim-erumenos. Bous Stephenoumenos" also recalls Ishmael's assertion, "Call me Ishmael," and Jack's, "Call me Jack-the-Bear." [U, p. 210; IM, p. 6] But in Ulysses Buck Mulligan finds Stephen's narcissism laughable, and he wounds Stephen emotionally with his verbal barbs when he grabs his own head and pretends that he is Zeus giving birth to Athena. And later Mulligan mocks: "Everyman his own wife" in "Scylla and Charybdis." [p. 494] Stephen's self-originating fantasy is further debunked in "Circe" when Bloom hallucinates giving birth to a baby during a mock virgin birth.

Stephen's assumption of the mask of artist-hero, then, serves as a prop for a nervous self-administered rite of initiation. Much as Rank's paranoid hero would reject the earthbound world of his father and seek an apostolic succession with spiritual fathers so as to create the world anew, Stephen uses his artistic world and his vision of freedom as a means to those ends. And indeed the act of creation itself comes for Stephen to symbolize a

self-administered rite, for he enters the spiritual
womb of his imagination in order to be reborn.

In Stephen Hero, Stephen had begun to outline
this rite via aesthetics:

> The artist, he imagined, standing in the
> position of mediator between the world of
> his experience and the world of his dreams
> "a mediator, consequently gifted with twin
> faculties, a selective faculty and a
> reproductive faculty. To equate these
> faculties was the secret of artistic
> success: the artist could disentangle the
> subtle soul of the image from its mesh of
> defining circumstances most exactly and
> "re-embody" it in artistic circumstances
> chosen as the most exact for it in its new
> office, he was the supreme artist. [pp.
> 177-78]

Much as the object reaches its separateness and
epiphany, so the psyche of the artist-hero is born,
reborn, that is, in the initiatory act of recreating
the world through art in a slow, dark birth. Stephen
defines his concept of epiphany in Stephen Hero with
the language of Aristotle and Aquinus:

> "This is the moment which I call epiphany.
> First we recognize that the object is one
> integral thing, then we recognize that it is
> an organized composite structure, a thing in
> fact: finally, when the relation of the
> parts is exquisite, when the parts are
> adjusted to the special point, we recognize
> that it is that thing which it is. Its
> soul, its whatness, leaps to us from the
> vestment of its appearance. The soul of the
> commonest object, the structure of which is
> so adjusted, seems to us radiant. The
> object achieves its epiphany." [p. 213]

As with the object, so with the conscience of the
artist. The two radiances are dependent. Both must
be recreated, birthed by the artist-hero. For in
Stephen Hero and A Portrait Stephen feels that he is
a foster child with no kinship to his biological
family: "He felt that he was hardly of the one blood
with them but stood to them rather in the mystical

266

kinship of fosterage, fosterchild, and foster-brother." [P, p. 350] Stephen even suggests to Cranly that Jesus was the son of God and not of Mary. And his paranoid fantasy reaches absurd heights with his definition of the artist as both priest and God, who, "like the God of the creation, remains within or behind or beyond or above his handiwork, invisible, refined out of existence, indifferent, paring his fingernails." [P, p. 483]

Such heroics, however, are satirized by Joyce, and the more restricted appearance of the heroic role is also partially debunked by Ellison's existential skepticism in Invisible Man. Yet the reasons for Stephen's and Jack's heroics partially stem from the same phenomena: incompetent parents. Christopher Lasch reveals that in the face of weak parents the child will often attempt to become the mother or father of himself. This causes the early narcissistic concepts of the parents experienced by the child in early infancy to linger on in the child's fantasy life and to serve as a defense against his realization of his parent's fallibility.[56]

Heinz Kohut has also shown that if the child cannot pass through oedipal identity-formation, he may think of himself as a god by means of a defensive narcissism, a regression to the "grandiose self."[57] Rank stated the problem somewhat differently years before. For Rank, as the child grows, the parent-child relationship may break down. The child then may regress to the happy time when the father appeared all powerful, the mother all good. Indeed, the lingering overvaluation of the parents continues as a defense. For Rank, two sets of parents emerge in the hero myth and in the neurotic, as well, and in the final phase of the hero myth:

these new and highborn parents are invested throughout with the qualities which are derived from real memories of the true lowly parents, so that the child does not actually remove his father but exaults him. The entire endeavor to replace the real father by a more distinguished one is merely the expression of the child's longing for the vanished happy time, when his father still appeared to be the strongest and the great-est man and the mother seemed the dearest

and most beautiful woman. The child turns
away from the father. as he now knows him.
to the father in whom he believed in his
earlier years. his imagination being in
truth the expression of regret for this
happy time having passed away. Thus the
overvaluation of the earliest years of
childhood again claims its own in these
fancies. [58]

As Schafer notes, Ellison leaves out the birth from
highborn parents in Invisible Man (as does Joyce).
but the grandfather offers a variation of that theme.
a variation which Rank accounted for. and the grandfather, indeed, becomes Jack's highborn father-
surrogate, much as Susie Gresham serves as his
spiritual guide as well. [59] Stephen, of course, links
himself to many elevated "parents": Thoth. Daedalus.
the Virgin, Shakespeare, Parnell, and Christ. Rank
reveals the neurotic base to all of this assertion of
ego:

> The paranoiac is apt to claim that the
> people whose name he bears are not his real
> parents. but that he is actually the son of
> a princely personage; he was to be removed
> for some mysterious reason, and was there-
> fore surrendered to his "parents" as a
> foster child. His enemies, however, wish
> to maintain the fiction that he is of lowly
> descent, in order to suppress his legitimate
> claims to the crown or to enormous riches. [60]

In short, the failure of the father to serve as
an adequate model forces the child to reactivate
archaic parent images; the hero must become the
father of himself, but in the process Rank tells us,

> by putting himself in the place of the
> father or the emperor--the anarchist
> complies more faithfully with the heroic
> character, by promptly himself becoming the
> persecutor of kings, and finally killing the
> king, precisely like the hero. [61]

Jack's recurrent desire to kill father-figures, i.e.,
Brockway, Bledsoe, and Brother Jack, result from his
project of becoming the father of himself, and it is

this violent paranoia Jack ultimately casts aside.
And finally, both Stephen and Jack begin to discover
humility as they put childish paranoia aside, as
they realize that they are "all in all." But Jack's
repudiation of the violent aspects of the heroic
posture does not rule out the fact that he does
embrace his grandfather's faith in the idealism of
the U.S. Constitution as a necessary replacement for
the debasement of that document. Jack does indeed
return to a highborn parent, symbolically, in a
bloodless act of existential violence: the affir-
mation of American democracy and equality of
opportunity and recognition--a dangerous revolutionary act in a society that has often forgotten its
revolution. And so Jack does ultimately accept the
self-originating fantasy implicit in the hero myth to
a degree. In a fatherless world the myth's existential, and, if we accept Rank's judgement, paranoid
appearance cannot be avoided. And in the Constitution, America defined itself, broke from its feudal
parents, and committed itself to making the fantasy a
reality.

The theme of truncated rites of passage occurs
obsessively and with near equal complexity in
Wright's works as well, and the possible influence
of Joyce on Wright's development of this theme also
needs to be argued.

As we might expect, rites of passage are
perverted in Wright's novels. Yet a Joycean
influence is less certain than is the case with
Ellison, although the few possible Joycean echoes
do need to be mentioned briefly. In Black Boy
Richard observes:

Whenever I thought of the essential
bleakness of black life in America, I knew
that Negroes had never been allowed to catch
the full spirit of Western Civilization,
that they lived somehow in it but not of it.
And when I brooded upon the cultural barren-
ness of black life, I wondered if clean,
positive tenderness, love, honor, loyalty,
and the capacity to remember were native
with man. I asked myself if these human
qualities were not fostered, won, struggled
and suffered for, preserved in ritual
from one generation to another. [p.33]

The pattern of ritual has clearly disintegrated in Wright's black America. When Richard is six, he wanders into a bar. The people inside force liquor down his throat and try to force a cigar into his mouth. One of the drunks asks Richard: "How do you feel, setting there like a man, boy?" [p. 27] Another man pays Richard to whisper obscene words in a woman's ear. Rather than exist in the perverse shadow of such ritual, Richard provides his own rites of passage. He beats some youths with sticks in order to walk the streets of Memphis freely. Later, he and his friends enter a train engine and pretend that they are engineers. And, much as Stephen Dedalus finally recoils from the rites of the Jesuit church, the rites of Richard's family church sicken Richard. In an episode highly reminiscent of Stephen's immersion into the apocalyptic imagery and the stale dogma of the Jesuit order, Richard is coerced by a preacher to join the church where he is warned of his soul's peril.

In Native Son the murder of Mary is a perverted, self-devised rite that gives Bigger a false sense of power:

> He had murdered and he had created a new life for himself. It was something that was all his own, and it was the first time in his life he had had anything that others could not take away from him. [p. 101]

This violent act causes him to feel a sense of equality:

> The knowledge that he had killed a white girl they loved and regarded as their symbol of beauty made him feel the equal of them, like a man who had been somehow cheated, but had now evened the score. [p. 155]

His compulsive need to administer his own violent rites results from a deep void within himself that seeks what America will not provide:

> a vast configuration of images and symbols whose magic and power could lift him up and make him live so intensely that the dread of being black and unequal would be forgotten . . . . [p. 256]

270

Near the conclusion of Native Son, Bigger confesses:

> "I didn't want to kill!" Bigger shouted.
> "But what I killed for, I am! It must've
> been pretty deep in me to make me kill!
> I must have felt it awful hard to
> murder. . . ." [pp.391-92]

Bigger must prove his "manhood" and claim his autonomy through violence in the ritual vacuum of America through a self-devised series of rituals.

In The Outsider the violence again is substituted for the absence of viable rites, but as in Native Son a direct Joycean influence is doubtful. In The Long Dream the influence may also be oblique. This novel, however, presents a more positive father, Tyree. Although Fishbelly does not regard his father's attempt to make a "man" out of him with any seriousness during their trip to the brothel, and although Fish provides his own rite of passage when he cuts the entrails out of the dying dog, the hope is offered in this novel that Tyree may endure in Fishbelly's memory as a positive image, that Fish may try to emulate him in the future. Yet, as in the worlds of Joyce and Ellison, rites of passage are truncated or absent; the emerging self must give itself birth through some form of self-administered rite. But in Wright's black America the attempt is abortive, and the influence of Stephen Dedalus' ordeal on the struggles of Wright's heroes can only be surmised.

If Wright laments both the alleged lack of rites of passage in America and the exclusion of blacks from any positive initiation into the mainstream of American life, Ellison, seemingly in the spirit of Joyce, tries to use this vacuum as a strength. For in America the black man is in a unique position, by virtue of his invisibility, to question all roles with a positive skepticism. The mutilation of fatherhood, the inability to successfully merge with the mainstream of America are not altogether tragic for Jack. For America has failed in Ellison's view to even approach an enactment of its professed ideals. And until Americans fulfill the meaning of their Revolution, it is unwise for anyone to be mainstreamed into the social order. Vet's advice to Jack to "Be your own father, young man," recalls

271

Stephen's ordeal and serves as the culmination of the "unsubstantial father" theme that Ellison partially picked up from his malcontent, Irish precursor. For like Joyce, Ellison ultimately seems to celebrate the disruption of European feudalism, a lesion that has jeopardized the old identities and plunged the American into a search for a more enlightened national and personal character than one might find in Europe. Norris' observation of Joyce's viewpoint in the Wake applies, in part, to Ellison's view as well:

> Redemption in Finnegans Wake does not result from the new covenant forged by the guilt of the sons, nor from a divine pardon. As in Christian mythology, redemption comes from a kind of grace, but here a grace that transforms chaos into play, the loss of identity into freedom, and the fall of man into a celebration. [62]

Shem's and Jack's descents into the coalholes are fortunate falls into human motivation and naked chaos, into ghostly rogues' galleries of human depravity and human possibilities, where identities are confounded but where an authentic human essense can be found.

CONCLUSION

Ellison's and Wright's heroes often echo Stephen's call for a "new humanity," a humanity that is both introspective and physical, yet one which transcends all ubiquitous, negative stereotypes. Dreaming of an Ireland of the future, young Joyce fostered the hope that his country might yet become the "Hellas of the North," a land free from the unnecessary repressions of the church and from the slave-mentality of many of its citizens. [CWJJ, p. 172] Ellison and Wright also create heroes who long for an end to colonialism, but more importantly, for an awakening of the oppressor and the oppressed from their respective mind-forged manacles. Jack hopes that America might finally apply the principles of its Revolution to save both itself and him, but he reflects nervously, "yes, but what is the next phase? How often I have tried to find it." [IM, p. 563] For these writers the next phase would seem to bask in the rational light of Hegel, Bruno, Vico, Frazer, Freud, and Jung; the next phase must forge a collective, rational conscience that might once and for all expose the vast heart of darkness, the human unconscious. "Yeow," says young Stephen when he contemplates being washed in rice water instead of in the blood of the lamb. Cross Damon seeks a similar liberation from the ice-grip of the Protestant Ethic when he contrasts the spirit of jazz with the deadening processes of the West:

> He came to feel that this music was the rhythmic flauntings of guilty feelings, the syncopated outpourings of frightened joy existing in guises forbidden and despised by others. He sensed how Negroes had been made to live in but not of the land of their birth, how the injunctions of an alien Christianity and the structures of white laws had evoked in them the very longings and desires that religion and law had been designed to stifle. He realized that this blue-jazz was a rebel art blooming seditiously under the condemnations of a Protestant ethic just as his own consciousness had sprung conditioned to defiance from his relationship to his mother, who had shrilly evoked in him exactly what she had

so desperately tried to smother. Blue-jazz was the scornful gesture of men turned ecstatic in their state of rejection; it was the musical language of the satisfiedly amoral, the boastings of the contentedly lawless, the recreations of the innocently criminal. [TO, p. 274]

Jack, too, finds his head ringing with such a subversive yet liberating syncopation in his coalhole.

The "plague will soon be over" Joyce's bluesy dreamer hopes, and a new play, hopefully less bloody, might be enacted by a rational, introspective man who has rebelled, not as Marx would have it, against the oppressor alone, but against the Hegelian "lord" residing in the minds of men. For the Hegelian influence on these writers is clear and it posits that the true heart of darkness is not only to be found in the American South or in the Joyce's Dublin, Wright's Chicago, or Ellison's Harlem, but in the minds of their heroes and in the minds of all men. Unlike Marx, with whose dialectics all three writers flirted, the real revolution to overthrow illegitimate authority and to establish a more legitimate one must be carried out through each hero's revolution of introspection. Bakunin's well nown denunciation of Marx was certainly known to Joyce:

I wonder how Marx fails to see that the establishment of a . . . dictatorship to perform, in one way or another, as chief engineer of the world revolution, regulating and directing a revolutionary movement of the masses in all countries in a machine-like fashion--that the establishment of such a dictatorship would be enough of itself to kill the revolution and distort all popular movements. [63]

As with Ellison, Joyce preferred democracy over all other forms of government, for only within such a system could a legitimate authority structure arise.

Indeed, the Wake is a kind of Hegelian epic, where according to Benstock the haves and the have-nots struggle against one another in the dreamer's mind.[64] And if Benstock is correct in assuming that as epic, the <u>Wake</u> parodies the epic founding of a new nation, then we must see this new country as a region within as well as without. For Benstock's Joyce, the Viconian wheel of history must, for a while at least, stop turning of its own inertia when the native and invader fuse into one man; when Shem and Shaun combine into Kevin, himself washed in rice water and a possible hero of Hegelian rational consciousness, a hero who realizes that man is all in all.[65] When Muta and Juva look toward the future at the close of the <u>Wake</u>, they contemplate a new, more rational age:

> Muta: "So that when we shall have acquired unification we shall pass on to diversity and when we shall have passed on to diversity we shall have acquired the instinct of combat and when we shall have acquired the instinct of combat we shall pass back to the spirit of appeasement?"

> Juva: "By the light of the bright reason which daysends to us from the high." [p. 270]

The boomerangs of history, or the "bommeringstroms," and battles of the native and invader, of the haves and the have nots , may become "Hegelstroms" when humanity hopefully spirals to the next phase, to a democritized world.

What Stephen discovers through introspection into his own brow, a brow he must tap to drive out the internalized images of priest and king; what Shem discovers in the coalhole of his mind--these are similar to the epiphanies or many of Wright's and Ellison's characters: the "devil" is in all of us, and, like Wheatstraw, we are all the devil's own son-in-law, not poor innocents polluted by corrupting lynchers of consciousness. Jack admits:

> I carried my sickness and though for a long time I tried to place it in the outside world, the attempt to write it down shows me that at least half of it lay within me. [<u>IM</u>, p. 562]

The entry into the coalhole also becomes a chthonic, self-enactment of a rite of passage, an initiation into a brotherhood of folk heroes, into a political understanding that the black person in America must, as Robert Bone argues, neither become an assimilationist nor a nationalist, but rather, maintain a respect for the honesty and self-determination of the American folk heritage, while at the same time lay claim to the national identity. Bone explains:

> The assimilationist demands that in the name of integration the Negro self be put to death. But Ellison regards this proposal as a projection of self-hatred. To integrate means to make whole, not to lop off or mutilate; to federate as equals, not to merge and disappear. Anything else is a denial not only of one's racial identity but of one's national identity as well. For slavery really happened on American soil, and it has made us both, Negro and white alike, what we are today.[66]

Yet in the coalhole of his mind, Jack learns that he has not only been a pawn in the white game of black definition, but that he too, after sorting out his past, is also capable of "white" crimes. For, like the Hegelian "bondsman," Jack chases out the "master within" with a strong dose of mea culpa. And in his half-conscious collusion with the stereotyped definitions of himself and his blackness, he, like the Hegelian "lord" and "bondsman," has violated his inner self, that "area in which a man's feelings are more rational than his mind," where a man's "will is pulled in several directions at the same time," and, like the "lord," he too has found the need for the scapegoat. [IM, p. 560] This is what the death of Tod has taught him: that he is not so unlike the policeman, or the nervous crowd that laughs at the dolls, or the boy with the Slavic eyes.

Richard Sennett's descriptions of Hegel's radicalism and the stages of the "bondsman's" growing consciousness apply to the ordeals of the heroes of these writers, to the heroic search for this "rational consciousness." He argues that when Hegel's "bondsman" is able to pity the master,

> a fundamental power perceived in the person of the authority can be broken: His or her

power to inspire fear. As long as one perceives an authority as the source of pain,
the authority is indeed potent and fearful.
What happens to the image of the person in
authority when this bond of fear is then
broken? Is an authority inevitably rendered
illegitimate? [67]

Jack's disciplined call for love at the close of the
novel echoes Bloom's admonition to the citizen in
Barney Kiernan's pub. Jack's call reveals that he
has reached the calm following the Hegelian mental
storm:

I denounce because though implicated and
partially responsible, I have been hurt to
the point of abysmal pain, hurt to the point
of invisibility. And I defend because in
spite of it all I find that I love. In
order to get some of it down I have to love.
I sell you no phony forgiveness, I'm a
desperate man--but too much of your life
will be lost, its meaning lost, unless you
approach it as much through love as through
hate. So I approach it through division.
So I denounce and I defend and I hate and I
love. [IM, 566-67]

The transformation of Jack is revealed, too, when he
sees Norton in New York. Norton's person no longer
inspires fear or awe in Jack, only a guarded pathos.
In the coalhole Jack realizes, as does the dreamer of
the Wake, that "the desprot slave wager and foeman
feodal unsheckled" can be seen as the components of
all men as "now one and the same person." [p. 354]
Jack's point in the Epilogue is that the black person
may have gone deeper into this Hegelian journey; that
black America might prod much of white America along
the journey so that a genuine nation might be formed.

Jack realizes on the lower frequencies that his
experience of racism is an extreme example of the
universal human condition mirrored in the dominance
of school, of factory, of political meeting or of
bedroom; that the problem of transformation from the
postures of dominance lies with the transformation of
the oppressed more so than with the overthrow of the
oppressor. Sennett reveals that it was so for Hegel
as well, for "young Hegel thought that the burden of

establishing conditions of liberty in society lay with the oppressed; no benevolent Platonic guardian, no necessary angel, would come to the rescue."

And Jack solves the essential Hegelian problem, that consciousness can only be formed where there is recognition, for Jack allows the ghost of his grandfather and the pantheon of remembered folk heroes, both real and fictional, to offer their recognition, to render him visible. As the Hegelian "bondsman," Jack realizes that he no longer needs to be recognized by the "lord," by the Bledsoes, the Nortons, the Brotherhood, in order to come into consciousness of an identity. This is the radical act that makes violent revolution of the type that Ras provokes appear superfluous. Jack's mea culpa arises from his long ago need for recognition by the illegitimate bearers of authority who would not recognize his emergence in a rite, but, like the Joycean father, impact and greedily hold onto authority and deny the novice a recognition of his maturity. Jack defines his consciousness, newly liberated, not as a distinct and ungraspable mental state to those outside that experience. And this experience might well be emulated, if not given its due respect, by much of white America. Jack contemplates his grandfather's advice:

> Was it that we of all, we, most of all, had to affirm the principle, the plan in whose name we have been brutalized and sacrificed--not because we would always be weak, not because we were afraid or opportunistic, but because we were older than they, in the sense of what it took to live in the world with others and because they had exhausted in us, some--not much, but some--of the human greed and smallness, yes, and the fear and superstition that kept them running. (Oh, yes, they're running too, running all over themselves.) Or was it, did he mean that we should affirm the principle because we, through no fault of our own, were linked to all the others in the loud, clammering semi-visible world, that world seen only as a fertile field of exploitation by Jack and his kind, and with condenscension by Norton and his, who were tired of being the mere pawns in the futile game of "making history". [IM, p. 561]

In Ellison's "Juneteenth" Daddy Hickman does affirm the principle in what must be described as a failed initiation rite for Bliss into the mysteries of the possibilities of American life in the form of a sermon supervised, according to white Bliss, by "The true father, but black, black." [p. 262] Hickman shouts of the redemptive suffering of blacks in American history, a suffering that has made the black man wiser, older, more mature, according to Ellison, than his oppressors. In fact, Hickman reveals: "Time will come round when we'll have to be their eyes; time will swing and turn back around." [p. 226] The vision that Hickman hands down is one of an America where blacks do not simply efface themselves in a cultural melting pot, but where the wisdom of blacks modifies more powerfully than at present the moral, intellectual, and aesthetic possibilities of American life. The "inner beat" intuited by black Americans, which counterpoints with the whine of "the merry-go-round" of American life, must become the beat of all Americans, and if this fails "Maybe we won't be that people but we'll be a part of that people, we'll be an element in them, Amen!" [p. 273] For this displacement from Africa, tragic as it was, was also redemptive, the harbinger of a new birth, the synthesis of a new people: "We had a new name and a new blood, and we had a new task. . ." [p. 273] And that task for Hickman involves nothing less than the rejuventation of American life by a full integration of black folk wisdom into the mainstream of American life. America awaits its rite of passage.

APPENDIX ON MYTH

Another aspect of the Joyce-Ellison connection involves the deliberate yet highly ambiguous parodies of classical sources these writers undertake with such analogous improvisation.

Of Ellison's use of literary allusion Archie Sanders has written:

> Steeped in the classics and fascinated by mythology, Ellison would naturally conclude as had Joyce. . . and others before him-- that the classical, Odyssean structure was the only framework suited to his conception of man and his life. [1]

Although this is quite true, we should not become carried away with matching characters and plots from the Odyssey, the Orestia, the Aeneid or from any other classical source with plot and character in Invisible Man or in Joyce's Ulysses in any point for point way. For the method of allusion in the works of Joyce and Ellison, more so even than in the works of T. S. Eliot, for example, is the method of the ambiguous near-miss rather than the exact analogue; and often a character, theme, or plot structure may have several possible classical echoes which may only add to the confusion. The resultant ambiguity created by their method of allusion evokes a sense of discontinuity rather than of continuity with the classics, of free improvisation and literary syncopation. Kenner has detailed much of this ambiguity in his study of the narrative voices in Ulysses. He reveals that unlike Eliot and Pound, Joyce uses mythic frames to evoke confusion rather than Eliotic order, to simulate a sense of the contemporaneity of the present rather than a sense of collapsed time. Indeed, Eliot's assertion that Ulysses attempts to order the "immense panorama of futility and anarchy" in modern life by means of a double vision whereby the events of the present repeat events reenacted over and over again in classical sources in order to set up "a continuous parallel between contemporaneity and antiquity" is misapplied, according to Kenner. [2] Eliot's analysis of Joyce's "mythological method" does not account for the deliberate ambiguities that such a method implies.

Ellison would follow the lead of Joyce by using allusion for the purposes of disordering rather than of ordering links with the past. For in the literary worlds of Joyce and Ellison, incertitude and protean flux have won the day; in such worlds, speech and thought, the clothing of the mind, are everchanging, often false; custom and archetypes, the stuff of the dio boia; ultimate philosophical questions, unanswerable. The continuity of history and myth with the present is strained. The scripts of the past must be rewritten, Eliot's rage for order scrapped. "Its history repeating itself with a difference" says Bloom. And as Camus said, the lonely artist can only paint colors on the void. Jack's oration at Tod's funeral therefore deliberately denies any affinity with the epic funeral oration for the fallen hero:

> "What are you waiting for me to tell you?"
> I shouted suddenly, my voice strangely crisp
> on the windless air. "What good will it do?
> What if I say that this isn't a funeral,
> that it's a holiday celebration, that if you
> stick around the band will end up playing
> 'Damit-the-Hell the Fun's All Over'? Or do
> you expect to see some magic, the dead rise
> up and walk again? Go home, he's as dead as
> he'll ever die. That's the end in the
> beginning and there's no encore. There'll
> be no miracles and there's no one here to
> preach a sermon. Go home, forget him. He's
> dead and you've got all you can do to think
> about you." [IM, pp. 443-44]

In the mature works of Joyce and Ellison, the interface of Graeco-Roman myth with a doubting 20th century inevitably creates more tensions than it resolves. In his eulogy to Tod, Jack simply refuses to mythologize Tod into a hero:

> He fell in a heap like any man and his blood
> spilled out like any blood; red as any
> blood, wet as any blood and reflecting the
> sky and the buildings and birds and trees,
> or your face if you'd looked into its
> dulling mirror--and it dried in the sun as
> blood dries. That's all. [p. 445]

Too many critics have attempted to "plug in" the plots of the Odyssey or the Aeneid into Ulysses and Invisible Man. An unacknowleged critical confusion has often resulted.

A critical dead end results, then, if exact parallels are sought between classical source material and the myth syncopated works of Joyce and Ellison. Rather, we need to keep time with the many comic near misses, the literary dissonances that result from the juxtapositions. For example, what overtones are heard when Ithaca or the Daedalian labyrinth of Crete are yoked together with Dublin or Harlem; when Bella and Carr in the "Circe" section, or Ras are interfaced with the Minotaur; when the initiatory descents of Stephen and Bloom into night-town or Jack's descents and ascents into the Golden Day, into the basement of Liberty Paints, into the Chthonian, into the bedroom of Sibyl, into the coalhole, and into the nightmarish landscape of his dreams are linked to the descents of Ulysses or Aeneas into their underworlds;[3] when Jack's Southern college is reminiscent of the land of the Lotus Eaters or the Isle of Calypso;[4] or when the letters that Bledsoe gives Jack resemble the bag of winds Aelous gives Ulysses (which Ulysses's crew and not Ulysses opens)?[5]

The parallels are close, but they are also strained. They begin to crack apart, miss the story-teller's beat, as if the narrators or the narrative voices of A Portrait, Ulysses or Invisible Man were so many exhausted Tiresias figures with memory lapses.[6] Is Ras, who Jack spears, to be likened to the suitor Antoninus who literally dies? Is Ras' nationalism Scylla to Hambro's international Charybdis? Or are the members of the Union meeting Scylla to Brockway's underworld with its whirlpool of goo?[7] Is Jack's grandfather to be likened to Ulysses, as Ellison hints, or to Anchises?[8] Are Mary Rambo and Molly Bloom composites of Penelope, Circe, Nausicaa, and maternal Athena?[9] Is Tod parallel to Elpenor, who falls off Circe's roof in the Aeneid?[10] Are one-eyed Brother Jack and Michael Cusak analogues for the Cyclops of the Odyssey? Are Stephen Dedalus and Jack composites of Daedalus, Icarus, Hamlet, Orestes, Telemachus? Is Rinehart Proteus? What kind of Homer is Homer Barbee?[11] Is Jack a composite of Ulysses, Orestes, Aeneas, Telemachus, and more? Can

283

Emerson's son be likened to Circe?[12]   As soon as the
analogue is brought into near focus it jumps back out
of focus again.

More dissonances: Can Jack be likened to Ulysses
when Jack walks through Harlem disguised with
sunglasses, when Jack experiences no homecoming, no
slaying of the suitors, no Penelope?[13] What suitors
does Bloom slay? Or does Molly slay most of them for
him in the "Penelope" section with her attacks on
the various Dubliners she hates. Are the "suitors,"
whom Stephen, Bloom, and Jack encounter, mainly these
heroes' own inner and unwanted impulses?

Like a wailing twelve bar blues, mythic parallels
are syncopated, put behind the beat or ahead, made
deliberately ambiguous, filled with ironies, gaps and
free improvisation that take us far from the
"melody," the classical sources.   Kenner again
explains the impulse behind Joyce's use of parody and
pastiche, an impulse that influenced Ellison as well:

> Pastiche and parody, these are modes which
> test the limits of someone's else's system
> of perception. Any 'style' is a system of
> limits; pastiche ascribes the system to
> another person, and invites us to attend to
> its recirculating habits and its exclusions.
> That is why Joyce, the student of Dublin
> limits, turned to sytlistic imitation so
> frequently.[14]

Ellison's parody of styles discussed in Shadow and
Act, the naturalistic, the expressionistic, and the
surreal, are windows of perception that Jack learns
from society, windows he must eventually discard.
Like the mythic frames, styles themselves can obscure
vision.   Joyce and Ellison create heroes who must
live out mythic scripts and perceptual modes only to
transcend them in their slow, dark births so that
they might name themselves, or at least try.
Ellison, again, on Invisible Man:

> The book is a series of reversals. It is
> the portrait of the artist as a rabble-
> rouser, thus the various mediums of
> expression. In the Epilogue the hero disco-
> vers what he had not discovered throughout
> the book: you have to make your own

decisions; you have to think for yourself. The hero comes up from underground because the act of writing an thinking necessitated it. He could not stay down there. [SA, pp. 178-79]

Parodies of myths, of styles, of characters are everywhere in the works of Joyce and Ellison. Masks such as Osiris, Orestes, Daedalus, Telemachus, Ulysses, Orpheus, Christ, the totem god, Finn Mac Cool, Shakespeare, Ham, Hamlet, Noah, Parnell are ghost-like flickerings that are reflected upon the broken glass of 20th century incertitude. All are discarded. Claude Lévi-Strauss helps explain why. He distinguishes between the strange hold of myth and introjected masks that haunts the present and a more open concept of history:

Mythology is static, we find the same mythical elements combined over and over again, but they are in a closed system, let us say, in contradistinction with history, which is, of course, an open system.[15]

To make history an "open system," a more profound system than Lévi-Strauss proposes, a realm of "possibilities," as Stephen and Jack agree, instead of a repetition-compulsion of the introjected past, may not be possible for all men, but perhaps it is feasible for the few anti-heroes of Joyce and Ellison. A key link in the Joyce-Ellison connection is the willing assumption of the positive values inherent in invisibility. The wake from the nightmare of myth and the repetition-compulsion is ultimately predicated on a creative grasp of the invisible state.

NOTES

Chapter I

[1]Ralph Ellison and James Alan McPherson, "Indivisible Man," The Atlantic Monthly. No. 6 (Dec. 1970), p. 59.

[2]William J. Schafer, "Ralph Ellison and the Birth of the Anti-hero," A Casebook on Ralph Ellison's Invisible Man, ed. Joseph F. Trimmer (New York: Thomas Y. Crowell, 1972), p. 232.

[3]Ralph Ellison, "Juneteenth," Quarterly Review of Literature, 13, Nos. 3-4 (1965), p. 271. All subsequent page references in the text will be made to this edition.

[4]Ralph Ellison, "The Little Man at the Chehaw Station," The American Scholar, 47 (Winter, 1977/78), p. 37.

[5]Ibid., p. 40.

[6]L. P. Curtis, Anglo-Saxons and Celts (Berkeley: Univ. of California Press, n. d.), p. 22.

[7]James Joyce, The Critical Writings of James Joyce, ed. Ellsworth Mason and Richard Ellmann (New York: Viking, 1959), p. 166.

[8]Quoted in Curtis, p. 30.

[9]James Joyce, A Portrait of the Artist as a Young Man, The Portable James Joyce, ed. Harry Levin (New York: Viking, 1959), p. 156. All subsequent page references in the text will be made to this edition.

[10]Richard Wright, "Introduction," Black Metropolis: A Study of Negro Life in a Northern City (New York: Harcourt, Brace and World, 1945), p. xxxi.

[11]E. Franklin Frazier, "The Pathology of Race Prejudice," The Black Sociologists: The First Half Century, ed. John H. Bracey, Jr., August Meier and Elliott Rudwick (Belmont, California: Wadsworth, n. d.), p. 82. It is relevant to look over some key insights into the psychology of race relations made by Wright. Here is a representative sample:

The fifteenth-, sixteenth-, and seventeenth-century
neurotic European, sick of his thwarted instincts,
restless, filled with self disgust, was looking for
not only spices and gold and slaves when he set out;
he was looking for an Arcadia, a Land's End, a
Shangri-La, a world peopled by shadow men, a world
that would permit free play for his repressed
instincts.

Living in a waking dream, generations of emotionally impoverished colonial European whites
wallowed in the quick gratification of greed, reveled
in the cheap superiority of racial domination, slaked
their sensual thirst in illicit sexuality, draining
off the dammed-up libido that European morality had
condemned, amassing through trade a vast reservoir of
economic fat, thereby established vast accumulations
of capital which spurred the industralization of the
West. Asia and Africa thus became a neurotic habit
that Europeans could forgo only at the cost of a
powerful psychic wound, ... (Richard Wright,
White Man, Listen! [New York: Doubleday, 1957], pp.
24-25. All subsequent page references in the next
will be made to this edition.)

So far my random observations compel me to the
conclusion that colonialism develops the worst qualities of character of both the imperialist and his
hapless victim. The European, on duty five hundred
miles from the Equator, in the midst of heat and
humidity, can never really feel at home and the
situation breeds in him a kind of hopeless laziness,
a brand of easygoing contempt for human life existing
in a guise that is strange and offensive to him.
Outnumbered, he feels safe only when surrounded by
men of his own race and color.

                    ***

And the native, when he looks at the white man
looming powerfully above him, feels contradictory
emotions struggling in his heart; he both loves and
hates him. He loves him because he sees that the
white man is powerful, secure, and in an absen-
timinded and impersonal sort of way, occasionally
generous; and he hates him because he knows that the
white man's power is being used to strip him slowly
of his wealth, of his dignity, of his traditions, and
of his life. Seeing that there is nothing that he
can do about it, he loses faith in himself and
inwardly quakes when he tries to look into the future
in terms of white values that are as yet alien to
him. Charmed by that which he fears, pretending to

288

be Christian to merit white approval, and yet, for
the sake of his own pride, partaking of the rituals
of his own people in secret, he broods, wonders, and
finally loses respect for his own modest handicrafts
which now seem childish to him in comparison with the
mighty and thunderous machinery of the white man.
(Richard Wright, Black Power: A Record of Reactions
in a Land of Pathos [New York: Harper, 1954], pp.
138-40. All subsequent page references in the text
will be made to this edition.)
   The steady impact of the plantation system on
our lives created new types of behavior and new patterns of psychological reaction, welding us together
into a separate unity with common characteristics of
our own. We strove each day to maintain that kind of
external behavior that would best allay the Lords of
the Land, and over a period of years this dual conduct became second nature to us and we found in it a
degree of immunity from daily oppression.
                    ***
   We black men and women in America today, as we
look back upon scenes of rapine, sacrifice, and
death, seem to be children of a devilish aberration,
descendants of an interval of nightmare in history,
fledglings of a period of amnesia on the part of men
who once dreamed a great dream and forgot. (Richard
Wright, 12 Million Black Voices: A Folk History of
the Negro in the United States, photo direction by
Edwin Rosskam [New York: Arno Press, 1969], pp.
41-42. All subsequent page references in the text
will be made to this edition.)

[12]"The Pathology of Race Prejudice," pp. 84-85.

[13]Joyce to Nora Barnacle Joyce, 27 October 1909, Letters,
Vol. II, ed. Stuart Gilbert (New York: Viking, 1966), p. 255.

[14]Ralph Ellison, Invisible Man (New York: Vintage, 1972),
pp. 345-46. All subsequent page references in the text will
be made to this edition. In Ellison's review of Gunnar
Myrdal's An American Dilemma, Ellison echoes Stephen Dedalus
again:
   In Negro culture there is much of value for America
   as a whole. What is needed are Negroes to take it
   and create of it "the uncreated conscience of their
   race." In doing so they will do far more, they'll
   help create a more human America.

[15]James Joyce, Ulysses (New York: Vintage, 1961), p.45.
All subsequent page references in the text will be made to
this edition.

[16]Gunther Anders, "Being without Time: On Beckett's Play
Waiting for Godot," Samuel Becket: A Collection of Critical
Essays, ed. Martin Esslin (Englewood Cliffs, New Jersey:
Prentice Hall, 1965), pp. 149-50.

[17]Georg Hegel, The Phenomenology of the Spirit, trans. A.
V. Miller (Oxford: Clarendon Press, 1977).

[18]Michel Fabre, The Unfinished Quest of Richard Wright
(New York: William Morrow, 1973), p. 111.

[19]In Shadow and Act Ellison describes his literary
interests during the Recession year of 1937: "I went to
Dayton, Ohio where my brother and I hunted and sold game to
earn a living. And at night I . . . studied Joyce, Stein,
Dosteievsky, and Hemingway." (New York, Vintage, 1972), p.168.

[20]Fabre, pp. 145-156.

[21]Ralph Ellison, "Recent Negro Fiction," New Masses (Aug.
5, 1941), p. 22.

[22]Fabre. p. 166. For more insights into the complexities
of the association of Ellison and Wright, see Joseph T.
Skerrett, "The Wright Interpretation: Ralph Ellison and the
Anxiety of Influence," The Massachusetts Review (Spring,
1980), pp. 196-212.

[23]"Recent Negro Fiction," p. 25.

[24]Ibid.

[25]Fabre, p. 278.

[26]John Hersey, "'A Completion of Personality': A Talk with
Ralph Ellison," Ralph Ellison: A Collection of Critical
Essays, ed. John Hersey (Englewood Cliffs, New Jersey:
Prentice-Hall, 1974), p. 14.

[27]Donald S. Connery, The Irish (New York: Simon and
Schuster, n. d.), p. 24.

[28]Ibid.

[29]F. L. Radford, "King, Pope, and Hero-Martyr: Ulysses and
the Nightmare of Irish History," JJQ, 15 (Summer, 1978), p.
296.

[30]Ibid., p. 274.

[31]Patrick O'Farrell, Ireland's English Question (New York: Shocken Books, 1971), p. 26.

[32]Quoted in Ibid., p. 25.

[33]Curtis, p. 34.

[34]Quoted in O'Farrell, p. 26.

[35]Quoted in Ibid.

[36]Quoted in Ibid., p. 153.

[37]Quoted in Ibid., p. 147.

[38]James Joyce, Stephen Hero (New York: New Directions, 1963), pp. 64-65. All subsequent page references in the text will be made to this edition.

[39]12 Million Black Voices, p. 128.

[40]James Joyce, Finnegans Wake (New York: Viking, 1969), p. 264. All subsequent page references in the text will be made to this edition.

[41]Ralph Ellison, "A Very Stern Discipline," Harpers Magazine (March, 1967), p. 78.

[42]John O'Brien, ed., Interviews with Black Writers (New York: Liveright, 1973), p. 70.

[43]Richard Wright, American Hunger (New York: Harper and Row, 1977), pp. 26-27. All subsequent page references in the text will be made to this edition.

[44]Richard Wright, Black Boy (New York: Harper and Row, 1966), p.215. All subsequent page references in the text will be made to this edition.

[45]Richard Wright, Native Son (New York: Harper and Row, 1966), p. 58. All subsequent page references in the text will be made to this edition.

[46]Winthrop Jordan, White over Black: American Attitudes Toward the Negro 1550-1812 (Baltimore: Penguin, 1969), pp. 11-12.

[47]William York Tindall, A Reader's Guide to James Joyce (New York: Noonday, 1959), p. 138.

[48]Harry Blamires, The Bloomsday Book (London: Methuen, 1972), p. 117.

[49]Ibid. p. 208.

[50]Adaline Glasheen, A Third Census of Finnegans Wake (Berkeley: Univ. of California Press, 1977), p. 115.

[51]Ralph Ellison, "And Hickman Arrives," Black Writers in America, ed. Richard Barksdale and Kenneth Kinnamon (New York: Macmillan, 1972), pp. 693-712.

[52]Susan L. Blake, "Ritual and Rationalization: Black Folklore in the Works of Ralph Ellison," PMLA, No. 1, 94 (Jan. 1979), p. 131.

[53]Glasheen, p. 182.

[54]Ibid., p. 115.

[55]Sigmund Freud, Totem and Taboo, The Basic Writings of Sigmund Freud, trans. and ed. A. A. Brill (New York: Modern Library, 1938), pp. 924-25.

[56]Michael Bakunin, God and State (London: Freedom Press, 1910), pp. 25-26.

[57]Radford, pp. 287-89.

[58]Quoted in Robert Orel, "The Two Attitudes of James Joyce," Irish History and Culture: Aspects of a People's Heritage, ed. Harold Orel (Lawrence, Kansas: Univ. of Kansas Press, 1976), pp. 316-17.

[59]For a discussion of the folklore elements in Wheatstraw's exchange which includes the appearance of the dog motif in "The Arkansas Traveler," see Gene Bluestein, The Voice of the Folk (Boston: (Univ. of Massachusetts Press, 1972), pp. 127ff. For an examination of Joyce's goddog motif and its linkage to St. Thomas Aquinas, see Tindall, p. 174.

[60]Richard Wright, The Outsider (New York: Harper and Row, 1965), p. 244. All subsequent page references in the text will be made to this edition.

[61]David Bakhish, Richard Wright (New York: Frederick Ungar, 1973), p. 53.

[62]Hugh Kenner, Dublin's Joyce (Boston: Beacon Press, 1956), p. 20.

[63]Ibid., p. 151.

[64]Ibid., p. 150.

[65]Giambattista Vico, The New Science of Giambattista Vico, trans. Thomas Goddard Bergin and Max Harold Fisch (Ithaca; New York: Cornell Univ. Press, 1948), p. 60.

[66]Margot Norris, The Decentered World of Finnegans Wake (Baltimore: The Johns Hopkins Univ. Press, 1976), pp. 99-100.

[67]Ibid., p. 92.

[68]Joseph Campbell and Henry Morton Robinson, A Skeleton Key to Finnegans Wake (Baltimore: Viking, 1972), p. 360.

[69]Frantz Fanon, Black Skin, White Masks, trans. Charles Lam Markmann (New York: Grove Press, 1967), pp. 38-39.

[70]Quoted in Richard Ellmann, James Joyce (New York: Oxford Univ. Press, 1965), p. 410.

[71]Ralph Ellison, "On Initiation Rites and Power: Ralph Ellison Speaks at West Point," ed. Robert H. Moore, Contemporary Literature, 15 (1974), p. 174.

[72]Bluestein, p. 134.

[73]Ibid.

[74]Norman O. Brown, Closing Time (New York: Random House, 1973), p. 109.

[75]For a good discussion of Ellison's use of affected dialog to deflate certain characters, see Lloyd W. Brown, "Ralph Ellison's Exhorters: The Role of Rhetoric in Invisible Man," pp. 289-303.

[76]Nancy Scheper-Hughes, Saints, Scholars and Schizophrenics: Mental Illness in Rural Ireland (Berkeley: Univ. of California Press, 1979), p. 152. She discusses the results of her interviews with parents in West Ireland, and one comment by a parent is telling: "You've got to slash them while they're still too young to remember it and hold it against you." (p. 154) She quotes J. Daly, one of the only child psychiatrists in Ireland:
The family home in Ireland is a novitiate for violence. Even from the cradle the child is made to feel rejection, hositility and open physical pain.

The infant is left to cry in the cot because his
mother does not want to "give in to him." Later he
is smacked with the hand or a stick. He is made to
go to bed early. He is not allowed to have his tea.
He is put into a room by himself. . . . In order to
invite this morale-breaking treatment from his
parents all the Irish child has to do is be normal.
(p. 154.)

This corporeal punishment is still encouraged in Irish schools
much as it was in Joyce's day. In any case, the Irish family
pattern that Joyce depicts conforms largely with the sociological stereotype. It appears that there is less maternal
ambivalence and more downright maternal hostility toward the
child than in many cultures outside Ireland, but it becomes
clear that a lack of mother love and resultant basic trust, as
well as the usual lack of a strong father, appear at the base
of the Joycean family pyramid.

[77]Ibid.

[78]Mark Shechner, Joyce in Nighttown (Berkeley: Univ. of
California Press, 1974), p. 36. Norman O. Brown's comments on
the appearance of the grandfather in fraternal social struc-
tures cast a good deal of light on the grandfather motif in
Invisible Man:

In fraternal organization, in the primitive mask
culture, the ancestors, the Eternal Ones of the
Dream, are distinct from the living. The son is an
ancestor reincarnated, but not a continuation of his
father; he is his grandfather (reincarnated), but not
his father. The distinction between generations, the
unity of the generations (the brothers) is preserved.
The rhythm is not continuity but alteration
(oscillation) between generations; my son is my
father reborn, and as such to be respected by me; the
integrity of the separate generations is preserved.
In patrilinear inheritance my son is a continuation
of me; I incorporate him, swallow him (Cronus
swallowing his children). In fraternal organization
my son was my father; in swallowing him I have
swallowed my father. So in patriarchy I become my
own father, pater sui; by parricide; and deny the
deed: the king never dies. (Norman O. Brown, Love's
Body [New York: Vintage, 1966], p. 103)

[79]See Gilles Deleuze, Masochism, trans. Jean McNiel (New
York: Faber and Faber, 1971), pp. 71ff. Deleuze discusses
the phenomena:

Masochism allows a kind of displacement through fantasy to take place. Oedipal incest is avoided whereas pre-sexual incest which insures rebirth is not. This displacement from the oedipal incestuous longings ends paralysis. The fetish becomes the phallus necessary for rebirth.

[80]See Melanie Klein, The Psychoanalysis of Children, trans. Alix Strachey (New York: Delta, 1976), pp. 176-193.

[81]"A Very Stern Discipline," p. 76. In the same interview Ellison goes on to clarify his regard for sociological theory:

> So when I look at my material I'm not looking at it simply through the concepts of sociology--and I do know something about sociology. I look at it through literature; English, French, Spanish, Russian-- especially 19th century Russian literature. And Irish literature, Joyce and Yeats, and through the international literature of the "twenties." And through the perspective of folklore. When I listen to a folk story I'm looking for what it conceals as well as what it states. I read it with the same attention I bring to Finnegans Wake or The Sound and the Fury because I'm eager to discover what it has to say to me personally. (p. 84)

[82]Ibid.

[83]Ibid., p. 76.

[84]Kenner, p. 169.

[85]Ibid., p. 167.

[86]Ibid.

[87]Ibid., pp. 164-65.

[88]Quoted in Frank Mc Connell, The Spoken Seen: Film and the Romantic Imagination (Baltimore: The Johns Hopkins Univ. Press, 1975), p. 46.

[89]Ibid., pp. 60-61.

[90]Ibid., p. 176ff.

[91]Ibid., p. 176.

[92]In his "Introduction" to Black Metropolis Wright quotes William James on the subject of recognition:

> No more fiendish punishment could be devised, were
> such a thing physically possible, than that one
> should be turned loose in society and remain abso-
> lutely unnoticed by all the members thereof. If no
> one turned round when we entered, answered when we
> spoke, or minded what we did, but if every person we
> met "cut us dead," and acted as if we were non-
> existent things, a kind of rage and impotent despair
> would ere long well up in us, from which the cruelest
> bodily tortures would be a relief; for these would
> make us feel that, however bad might be our plight,
> we had not sunk to such a depth as to be unworthy of
> attention at all. (Quoted, p. xxxii)

[93]See Joel Kovel, White Racism: A Psychohistory (New York: Pantheon, 1971), pp. 239ff for an interpretation of the racial allegory in "The Whiteness of the Whale" chapter of Moby Dick.

[94]Richard Wright, "The Man Who Lived Underground," Black Voices: An Anthology of Afro-American Literature, ed. Abraham Chapman (New York: New American Library, 1968), pp. 128, 147. All subsequent page references in the text will be made to this edition.

[95]Morton Levitt, "The Family of Bloom," New Light on Joyce (Bloomington: Univ. of Indiana Press, 1972), pp. 141-43.

[96]Ellmann notes that in the early drafts of A Portrait Joyce wished that Stephen remain nameless. Richard Ellmann, The Consciousness of Joyce (Toronto: Oxford Univ. Press, 1977), p. 12.

[97]"Indivisible Man," pp. 50-51.

[98]Lord Raglan, The Hero (Westport, Connecticut: Greenwood Press, 1975), pp. 41-45.

[99]Katherine Briggs, The Vanishing People: Fairy Lore and Legends (New York: Pantheon Books, 1978), pp. 21-22.

[100]Ibid., pp. 33, 85, 83.

[101]Robert S. Boyle, "Astroglodynamologos," New Light on Joyce, p. 138.

[102]Ibid., p. 132.

[103]Fyodor Dostoevsky, Notes from Underground (New York: Thomas Y. Crowell, 1969), p. 30.

NOTES

Chapter II

[1]"On Initiation Rites and Power: Ralph Ellison at West Point," p. 172.

[2]Quoted in James Joyce, p. 394.

[3]Ibid., p. 460.

[4]Richard Ellmann, Ulysses on the Liffey (New York: Oxford Univ. Press, 1972), p. 60.

[5]Richard Sennett, Authority (New York: Alfred A. Knopf, 1980), pp. 125-164.

[6]Gordon Allport, The Nature of Prejudice (Garden City, New York: Doubleday, 1958), pp. 147-48.

[7]O'Farrell, p. 8.

[8]For a defense of the strengths of black family life in America, a primary source is Andrew Billingsley, Black Families in White America (Englewood Cliffs, New Jersey: Prentice Hall, 1968), Billingsley attacks the Moynihan report for "singling out instability in the Negro family as the causal factor for the difficulties Negroes face in the white society. It is quite the other way around." p. 199.

[9]Leslie Fiedler, Love and Death in the American Novel (New York: Dell, 1960), p. 337. Ellison refers to Fiedler in Shadow and Act, p. 51.

[10]Barbara Tomasi, "The Fraternal Theme in Joyce's Ulysses," American Imago, 30 (Summer 1973), p. 182.

[11]See Mark L. Troy, Mummeries of Resurrection: The Cycle of Osiris in Finnegans Wake (Stockholm, Upsala, 1976).

[12]James Joyce, Dubliners, The Portable James Joyce. This and all subsequent page references in the text will be made to this edition.

[13]The Consciousness of Joyce, p. 57.

[14]Tomasi, p. 191.

[15]Richard Wasson, "Stephen Dedalus and the Imagery of Sight: A Psychological Approach," Literature and Psychology. 15 (Fall 1965). p. 199.

[16]Ibid.. pp. 196-97.

[17]Ibid.. p. 199.

[18]Ibid.. p. 196.

[19]Ibid.. p. 197.

[20]Ibid.

[21]Ibid.. p. 198.

[22]George E. Kent. "Ralph Ellison and Afro-American Folk and Cultural Tradition." Ralph Ellison: A Collection of Critical Essays. p. 166. Kent argues:

> He unites the invisible narrator and the nude blonde as victims and makes out of her a symbol implying the mystery of freedom. similar to James Joyce's use of woman in A Portrait of the Artist as a Young Man: "She seemed like a fair bird-girl girdled in veils calling to me from the angry surface of some gray and threatening sea."

[23]Wasson, p. 199.

[24]This "authentic" singing anticipated the brown girl's singing a cappella during the chapel service.

[25]Bluestein, pp. 130-131. Sheldon R. Brivic has argued that Stephen's search for the "unsubstantial image" is really an erotic search for Emma, and, ultimately, for the lost maternal paradise of infancy. Brivic explains:

> But if Stephen does not know what he seeks, he does provide details indicating the object of his desire. He will meet it "perhaps at one of the gates or in some more secret place . . . surrounded by darkness . . . ." Thus, he associates his "image" with the womb. And he clearly associates it with tenderness and security. He also says, "They would meet as if they had known each other . . .," and later, when he feels tempted by E_.C_., he says, "He heard what her eyes said to him . . . and knew that in some dim past, whether in life or in revery, he had heard

their tale before." (p. 69) Both in his vague state of unspecified desire and in the late stage in which he focuses his emotion on E .C ., he senses that the object of his desire is one with which he has somehow been familiar for a long time, one he knew in the "dim past." This is obviously his mother. But the idea of mother has now been repressed and the distant goal of longing has been sublimated into a spiritual ideal associated with transfiguration. It is this maternal ideal which Stephen pursues as he wanders in ever widening circles throughout the rest of the Portrait. (Sheldon R. Brivic, "From Stephen to Bloom," in Psychoanalysis and the Creative Process, ed. Frederick Crews [Cambridge: Winthrop, 1970], pp. 118-168.

Leopold Bloom or "Poldy" is comically treated as a big infant in "Circe," and Molly's attitude toward this "manchild in the womb" is similar to Bloom's own fantasies. Joyce argued that Bloom revealed the same type of impotency as the other Dubliners, although certainly in a more benign and controlled way. Bloom, of course, serves as a father for "fatherless" Stephen, and for this reason Ulysses becomes only partially therapeutic. As lovable as Poldy is, he bears the paralytic scars of oppression and cannot successfully serve as the less physical father Stephen needs. Nevertheless, his influence on Stephen and on many readers is humanizing, to say the least. Yet, Bloom wishes to "use" Stephen masochistically if his plan is to offer Stephen to Molly as a substitute for his own lack of potency and for the animalism of Boylan. Poldy's love is clearly incestuous as Joyce himself, no doubt, knew. Poldy relishes his infant-like submission to Zoe and sputters "Laughing witch! The hand that rocks the cradle." She answers "Babby." (p. 550) Bloom appears in "babylinen and pelisse, bigheaded, with a caul of dark hair," and "fixes his big eyes on her fluid slip and counts its bronze buckels" in baby talk. (p. 551) The gigantism that surrounds both Bloom's description of Bella and Joyce's description of Molly is similar to the way the small infant may perceive the massive body of his mother. The fact that Bloom, as an infant, discovers the smells of other men that have possessed Zoe, seems to harken back to the child's discovery that the mother does not exist exclusively for him. Oedipus looms again. The Nymph's association with Photo Bits implies a linkage between she and Molly with the hint then of father-daughter incest or at least of the unconscious desire for it. The linkages Bloom makes between food and sex reveal, in psychoanalytical terms, a fixation on the food giving function of the mother. The linkage of food and sex is grossly made by Lenehan and Boylan in "Circe" and elsewhere in Ulysses, as

well. (pp. 564-565) A most surprising coincidence also
reveals the incestuous desire of Bloom to be "man-child in the
womb." As Blamires notes, Zoe's last name is Higgins. This
is also the maiden name of Bloom's mother. In addition,
Blamires notes "If then Zoe is really Fanny Higgins, she has
exactly the same name as Bloom's grandmother."

Stephen too is a victim of the incest bond. He ends up in
the fetal position at one point in "Circe." (p. 609) Yet he
differs from the other Dubliners, because he struggles to
break the bond, a bond both moral as well as unconsciously
sexual, by means of his rather weak non serviam. Stephen is
appropriately linked with Oedipus and the theme of solving the
riddle. Stephen must say the word which may be "father."

26Love's Body, p. 11.

NOTES

Chapter III

[1]W. E. B. DuBois, <u>Souls of Black Folk</u> (Chicago: A. C. McClure & Co., 1903), p. 3.

[2]George Novak, ed., <u>Existentialism versus Marxism:</u> <u>Conflicting Views on Humanism</u> (New York: Dell, 1968). p. 10.

[3]Kenner. pp. 161ff.

[4]Quoted in McConnell. p. 46.

[5]Kovel. p. 264.

[6]<u>Ibid.</u>. p. 265.

[7]<u>Ibid.</u>. p. 132.

[8]<u>Ibid.</u>. p. 135.

[9]<u>Ibid.</u>. pp. 127-28.

[10]<u>Ibid.</u>, p. 155.

[11]<u>Ibid.</u>, p. 184.

[12]McConnell, pp. 47-48.

[13]<u>Ibid.</u>, p. 62.

[14]<u>Ibid.</u>, p. 52.

[15]<u>Ibid.</u>, p. 47.

[16]<u>Ibid.</u>, p. 176.

[17]<u>Ibid.</u>, p. 175.

[18]<u>Ibid.</u>, pp. 182, 177.

[19]Morris Beja, "'Dividual Chaoses': Case Histories of Multiple Personality in <u>Finnegans Wake</u>," <u>JJQ</u> (Spring 1977), p. 241.

[20]Ibid., pp. 241ff.

[21]E. M. Kist, "A Langian Analysis of Blackness in Ralph Ellison's Invisible Man," Studies in Black Literature, No. 7, ii, pp. 19ff.

[22]Ibid., p. 20.

[23]Ibid.

[24]R. D. Laing, The Divided Self (New York: Penguin, 1969), p. 113.

[25]Alan R. Spiegel, Fiction and the Camera Eye: Visual Consciousness in Film and the Modern Novel (Charlottesville, Virginia: Univ. Press of Virginia, 1976), pp. 63-64.

[26]Ibid., p. 66.

[27]Ibid., p. 68.

[28]Ibid., p. 64ff.

[29]Quoted in Colin Turbayne, The Myth of Metaphor (Los Angeles: Univ. of Southern California Press, 1970), p. 205.

[30]Ibid.

[31]Ibid.

[32]Harry Levin, James Joyce (New York: New Directions, 1960), p. 88.

[33]Henri Bergson, Creative Evolution. trans. Arthur Mitchell (New York: The Modern Library. 1964). p. 332.

[34]Spiegel, p. 3.

[35]Ibid., pp. 113-16.

[36]The Consciousness of Joyce, p. 63.

[37]Leo Knuth, "Finnegans Wake as a Product of the Twenties," JJQ, 11 (Summer 1974). pp. 318-19.

[38]McConnell. pp. 57-63.

[39]Spiegel. pp. 140-41.

[40]Ibid., p. 142ff.

[41]We should well recall Stephen's fears in A Portrait that he might become a subject for electrocution.

[42]Tony Tanner, "The Music of Invisibility," Ralph Ellison: A Collection of Critical Essays. p. 83.

[43]Marcus Klein. After Alienation (Freeport. New York: Books for Libraries Press, 1970), p. 134. Part of the grim pathology created by oppression involves the need to assume several fantasy masks that may elevate the "servant" from his sense of inferiority, or give him the hope of transcending his predicament. Joyce admitted his own need for masks. He revealed his own unstable sense of identity when he discussed his use of masks and the "trickster" side of his personality in a letter to Nora: "Can you not see the simplicity which is at the back of all my disguises? We all wear masks." Earlier in this letter Joyce wrote of his disdain for the "system" in Ireland that killed his mother. He related: "My mind rejects the whole present social order and Christianity--home, the recognized virtues, classes of life, and religious doctrines." (Letters, II, pp. 48, 50) In another letter to Nora, Joyce again referred to the "trickster" element in his personality:
. . .how is it that I cannot impress you with my magnificent poses as I do other people: You see through me, you cunning little blue-eyed rogue, and smile to yourself knowing that I am an imposter and still you love me. (Letters, II, p. 279)

[44]Fanon, pp. 26-27.

[45]Ibid., pp. 212-13.

[46]Norris, p. 78.

[47]Soren Kierkegaard, The Sickness Unto Death, trans. Howard and Edna Hong (New York: Princeton Univ. Press, 1980), p. 83.

[48]Hugh Kenner, Joyce's Voices (Berkeley, California: Univ. of California Press, 1978), p. 52.

[49]Ibid., p. 53.

[50]Laing, p. 59.

[51]Eldridge Cleaver, Soul on Ice (New York: Dell, 1968), p. 181.

[52]Ibid., p. 186.

[53]Joyce also juxtaposes his plantation country with Griffith's film, or, as he puts it, the "birth of an otion," (FW, p. 309.)

[54]McConnell, p. 180.

[55] Ibid., p. 181.

[56]Laing, pp. 35ff.

[57]See Glasheen, p. 244.

[58]The name "Bigger" may be derived in part from Joyce's primal Viconian man "joebiggar" who appears in the Wake:
The brontoichthyan form In the name of Anem this carl on the kopje in pelted thongs a parth a lone who the joebiggar be he? Forshapen his pigmaid hoagshead, shroonk his plodsfoot. He had locktoes, this shortshins, and Obeold that pectoral, his mammamuscules most mousterious." (FW, pp. 7, 15)

[59]Robert E. Abrams, "The Ambiguities of Dreaming in Finnegans Wake," American Literature, No. 49 (1978), p. 593.

[60]Ibid., p. 600.

[61]Ibid., p. 594.

[62]Ibid.

[63]Norris. p. 91.

[64]Ibid.

[65]Kovel. pp. 109-110.

[1]Sigmund Freud, Moses and Monotheism. Selected Essays.
Vol. XXIII. p. 159.

[2]Ralph Ellison "Tell It Like It Is Baby " The Nation
201 (September 1965). p. 136.

[3]"The Little Man at the Chehaw Station." pp. 36-37.

[4]"On Initiation Rites and Power: Ralph Ellison Speaks at
West Point." p. 178.

[5]"A Very Stern Discipline." p. 80.

[6]Richard Wright. The Long Dream (New York: Ace Books.
1958). p. 102. This and all subsequent page references in the
text will be made to this edition.
    In Savage Holiday. Wright gives us a complex and heavy
handed examination of the resiliency of Freudian archetypes.
There is evidence of a slight Joycean influence in Savage
Holiday. and it is necessary to note the echoes of Totem and
Taboo in this most Freudian novel. For the frontpiece of the
first section includes the following excerpt from Freud's
work: "In the very nature of a holiday there is excess; the
holiday mood is brought about by the release of what is
forbidden." Less than subtle echoes of Freud's theory run
throughout this novel. Retiring Erskine finds himself
included in a primal family vestige when President Warren
hypocritically speaks of the insurance staff as "brothers and
sisters" under the protection of fatherly Warren. Erskine's
supposition that Warren will replace Erskine's old position
with Warren's 23-year old son Robert causes a return of the
repressed in Erskine which leads to his assumption of the role
of the primal father, a father who is threatened by his young
replacement. The fact that Erskine feels guilt for the death
of Tony Blake, who falls from the balcony at the sight of
Erskine's hairy, nude body reveals, in the logic of the novel,
that Erskine has fulfilled his subliminal wish to kill young
Warren through the death of Tony. On the unconscious level,
then, young pistol wielding Tony has been castrated, killed as
a surrogate for Robert, by Erskine, the nude, hairy, primal
father imago. Erskine also is haunted by a dream where the
trees in his phallic forest are being cut. One of those dream

trees nearly crushes Erskine's dream self. He must, on the unconscious level, castrate or be castrated. To complicate matters further, however, the death of Tony is equated in the novel to the symbolic death of Erskine, for Tony serves as the unconscious symbol of Erskine's child self while Mabel serves as the surrogate image of Erskine's mother. When a child, he, too, fatherless like Tony, had to witness his mother's lovers, and intuit her rejection of his need for exclusive love. And the "irresistably unreal" moment of Tony's plunge puts Erskine in the ancient realm of primal murder. He not only feels that he too has hurtled through space, but he wishes Tony dead. The event has all been a "wild dream" that has sprung ancient, buried archetypes, wishes, that to the Freudian superego are the same as an actual deed, for such is the implication of the quote from Reik that Wright places on the frontpiece of the second chapter ". . . is there really such a world of difference between the wish and the dead?"

Erskine's act of scaring Tony into a fall, consciously, is an innocent event; Erskine should feel no guilt. But he wonders again about the deeper level of the nightmarish incident, about Tony's perception of his naked body:

> Erskine realized that a child's mind was a strange
> shadowland, and what seemed ordinary to adults would
> loom as something monstrous or fearful to Tony who
> had lived in a world of Indians, horses, bombing
> planes, soldiers, whales, and perhaps things never
> seen on land or sea. What, then, had Tony asso-
> ciated him with that seemed so fantastic, frightful?
> Why had the sudden sight of him--huge, hairy,
> sweating, panting--sent Tony reeling?

And Erskine wonders also why guilt should knaw at him for his apparently neutral act of entering the Blake apartment to spare the other apartment dwellers a glimpse of his nudity. Wright's constant need to inform the novel with raw Freudian analogues forces the reader's conclusion: On the unconscious level Erskine, as primal father, has castrated the threatening son, and the "son's" identity with Erskine has allowed Erskine the release, on one level, of symbolic suicide, a longed for death, and on another, the fantasy that he now is both the mother's son and the possessor of the mother. He will now be able to seek revenge on his mother-surrogate Mabel for the rejection he experienced with his real mother, as Wright blends Totem and Taboo with other psychological projections. In Erskine's unconscious logic, it is Mabel who through neglect really killed the child's soul, so that the child's physical death is a blessing. Erskine-Orestes can thus punish Mabel for her rejection of Tony, and, on the deeper level, Erskine can fulfill his infantile sadistic wish to destroy the lingering image of his own mother?

> What puzzled him was that it was like a waking dream
> . . . some fantasy of his own mind, just as he had
> objectified a fantasy in the mind of poor little
> Tony. . . . That was why Mabel had such powerful
> hold over him.

Wright's allusion to Euripides' version of the Orestia on the frontpiece of the third chapter, his use of the motif of the waking nightmare, Erskine's dream experiences of the rotting female corpse, his fears of the devouring, phallic nature of the mother image, along with his use of Totem and Taboo all appear to be possible Joycean echoes which reveal Wright's obsession with the psychological boomerangs of the unconscious that transcend race. (Richard Wright, Savage Holiday [New York: Avon, 1954])

[7]Totem and Taboo. pp. 915ff.

[8]Ibid.. p. 811.

[9]Ibid.

[10]Ibid.

[11]Moses and Monotheism. pp. 80ff.

[12]Totem and Taboo. p. 920.

[13]Ibid.. p. 922.

[14]Ibid.

[15]Ibid.. p. 923.

[16]Ibid.. p. 924.

[17]Ibid.. p. 925.

[18]Ibid.. p. 807.

[19]Moses and Monotheism. p. 113.

[20]Campbell and Robinson, p. 169.

[21]Norris, p. 43.

[22]James B.Vickery, The Literary Impact of The Golden Bough (Princeton: Princeton Univ. Press. 1973). pp. 334-35.

[23]Norris. pp. 62ff.

[24]Vico, p. 221.

[25]Norris, p. 120.

[26]Vico, p. xxvi.

[27]Norris, p. 56.

[28]Ibid.

[29]Ibid., p. 57.

[30]Ibid.

[31]Ellison has argued that a strength of the Afro-American experience lies in its integration of African and European elements.

> Thus it would seem to me that any objective approach
> to its dynamics would lead to the basic conclusion
> that here in the U.S., at least, culture has success-
> fully confounded all concepts of race. American
> culture would not exist without its Afro-American
> component, or if it did, it would be quite different.
> (Ralph Ellison, "Study and Experience: An Interview
> with Ralph Ellison," with Michael Harper and Robert
> Stepto, The Massachusetts Review 18 [1977], p. 424)

Ellison must have noted the analogies between the confusion of lineages and race in Ireland, and Joyce's conclusions on internationalism versus in-group loyalty may well have influenced Ellison's own integrative outlook.

[32]Bernard Benstock, Joyce-again's Wake (Seattle: Univ. of Washington Press, 1965), pp. 198-99.

[33]In Interviews with Black Writers, Ellison alludes to his reaction to Vico and Joyce in regard to the metaphor of history:

> Vico, whom Joyce used in his great novels, described
> history as circling. I described it as a boomerang
> because a boomerang moves in a parabola. It goes and
> it comes. It is never the same thing. There is
> implicit in the image of old idea that those who do
> not learn from history are doomed to repeat its
> mistakes. History comes back and hits you. But you
> really cannot break down a symbol rationally. It
> allows you to say things that cannot really be said.
> (p. 73)

[34]See Sir James Frazer, The Golden Bough, Vol. xi, p. 243. In "Scylla and Carybdis" Bloom describes the sun as a

wheelbarrow: "Day. Wheelbarrow sun over arch of bridge." (p. 217) For a more detailed look at this Egyptian god and its transmission, see Robert K. G. Temple, The Sirius Mystery (New York, St. Martins Press, 1976), pp. 198-99.

[35]See Lévi-Strauss, The Savage Mind (Chicago: Univ. of Chicago Press, 1966), pp. 16-36.

[36]This punning recalls MacBeth's "Tomorrow, and tomorrow, and tomorrow . . ." soliloquy and the cyclic repetition of human life.

[37]See Frederick L. Radford, "The Journey Towards Castration: Interracial Sexual Stereotypes in Ellison's Invisible Man," American Studies, 4, pp. 227-331. He also discusses the theme of taboo.

[38]Totem and Taboo, p. 832.

[39]In an interview, John O'Brien asked Ellison:
When I read Reverend Barbee's speech I was reminded of the sermon that Stephen Dedalus hears when he's on retreat in A Portrait of the Artist as a Young Man. Did you perhaps have Joyce's satire in mind when you composed Barbee's speech?
Ellison appears to hedge the question:
Sure, I had read Joyce. I had read A Portrait any number of times before I thought I could write a novel. But I was also concerned with the problem of heroism and with the mythology of the hero. I have read Rank's The Myth of the Birth of the Hero. (Interviews with Black Writers. pp. 73-74)

[40]The numerals on the containers at Liberty Points appear to be a parody of mystical numbers: "SKA-3-69." (p. 155)

[41]Vickery, p. 358.

[42]Ibid., p. 256.

[43]Love's Body. p. 29.

[44]"King. Pope. and the Hero-Martyr: Ulysses and the Nightmare of Irish History." pp. 315-16.

[45]Articles by Fiedler were appearing at the time Ellison was revising Invisible Man.

[46]Love's Body. p. 29.

[47]Vickery, p. 358.

[48]Ibid., p. 405.

[49]Totem and Toaboo, p. 914.

[50]Ibid., pp. 914-15.

[51]It is for this reason that Joyce puns "Pater Noster" with "Panther monster." See Closing Time, p. 61.

[52]Vickery, p. 341.

[53]The Golden Bough. ix. p. 312.

[54]Ibid.. ix. p. 306.

[55]Ibid.. p. 307.

[56]Totem and Taboo. p. 922.

[57]For a fuller discussion see Vickery, pp. 358ff.

[58]Ibid., pp. 411, 408-422, 432.

[59]See Chester G. Anderson. "On the Sublime and Its Anal-Urethral Sources in Pope. Eliot. and Joyce." Modern Irish Literature: Essays in Honor of William York Tindall. ed. Raymond S. Porter and James D. Brophy. (New York: Twayne Publishers. Inc.. 1972). p. 248 for more information on the bull totem.

[60]Ralph Ellison, "Flying Home," Black Writers of America: A Comprehensive Anthology. pp. 254-270. All page references in the text will be made to this edition.

[61]Joseph F. Trimmer. "Ralph Ellison's 'Flying Home.'" Studies in Short Fiction. 9 (1972). p. 181ff.

[62]Ibid.. p. 181.

[63]Ibid.. p. 181-82.

[64]Ibid.. p. 182.

[65]Stephen undergoes several such awakenings in A Portrait. especially when he enters the streets of nighttown which are lined with prostitutes.

[66]See The Long Dream. pp. 96-97.

[67]See Eleanor R. Wilner. "The Invisible Black Thread: Identity and Nonentity in Invisible Man." CLAJ. XIII. 3. 1971. p. 242ff. The following excerpts from her study are informative:

> There is no way to resolve the various roles which Tod may play for this work. since they tend to work against each other. It is as if the narrator were trying to be superior to the tragic heart of his own vision. as if he were trying to venerate and deprecate the same character. Perhaps the death of Tod may be the author's way of disposing of the difficulties he presents. a psychological suicide of a certain kind. a fictional murder to embrace an ontological position. It is true. anyway. that Tod who of all the characters is perhaps the most admirable. is a character whose pride the narrator both admires and fears. and whose death marks. for the narrator. a reduction of ego. the end of a certain set of possibilities. (p. 253)

***

> After this first outburst of rage. the book turns away from the terrors of the passions raised by an assertive self-recovery. Perhaps it is only Tod who bears the burden of this depth. Tod who may serve as a kind of alter ego. a man whose integrity leaves nothing out. It is Tod, not the narrator, who opposes Ras, but at the same time admits to being tempted by his emotionally releasing rage; and it is Tod who turns. as the last act of his life. against the authority which has always oppressed and opposed him. It is Tod, then, as he has been shown who carries the black identity, and the human dilemma; he may be the vicarious bearer of the narrator's repressed identity, plummed at a distance from himself, observed in that indefinite way of the dimly comprehended inner truth, and destroyed in the very way that the narrator fears his emotions would destroy him. (p. 256)

[68]Totem and Taboo, p. 852. The "nigger"-"trigger" rhyme recalls the McTrigger motif in Ulysses, p. 171.

[69]One-eyed Brother Jack, a possible Saturn figure, recalls Mr. Eugenides from Eliot's The Waste Land.

[70]For other applications of Frazer's mythopoeic eye by Ellison see Ralph Ellison, "Cadillac Flambé," American Review, 10 (February 1973), pp. 249-269.

71Philip Reiff, "Freud and the Authority of the Past," Explorations in Psychohistory: The Wellfleet Papers, ed. Jay Lifton with Eric Olson (New York: Simon and Schuster, 1974), pp. 107-108.

72Love's Body. p. 119.

NOTES

Chapter V

[1]Mircea Eliade. <u>Rites and Symbols of Initiation: The</u>
<u>Mysteries of Birth and Rebirth</u> (New York: Harper and Row.
1958). pp. 127-28.

[2]<u>Ibid</u>.. p. 128.

[3]<u>Ibid</u>.

[4]<u>Ibid</u>.

[5]<u>Ibid</u>.. p. xiv.

[6]<u>Ibid</u>.

[7]<u>Ibid</u>.. p. 9.

[8]<u>Ibid</u>.. p. 134.

[9]Vickery. pp. 341-42.

[10]<u>Ibid</u>.. p. 342.

[11]Eliade. p. 78.

[12]<u>Ibid</u>.. p. xiii.

[13]<u>Ibid</u>.

[14]Quoted in William Fitzpatrick. "The Myths of Creation--
Joyce. Jung and <u>Ulysses</u>." <u>JJQ</u>. 2 (Winter 1974). p. 125.

[15]Kenner, p. 259.

[16]Fitzpatrick, p. 128.

[17]<u>Ibid</u>., p. 131.

[18]<u>Ibid</u>., p. 136.

[19]Ellison has the Harlem riot occur on Thursday. and the
archaic "Thorsday" implies initiation thunder.

[20]Ralph Ellison. "Mr. Toussaint." Negro Story Magazine. No. 1 (October-November 1944), p. 4. This and all subsequent page references will be made to this edition.

[21]Klein, p. 99.

[22]"Ralph Ellison's 'Flying Home.'" p. 176.

[23]Ibid.. p. 177.

[24]Eliade. p. 56. See also Raglan. pp. 226. 267.

[25]For a folklore analogue to the buzzard image see Blake, p. 124.

[26]"Ralph Ellison's 'Flying Home,'" p. 179.

[27]Ibid., pp. 181-82.

[28]"On Initiation Rites and Power: Ellison at West Point," p. 174.

[29]Ibid., p. 176.

[30]See Chester G. Anderson, "Baby Tuckoo: Joyce's 'Features of Infancy'" Approaches to A Portrait, ed. Thomas F. Staley and Bernard Benstock (Pittsburg: Univ. of Pittsburg Press, 1976), pp. 144-45. He interprets the series of abortive rebirths that provide much of the overall structure of A Portrait as indicative of Stephen's maternal curse:
> Such fantasies of rebirth, or parentless or virgin
> births, and of reconstructing the body seem always to
> provide reassurance that the sadistic attacks on the
> mother have not succeeded in destroying her and that
> therefore the talonic revenge against the infant's
> own body has not been wreaked.
Ellison borrows the circular structure for his novel but leaves out much of the psychological motivation.

[31]Eliade, pp. 22-23 notes how beasts of prey serve symbolically in initiation rites.

[32]Klein, p. 108.

[33]Ibid., p. 109.

[34]"The Journey Towards Castration: Interracial Stereotypes in Ellison's Invisible Man," pp. 228-29.

[35]See Blake, p. 123 who discusses the symbolic meaning of the castration in Ellison's "The Birthmark."

[36]*Interviews with Black Writers*, p. 75.

[37]Otto Rank, *The Myth of the Birth of the Hero, Nervous and Mental Disease Monographs*. No. 8 (1914) p. 69.

[38]Vickery, pp. 365-66.

[39]Trudier Harris, "Ellison's 'Peter Wheatstraw': His Basis in Black Folk Tradition," *Mississippi Folklore Register*. No. 2 (Summer 1975). pp. 117ff.

[40]Eliade. pp. 15-16.

[41]*Ibid.*. pp. 34-35.

[42]William J. Schafer. "Ralph Ellison and the Birth of the Anti-Hero." *Ralph Ellison: A Series of Critical Essays*. pp. 120-21.

[43]See Floyd Horowitz. "Ralph Ellison's Modern Version of Brer Bear and Brer Rabbit in *Invisible Man*." *A Casebook on Ralph Ellison's Invisible Man*. ed. Joseph Trimmer (New York: Thomas Y. Crowell. 1972). pp. 273-280.

[44]Eliade. p. 28.

[45]See Isaac Sequeira. "The Uncompleted Initiation of the Invisible Man." *Studies in Black Literature*. 6 (1975). p. 12. Sequeira suggests that the burst water main that sprays Jack during the Harlem riot is a baptismal image. on the mythic level.

[46]See "The Invisible Black Thread: Identity and Nonentity in *Invisible Man*," on the rabbit and trickster motifs, pp. 243ff. Interestingly enough, Joyce puns the history of human oppression as "harestory." (*FW*. p. 288) Wilner offers a concise description of the rabbit motif:
Odysseus. the picaro. and Brer Rabbit are all soul brothers: champions of the underdog, the little man's hero under every unjust regime in history-- including nature's own. The rabbit, like the oppressed man, is without weapons in the order of things; left unprotected, he uses his very condition of helplessness as his mask; like Odysseus, his ruse is to be "Nobody." In a typical version of the African hare tales, the hare, servile and fawning,

offers to pick fleas from the lion's tail and then
buries the tail, so rendering the king of beasts
helpless while he makes off with the lion's kill.
However, because the odds are against him, the hare
is sometimes caught and beaten, and it is usually
when he takes himself seriously that the worst happens. In the American version, it is the tar baby
which makes Brer Rabbit; loving and embracing in a
sense, his own image, he is caught. That is why
self-irony is the price of his [sic] he is not in a
position fully to afford himself. (p. 245)

[47]Schechner, p. 43.

[48]Ibid.

[49]Ibid.

[50]Lawrence Clipper, "Folkloric and Mythic Elements in
Invisible Man," CLAJ, xxii. pp. 229-240.

[51]Schechner. p. 44.

[52]Ibid.. p. 45.

[53]Ibid.

[54]Ibid.

[55]Ibid.

[56]See Christopher Lasch. Haven in a Heartless World (New
York: Basic Books. 1977). pp. 167ff.

[57]See Heinz Kohut. The Analysis of the Self (New York:
International Universities Press. 1971).

[58]Rank. p. 71.

[59]Schafer. p. 125.

[60]Rank. p. 93.

[61]Ibid.. p. 95.

[62]Norris. p. 64.

[63]Quoted in Sennett. p. 189.

[64]Benstock. pp. 165-67.

[65]*Ibid.*

[66]Robert Bone. "Ralph Ellison and the Uses of the Imagination." *Ralph Ellison: A Collection of Critical Essays.* p. 112.

[67]Sennett. p. 154.

NOTES

Appendix

[1] Archie D. Sanders. "Odysseus in Black: An Analysis of the Structure of Invisible Man." CLAJ. 13 (March 1979). p. 218.

[2] Hugh Kenner. Joyce's Voices (Berkeley: Univ. of California Press. 1978). pp. 1-2.

[3] Charles W. Scruggs. "Ralph Ellison's Use of The Aeneid in Invisible Man." CLAJ. 17 (March 1974). pp. 368ff.

[4] Sanders. p. 222.

[5] Ibid.. pp. 222-23.

[6] Ibid.pp. 227-28.

[7] John Starke. "Invisible Man: Ellison's Black Odyssey." NALF. 7 (1973). pp. 60ff.

[8] Scruggs. pp. 370-71.

[9] Sanders. p. 225.

[10] Starke. p. 63.

[11] Ibid.. p. 226.

[12] Ibid.. p. 223.

[13] Sanders. p. 228.

[14] Joyce's Voices. pp. 81-82.

[15] Claude Lévi-Strauss. Myth and Meaning (New York: Schocken. 1979). p. 40.

318

INDEX

319